THE PAN-GERMA
RADICAL NATIONA
INTERWAR GERM

The Pan-German League and Radical Nationalist Politics in Interwar Germany, 1918–39

BARRY A. JACKISCH
University of Saint Francis, USA

Routledge
Taylor & Francis Group

LONDON AND NEW YORK

First published 2012 by Ashgate Publisher

2 Park Square, Milton Park, Abingdon, Oxon OX14 4RN
711 Third Avenue, New York, NY 10017, USA

Routledge is an imprint of the Taylor & Francis Group, an informa business

First issued in paperback 2017

British Library Cataloguing in Publication Data
Jackisch, Barry A.
  The Pan-German League and radical nationalist politics in interwar Germany, 1918-39.
  1. Alldeutscher Verband. 2. Deutschnationale Volkspartei. 3. Nationalism--Germany--History--20th century. 4. Right-wing extremists--Germany--History--20th century. 5. Germany--Politics and government--1918-1933.
  I. Title
  320.5'4'0943'09042-dc23

Library of Congress Cataloging-in-Publication Data
Jackisch, Barry A.
  The Pan-German League and radical nationalist politics in interwar Germany, 1918-39 / Barry A. Jackisch.
    p. cm.
  Includes bibliographical references and index.
  ISBN 978-1-4094-2761-2 (hbk)
(ebook) 1. Germany--Politics and government--1918-1933. 2. Germany--Politics and government--1933-1945. 3. Alldeutscher Verband--History--20th century. 4. Pangermanism--History--20th century. 5. Radicalism--Germany--History--20th century. 6. Nationalism--Germany--History--20th century. 7. Right-wing extremists--Germany--History--20th century. 8. Nationalsozialistische Deutsche Arbeiter-Partei--History. 9. Politicians--Germany--History--20th century. 10. Politicians--Germany--Biography. I. Title.
  DD240.J315 2012
  320.54094309'041--dc23

                                                                    2012006248

ISBN 978-1-4094-2761-2 (hbk)
ISBN 978-1-138-11598-9 (pbk)

Contents

Acknowledgments

This book would never have been completed without the support and encouragement from a wide range of institutions and people.

First of all, I am deeply indebted to the mentors, colleagues, and friends who have helped to make this project possible. I would like to express my sincerest gratitude to the original members of my dissertation committee: William Sheridan Allen, Georg Iggers, and John Naylor; a PhD student simply could not have asked for a better group of advisors. As my outside reader, Larry Eugene Jones provided invaluable expertise and insight into all aspects of the world of Weimar-era party politics and I continue to benefit significantly from his ongoing advice and encouragement. I have received invaluable support from colleagues at my two fulltime university positions. At Gannon University: Timothy Downs and Mark Jubulis. In my current position at the University of Saint Francis: Phyllis Gernhardt, Monique Gregg, Jason Jividen, David Mullins, Thomas Schneider, and Matthew Smith. My work has also benefitted from constructive criticism and suggestions from colleagues in the field of German history including: Hermann Beck, Roger Chickering, Clifton Ganyard, Karl Meyer, Dietrich Orlow, William Patch, Jim Retallack, and Raffael Scheck. In particular, I want to thank Richard Frankel and Steven Pfaff for their friendship, expertise, advice, and support.

The research for this book was made possible by the generosity of the German Academic Exchange Council (DAAD) and funds from the State University of New York-Buffalo, Gannon University, and the University of Saint Francis. My thanks go to the German archivists whose expertise and professionalism helped make all aspects of my research productive and enjoyable. Thanks also to the interlibrary loan staff of the various American institutions listed above for their help.

I am grateful to the editors, staff, and anonymous readers at Ashgate Publishing for their expert work on this book. They have improved this project in many ways and have been a pleasure to work with throughout the publishing process.

Finally, I wish to thank those closest to me for their support over many years. My parents Frederick and Emilie Jackisch, my sister Rhonda, and my brother Paul instilled in me a life-long interest in learning and encouraged me in all of my endeavors. I will always be grateful for your support and the innumerable ways that you have strengthened and uplifted me throughout my life. I dedicate this book to my wife Ami. Your love, support, and friendship have helped me through many trying times and have given me the strength and clarity to see this project to its completion. You have made all the difference.

Introduction: The Pan-German League and the German Right

In early March 1939 Nazi Germany's secret state police, the Gestapo, launched coordinated raids to shut down the Pan-German League's national headquarters, as well as its numerous regional and local offices throughout Germany. Acting with Adolf Hitler's knowledge and approval, the Gestapo brought an abrupt end to the organization's nearly 50-year history.[1] The regime's official explanation for this action stated that the League had been terminated and its publications banned in accordance with Article 1 of the 1933 "Law for the Protection of the People and the State."[2] Classified state security documents reveal that the Nazi state had grown increasingly concerned about the Pan-German League's activities after the Nazi seizure of power in 1933. In fact, for roughly six years from 1933 until 1939, the Third Reich's security forces kept track of the League's actions and compiled a detailed record of activities that the Gestapo viewed as potentially threatening to the regime.[3]

These facts will likely surprise many readers unfamiliar with the Pan-German League's later history. It may seem odd that the League survived in any form after 1933 and, in fact, lasted until 1939. Stranger still might be the fact that Hitler's regime would move so swiftly and decisively to shut down the Pan-German League, a leading radical nationalist organization that seemed to share many of the regime's general goals. Yet, this is precisely what happened to one of Germany's oldest and best known right-wing organizations only months before the outbreak of World War II. Why this happened, and how the Pan-German League reached this point, is the focus of the following study.

---

[1]   See the official correspondence approving the Pan-German League's dissolution in the unpublished records of the Reich Chancellery, record number R43 (Reichskanzlei—hereafter "R43") II/829, Bd. 3, in the Bundesarchiv Berlin (hereafter "BARCH"), 5–11.

[2]   BARCH R43 II/829, Bd. 3, 12.

[3]   For a detailed Gestapo report on the League's meetings, speeches, and rallies throughout Germany and its alleged "anti-governmental" activities, see the file on the Pan-German League from the Moscow Special Archive in the records of the Gedenkstätte Deutsche Widerstand, Berlin: Sonderarchiv Moskau (Moscow Special Archive—hereafter "SM") 500-3-569 "Alldeutscher Verband," 1–3, 27–44, and 139–160.

Scholars have devoted considerable attention to the Pan-German League's political influence before 1918 and to its overall importance for the development and dissemination of radical nationalist ideology.[4] However, the League's history after World War I until its dissolution in 1939 has attracted relatively less scholarly attention.[5] This study seeks to address that deficiency. It argues

---

[4]   On the League's history in Imperial Germany see: Roger Chickering, *We Men Who Feel Most German: A Cultural Study of the Pan-German League, 1886–1914* (Boston, 1984); Rainer Hering, *Konstruierte Nation. Der Alldeutsche Verband 1890 bis 1939* (Hamburg, 2003); Michael Peters, *Der Alldeutsche Verband am Vorabend des Ersten Weltkrieges (1908–1914)* (Frankfurt am Main, 1992); Günter Schödl, *Alldeutscher Verband und deutsche Minderheitenpolitik in Ungarn 1890–1914: Zur Gechichte des deutschen "extremen Nationalismus"* (Frankfurt am Main, 1978); and Mildred S. Wertheimer, *The Pan-German League, 1890–1914* (New York, 1924). A number of Pan-German commissioned, or ideologically colored accounts largely from the Nazi era also exist, including: Otto Bonhard, *Geschichte des Alldeutschen Verbandes* (Leipzig, 1920); Josephine Hussmann, *Die Alldeutschen und die Flottenfrage* (Diss. Phil., Freiburg, 1945); Dietrich Jung, *Der Alldeutsche Verband und die Marokkofrage* (Diss. Phil., Bonn, 1934); Siegfried Wehner, *Der Alldeutsche Verband und die deutsche Kolonialpolitik der Vorkriegszeit* (Diss. Phil., Greifswald, 1935); and Lothar Werner, *Der Alldeutsche Verband 1890–1918* (Berlin, 1935). For East German accounts of the League's pre-war activities, see: Edgar Hartwig, *Zur Politik und Entwicklung des Alldeutschen Verbandes von seiner Gründung bis zum Beginn des Ersten Weltkrieges (1891–1914)* (Diss. Phil., Jena, 1966), and Gerald Kolditz, *Die Ortsgruppe Dresden des Alldeutschen Verbandes von ihrer Entstehung bis zum Verbandstag 1906* (Diplomarbeit, Berlin, 1989). The League's chairman Heinrich Claß published his own account of the League's activities in the broader context of the German Right before and during World War I: Heinrich Claß, *Wider den Strom. Vom Werden und Wachsen der nationalen Opposition im alten Reich* (Leipzig, 1932). Finally, the author recently became aware of a newly published biography of the Pan-German chairman Heinrich Claß but was not able to include it in this study: Johannes Leicht, *Heinrich Claß 1868-1953. Die politische Biographie eines Alldeutschen* (Paderborn, 2012).

[5]   Several studies have addressed various aspects of the League's post-World War I history. The two earliest accounts are: Alfred Kruck, *Geschichte des Alldeutschen Verbandes 1890–1939* (Wiesbaden, 1954); and Brewster S. Chamberlin, *The Enemy on the Right. The "Alldeutsche Verband" in the Weimar Republic, 1918–1926* (Diss. Phil., University of Maryland, 1972). However, neither of these studies had access to all of the important archival source collections used extensively together for the first time in this study. As a result, both Chamberlin and Kruck were unable to explain the full extent of the League's influence on the major right-wing organizations, or the League's broader significance in the development of the German Right in the Weimar period. One East German study for the post-1918 period is marred by serious ideological assumptions evident even in its title: Willi Krebs, *Der Alldeutsche Verband in den Jahren 1918 bis 1939: ein politisches Instrument des deutschen Imperialismus* (Diss. Phil., Berlin, 1970). Another East German article offers limited insight in to the relationship between the Pan-Germans and the Nazi movement: Joachim Petzold, "Claß und Hitler. Über die Förderung der frühen Nazibewegung durch den Alldeutschen Verband und dessen Einfluß auf die Nazi Ideologie," *Jahrbuch für Geschichte*, 21, 1980, 247–288. Finally, Rainer Hering provides an overview of the League's role in Weimar politics in: Hering, *Konstruierte Nation*, 138–153.)

that the Pan-German League's history during the Weimar Republic and the first years of the Nazi dictatorship offers important new insights into the political history of German radical nationalism and the transformation of the German Right in the Weimar era.

The Pan-German League's pre-1918 history is generally well known. Founded in 1891 as a political pressure group critical of the German government's foreign and domestic policy decisions, the Pan-Germans were an openly expansionist organization that called for German colonies and spheres of influence throughout the world and the creation of a strong navy to reinforce Germany's newly gained status abroad. In domestic politics, the League supported an authoritarian monarchy and opposed the growth of parliamentary democracy. The League also sought to combat what it regarded as the pernicious influence of a myriad of "un-German" elements, particularly Slavs, often Catholics, and ultimately, Jews.[6] In addition, the Pan-German League was a driving force behind the annexationist war aims movement during World War I, and many of its members participated in the short-lived Fatherland Party (*Vaterlandspartei*) in 1917–1918.[7] The League was one of the only major right-wing organizations to survive the upheavals of the German Revolution in 1918–1919, and it reached its highest active membership total of about 38,000 in 1922.[8]

Throughout its history, the Pan-German League drew the vast majority of its members from the social strata identified by the German terms *Bildung und Besitz*, or the propertied and educated middle class.[9] However, several members of the nobility joined the League at various points before and after World War I and they remained an influential, although relatively small, part of the League's membership. During the Weimar period, a number of these aristocrats became close confidants of League chairman Heinrich Claß and they figured prominently in the Pan-German League's leadership structure.[10]

---

[6] Roger Chickering offers an excellent analysis of the League's ideological construction of a world of enemies that threatened the German Volk. See: Chickering, *We Men Who Feel Most German*, esp. 122–132.

[7] On the League's participation in the Fatherland Party, see: Heinz Hagenlücke, *Deutsche Vaterlandspartei. Die Nationale Rechte am Ende des Kaiserreiches* (Düsseldorf, 1997).

[8] The League's leaders discussed the organization's membership at a 1928 meeting of the Business Management Committee. The minutes of this meeting are located in the Pan-German League's unpublished records (hereafter "R8048 Alldeutscher Verband") in the Bundesarchiv-Berlin ("BARCH"). See: Sitzung des Geschäftsführenden Ausschusses (hereafter "SGA") 1/2 Dezember 1928-Berlin, BARCH R8048/156, 55–56.

[9] A comprehensive analysis of the League's pre-war membership is available in: Chickering, *We Men Who Feel Most German*, 102–121.

[10] For the composition of the League's post-war leadership, see: "Handbuch des Alldeutschen Verbandes – 1921," BARCH R8048/533, 105. Influential Pan-German nobles included Axel

Thus the League's membership counted social and political elites including nobles, industrialists, and high-ranking military officers as well as middle-class professionals like teachers, doctors, lawyers, civil servants, and small business owners.

During the Weimar era, the Pan-Germans approached the momentous political events of their time with a generally elitist attitude toward society and politics. The League sought to establish an authoritarian government of its choosing composed of leading nationalist politicians whom they believed would rescue the German people from the allegedly incompetent and disastrous Weimar Republic. However, the Pan-Germans believed that this goal could not be achieved through demagogy and the mass rallies that became such a prominent part of Weimar politics. Instead, the League's leaders preferred to pursue their political goals by working behind the scenes to gain influence over other, often larger, right-wing organizations.

Because of the League's elitist strategy and its disdain for Weimar-era mass politics, scholars have often underestimated the Pan-German League's influence after 1918, dismissing the group as an increasingly irrelevant relic of the Wilhelmine era. However, the League's leaders, especially its long-time chairman Heinrich Claß, continued to cultivate contacts at the national, regional, and local level with a wide range of rightist organizations. These contacts allowed the League to exercise an influence over the course of German right-wing politics that far exceeded its numerical strength.[11]

Most existing studies of the Pan-German League have focused more on the group's radical nationalist ideology than on its specific role in right-wing politics. Historians' early concentration on the League's extremist stance—including its early adoption of racial anti-Semitism, German identity based on blood rather than geography, and a paranoid hatred of parliamentary democracy and the political Left in all its forms—has led to the notion that the Pan-German League's

---

Freiherr von Freytagh-Loringhoven, Konstantin Freiherr von Gebsattel, Gertzlaff von Hertzberg-Lottin, Otto Fürst zu Salm-Horstmar, and Leopold von Vietinghoff-Scheel. On the radicalization of the German nobility after World War I and the role of aristocrats in nationalist organizations including the Pan-German League see: Stephan Malinowski, *Vom König zum Führer. Sozialer Niedergang und politische Radikalisierung im deutschen Adel zwischen Kaiserreich und NS-Staat* (Berlin, 2003).

[11]   Historian Annelise Thimme correctly asserted already in 1969 that the League's influence was far greater in the Weimar period than historians had assumed. In her study of the German National People's Party (DNVP) in 1918, she refers to Pan-German leaders as "secularized sectarians" for their elitist, narrow-minded devotion to the righteousness of their cause. See: Annelise Thimme, *Flucht in den Mythos: Die Deutschnationale Volkspartei und die Niederlage von 1918* (Göttingen, 1969), 58. A similar argument can be found in: Michael Stürmer, *Koalition und Opposition in der Weimarer Republik 1924–1928* (Düsseldorf, 1967), 190–196.

primary historical importance was as an ideological precursor of National Socialism. Scholars established this linkage between the Pan-German League and Hitler's movement shortly after World War II in an attempt to understand Nazism's origins. Friedrich Meinecke's *The German Catastrophe* is one early example of this type of argument.[12] In pointing out the connection between the Pan-Germans and Nazism, Meinecke posed the following rhetorical question: "Can one doubt any longer that the Pan-Germans and the Fatherland Party are an exact prelude to Hitler's rise to power?"[13]

This interpretation has also been central to studies that find strong right-wing ideological continuity stretching from Imperial Germany, through the Weimar Republic, to the Third Reich. George Mosse's history of the crisis of German ideology clearly takes this approach. While Mosse acknowledged that the Pan-German League and Hitler's movement were not completely synonymous, he emphasized the League's considerable ideological influence on Nazism after 1918. "Through [the League]," Mosse writes, "völkish ideas found firm footing within the establishment itself; and thus this organization must be ranked with the Youth Movement and the educational system as the chief transmitters of the Germanic ideology from the prewar to the postwar world."[14] Mosse's account clearly reinforces the important ideological link between the Pan-German League and the National Socialists.

More recently, archivist and historian Rainer Hering has examined the Pan-German League through the lens of Benedict Anderson's theory of the nation as an "imagined community."[15] According to Hering, the Pan-German League prepared the way for racist thinking in modern Germany and, therefore, it represented a significant organizational and ideological constant of the radical nationalist movement stretching from Imperial Germany through the Third Reich.[16] Quoting the well-known German historian Fritz Fischer, Hering concludes that the Third Reich was no "accident" (*Betriebsunfall*), but rather the

---

[12]   Friedrich Meinecke, *The German Catastrophe: Reflections and Recollections* (English edition: Boston, 1963—originally published in 1950).

[13]   Ibid., 30. For a definitive history of the Fatherland Party that disagrees with Meinecke's assessment see: Hagenlücke, *Deutsche Vaterlandspartei*, esp. 13–19 and 408–410.

[14]   George Mosse, *The Crisis of German Ideology: Intellectual Origins of the Third Reich* (New York, 1964), 225. Two recent works also stress general lines of continuity between pre- and post-war German right-wing thought stretching to National Socialism: Thomas Rohkrämer, *A Single Communal Faith? The German Right from Conservatism to National Socialism* (New York and Oxford, 2007); and Peter Walkenhorst, *Nation-Volk-Rasse: Radikaler Nationalismus im Deutschen Kaiserreich 1890–1914* (Göttingen, 2007), esp. 333–342.

[15]   Hering, *Konstruierte Nation*.

[16]   Ibid., 12 and 15.

realization of the nation's most extreme historical developments stretching back before 1918, including the radical nationalist vision of the nation espoused by the Pan-German League.[17]

All of these accounts generally emphasize a strong line of continuity between the Pan-German League's radical nationalist ideology and the establishment of the Third Reich. They stress the similarity of ideas and worldview between the Pan-Germans and the Nazis and they explain Hitler's rise to power in the context of the long-term impact of radical nationalist agitation and ideology stretching back before 1918. However, this interpretation of the Pan-German League does not explain the surprising and substantial political friction that existed between the League and other prominent rightist groups, especially the Nazi Party, in the Weimar period. The present study takes these political conflicts seriously and therefore places the Pan-German League's history within a different historiographical tradition that stresses the division of the German Right as a key component of Hitler's rise to power.

Over the last two decades, several historians have begun to challenge the explanatory power of studies focused on right-wing continuity from Imperial Germany to the Third Reich. These scholars suggest that Hitler's rise to power was much more complicated and resulted at least in part from the political fragmentation and infighting among prominent right-wing organizations. For example, Geoff Eley contends that while the Pan-German League was indeed an important and early proponent of radical völkisch ideology in the pre-1918 period, it was only one of many groups after the war that espoused such ideas. Eley points out that by the early 1920s, the Wilhelmine radical nationalist legacy had become the common property of the German Right. This remained, however, primarily an ideological achievement because of the substantial political divisions that undermined the emergence of a coherent, unified, and effective right-wing movement.[18] The failure to organize an effective, unified right-wing political movement in the Weimar Republic's early years also helps explain Hitler's contempt for the members of the established political Right and the relative ease with which the Nazi movement eventually supplanted them.[19]

More recently, Larry Eugene Jones has argued that the German Right was actually deeply divided when it came to specific strategies for securing political

---

[17]   Ibid., 29 and 488.

[18]   Geoff Eley, "Conservatives and Radical Nationalists in Germany: The Production of Fascist Potentials, 1912–1928," in Martin Blinkhorn (ed.), *Fascists and Conservatives: The Radical Right and the Establishment in Twentieth-Century Europe* (London, 1990), 50–70, esp. 65.

[19]   Ibid., 65. On the lack of political cohesion within the so-called "völkisch" movement and its attitude toward National Socialism, see: Uwe Puschner, *Die Völkische Bewegung im wilhelminishen Kaiserreich. Sprache-Rasse-Religion* (Darmstadt, 2001), 9–12.

power. This division and infighting prevented the emergence of a stable moderate conservatism and allowed Nazism to co-opt the radical nationalist campaign against the Weimar system. In the Republic's final years, Jones argues, the established Right became so divided that it could no longer muster any effective alternative to Hitler's radicalism and broad populist appeal. This forced the traditional Right into a position of political weakness in their negotiations with Hitler. In this regard, Jones maintains that the political division of the German Right was just as significant a precondition for Hitler's seizure of power as was the dissolution of the liberal parties or the division of the Marxist Left in the Weimar period.[20]

Finally, Hermann Beck's recent study of the relationship between German conservatives and the Nazis during the "seizure of power" further reinforces the importance of political conflict and division between Hitler's movement and the non-Nazi Right.[21] Beck stresses the strongly revolutionary, anti-bourgeois thrust of National Socialism and its sometimes violent attacks on the established political Right, especially its conservative coalition partners in 1933. Although Beck's study focuses primarily on the months surrounding Hitler's appointment as chancellor in January 1933, it raises important questions about the broader relationship between the Nazi movement and the non-Nazi right-wing establishment.

The following study of the Pan-German League offers further evidence of the significant political conflict that existed not only within the German Right during the first decade of the Weimar era, but also between the forces of the non-Nazi Right and Hitler's movement in the Republic's final turbulent years. Because of historians' long-standing focus on the general ideological similarities between the Pan-Germans and other prominent rightist organizations after 1918, scholars have, to this point, largely overlooked or downplayed the substantial political differences between the League and other right-wing groups. Our understanding of the Pan-Germans' role in the history of the Weimar-era German Right is, therefore, incomplete if we dismiss these numerous and often intense right-wing power struggles merely as personal disputes or irrational squabbles over minor political fiefdoms. Rather, these conflicts, in which the

---

[20] Larry Eugene Jones, "The Limits of Collaboration: Edgar Jung, Herbert von Bose, and the Origins of the Conservative Resistance to Hitler, 1933–34," in Larry Eugene Jones and James N. Retallack (eds), *Between Reform, Reaction, and Resistance: Studies in the History of German Conservatism from 1789 to 1945* (Providence, 1993), 465–501, esp. 468. More recently see: Jones, "German Conservatism at the Crossroads: Count Cuno von Westarp and the Struggle for Control of the DNVP, 1928–1930," *Contemporary European History*, 18/2, 2009, 147–177, esp. 177.

[21] Hermann Beck, *The Fateful Alliance: German Conservatives and Nazis in 1933: The Machtergreifung in a New Light* (Oxford and New York, 2008).

Pan-German League was directly involved, deeply divided the German Right at important moments throughout the Weimar period. The political division and infighting ultimately contributed to Hitler's success in 1933 in ways that historians are beginning to appreciate more fully.

This study will examine the Pan-German League's role in the broader context of the German Right in the following chapters. Chapter 1 traces the League's reaction to Germany's defeat in World War I and the government's collapse in the following months. The League assembled for the first time in the post-war period at Bamberg in Upper Bavaria in late February 1919. Here the League's leaders drafted the group's post-war manifesto known as the "Bamberg Declaration." They outlined their demands for an authoritarian government that would replace the emerging republican system. At this Bamberg meeting, the League also created the influential, and explicitly anti-Semitic, mass organization called the German Völkisch Offensive and Defensive League (*Deutschvölkischer Schutz- und Trutzbund*). The chapter concludes by surveying the Pan-German League's early stance on party politics, and the League's role in the planning and outcome of the Kapp Putsch in March 1920.

Chapter 2 examines the League's intensely acrimonious relationship with the German Völkisch Freedom Party (*Deutschvölkische Freiheitspartei* or DVFP), a major north German right-wing extremist organization. In spite of many apparent ideological similarities, the League and the DVFP's leaders became embroiled in a widely publicized feud that was exacerbated by the angry, paranoid climate of extremist right-wing politics in the immediate post-war period. The League's tense relationship with the increasingly eccentric, but still widely respected war hero Erich Ludendorff also contributed to the broader struggle with the DVFP. This prolonged conflict between 1920 and 1925 played a crucial role in the disintegration of the northern German radical nationalist movement and had a profound impact on the development of right-wing politics as a whole in the Weimar Republic's first decade.

While the Pan-Germans attempted to resolve the growing conflict with the DVFP in northern Germany, they kept a close watch on southern radical nationalist groups as well. Chapter 3 explores the League's relationship, particularly through its chairman Heinrich Claß, to Adolf Hitler and the Nazi Party through April 1924. In spite of the growing political conflict with other northern right-wing groups, the Pan-Germans remained intensely interested in the emergence of the Nazi Party and its potential impact on the radical nationalist cause. From early 1920 until Hitler's failed "Beer Hall Putsch" in November 1923, Heinrich Claß and other leading Pan-Germans had a series of direct discussions with Hitler in Munich and Berlin that covered a wide range of issues. The Pan-German leadership also tried unsuccessfully to gain Hitler's allegiance and encourage the Nazi Party's expansion to Berlin and northern Germany through limited financing and political influence. However, these early efforts to persuade Hitler failed entirely. In the wake of the Beer Hall Putsch and Hitler's subsequent trial, relations between the Pan-Germans and the Nazi movement collapsed. As a result, the League shifted its focus almost entirely to a systematic attempt to gain control over Germany's largest national right-wing political party, the DNVP (*Deutschnationale Volkspartei* or German National People's Party). This decision would have a fateful impact on the development of German conservatism and the overall stability of the Weimar Republic.

Chapter 4 examines the background and development of the conservative DNVP and its ties to the Pan-German League through 1925. Until the rapid rise of the Nazi Party in 1929–1930, the conservative DNVP was by far the largest right-wing party in German politics. From its inception, however, it was deeply divided between a more moderate conservative majority and an intransigent, radical nationalist wing that rejected out of hand any accommodation with the republican system. The Pan-Germans were an influential part of this later group. Beginning already in 1924, the League attempted to drive the party away from governmental participation and into a permanent stance of nationalist opposition. The Pan-Germans played a significant role in the party's embarrassing public split over the Dawes Plan vote, its withdrawal from the 1925 Luther government, and the DNVP's lack of unity regarding Gustav Stresemann's foreign policy. These crucially important events undermined Germany's largest conservative party and sapped its effectiveness as a potentially reliable coalition partner.

The Pan-German League's efforts to radicalize the DNVP only intensified after 1925. Chapter 5 examines in detail the League's role in the campaign to promote Alfred Hugenberg as party chairman. During this period, the Pan-Germans mounted a concerted campaign to force the party away from any further accommodation with the Weimar Republic. The Pan-Germans hoped that with the radical Hugenberg's election as party leader, the DNVP could serve as a larger popular platform for the dissemination of Pan-German policy to the wider public. The DNVP's fairly loose national structure and the relative strength of its regional and local chapters allowed the Pan-Germans to focus their effort not only on high-level party contacts, but also on a "grassroots" reorientation of the party. This effort paid off in October 1928 with Hugenberg's election as party chairman.

The Pan-German League's broader attempt to rid the party of its last remaining moderate conservatives continued through 1930 with disastrous consequences. As Chapter 6 demonstrates, the Pan-Germans retained some influence over the DNVP and the German Right more broadly in the final stages of the Weimar Republic, primarily through their political contacts at the national level. In December 1929 and again in July 1930, nearly all moderate conservatives split from the DNVP, leaving the radical Hugenberg with a considerably smaller, but more tightly organized party than ever before. This represented the triumph of the Pan-German position within the party, but it was a disaster in a broader political sense for the stability of the Weimar system. The Pan-German influenced purge of a nascent moderate, responsible conservatism within the DNVP was a terrible setback for coalition strategies in the Weimar Republic and ushered in a new era of increasingly radical anti-democratic politics on the German Right as a whole between 1930 and 1933. The DNVP's loss of political influence and popular support under Hugenberg's leadership also made possible Hitler's emergence as the dominant political force on the German Right. Although the Pan-German League survived the Nazi seizure of power intact, it would not be long before the regime moved against the League and ended its existence permanently in 1939.

This study is based on a broad range of archival sources that provide insight into the League's activities after 1918 from a number of important perspectives. The most significant single source is the League's own document collection, which the last chairman Heinrich Claß turned over to the German National Archive (*Reichsarchiv*) in 1942. These records now reside in the German Federal Archive (*Bundesarchiv*) in Berlin. The Federal Archives in Berlin and Koblenz also hold valuable collections from government departments, political parties, and groups (including the DNVP), as well as the personal papers of leading nationalist politicians with whom Pan-German leaders had frequent contact like Alfred Hugenberg. Furthermore, the Federal Archives in Koblenz retain the unpublished portion of Heinrich Claß's memoirs covering the period from 1918 until the mid-1930s. This source is particularly valuable in unlocking Claß's personal role in the Weimar era, as well as his relationship to Adolf Hitler and the Nazi movement.

The papers of Kuno Graf von Westarp, held in private possession on the family estate in Gaertringen near Stuttgart, contain a great deal of valuable information concerning the Pan-German League's ties to the DNVP at the national and local level. Likewise, Gustav Stresemann's papers in the Political Archive of the German Foreign Office (*Politisches Archiv des Auswärtigen Amtes*) shed light on the Foreign Minister's relationship to the Pan-Germans and the DNVP around the critical time of the Locarno Accords negotiations in 1925–1926. The Gestapo files from the Moscow Special Archive (*Sonderarchiv Moscow*) in the Memorial Center for the German Resistance (*Gendenkstätte Deutscher Widerstand*) are invaluable for reconstructing the Nazi regime's attitude toward the Pan-Germans in the Third Reich.

This project also benefits from several regional archival collections that allow for a closer investigation of the League's activities at the local level. The most comprehensive and informative of these collections is certainly the detailed records of the Pan-German League's local group (*Ortsgruppe*) Dresden in the Dresden City Archives (*Stadtarchiv Dresden*). These Pan-German documents are supplemented by the detailed personal papers of DNVP member Albrecht Phillip, available in the Saxon Main State Archives in Dresden (*Sächsisches Hauptstaatsarchiv Dresden*). In addition to Dresden and eastern Saxony, this study draws selectively on local records from Osnabrück, Stuttgart/Württemberg, and Darmstadt. These documents provide an added dimension to the League's activities at the national level, and help explain in greater detail the League's relationship to other major right-wing organizations.

Ultimately, this study demonstrates that the Pan-German League was an influential factor in the history of the German Right in the Weimar Republic. While the League's influence before 1918 is widely acknowledged, its role after World War I has been more often assumed than thoroughly explored. The Pan-German League played an important role in the political division of the German Right in the Weimar Republic, which contributed to Hitler's ultimate seizure of power. Although it operated in a radically different political environment after 1918, the Pan-German League was arguably just as significant for the development of right-wing politics after World War I as it had been before.

Chapter 1

In the Wake of War and Revolution

By October 1918, it was increasingly clear that Germany had lost World War I; what would happen to the country in the following weeks and months was much less certain. Millions of Germans called for an end to the bloodshed on the battlefield and privations on the home front, even with the certain prospect of German defeat. By no means, however, did the war's end come as a relief to all segments of the German population. Millions still greeted the reality of German defeat with stunned disbelief. It seemed impossible that an army that had forced a decisive German victory against the Russians in the East and gained large tracks of territory in its spring offensive in the West had been defeated and teetered on the verge of complete collapse. To those groups who had pinned such great hopes on the war at its beginning, and had kept faith in ultimate Germany victory until the bitter end, the defeat was a crushing blow. On 19–20 October 1918, one of the most prominent of these groups, the Pan-German League, gathered for its last wartime meeting in Berlin.

To those League members who traveled to the October gathering, Germany's position appeared bleak indeed. Nonetheless, several of Germany's most prominent pre-war radical nationalists were in attendance, including the chairman of the Pan-German League Heinrich Claß, German Army League leader General August Keim, Lübeck's nationalist mayor Dr. Johann Neumann, and the well-known Munich publisher J.F. Lehmann.[1] The meeting's final resolution, meant for public release, in no way reflected the dire reality of Germany's position in relation to the Allied powers. In addition to overestimating the strength and quality of Germany's fighting forces remaining in the West, the resolution singled out Prince Max von Baden's interim government as the single most harmful and dangerous element to the German nation. The League argued that Germany's ceasefire request had only strengthened Allied arrogance and contempt, while the government's intention to abandon important parts of the German Reich was a clear indication of its willingness to preside over the dismemberment and destruction of Germany as a whole.[2] The Pan-Germans called for a government of "national defense" that

---

[1] SGA, 19–20 October 1918, BARCH R8048/121, 55.

[2] For a complete draft of this resolution see ibid., 67–68.

would reawaken all the powers of the German people and would "passionately announce ... the demands of national honor which would, in turn, reestablish the spirit of August 1914 ... and demonstrate that Germany's resistance is far from exhausted." Heinrich Claß admonished his fellow members to "stay at your posts and do your duty."[3]

These hollow phrases reveal a great deal about the Pan-German League in the immediate post-war period. Indeed, the League's hopeless calls in October 1918 for national revival and the "spirit of 1914" indicate just how desperate they were to alter the war's outcome. Incapable of changing the inevitable, the League vented its frustration and anger against the new republican system. The Pan-Germans quickly sought to build a united völkisch movement from the fractured forces of the wartime German Right. Heinrich Claß and other League leaders believed that this new movement could strike against Germany's fragile democratic system and eventually establish some form of a völkisch dictatorship. In spite of this early confidence, the League's expectations for a united völkisch movement in the Weimar period were as unrealistic as their desperate calls for Germany's reawakening at the close of World War I.[4]

The Bamberg Declaration

The war's end and the stark reality of German defeat left the Pan-German League, as well as other large segments of the German Right, adrift in search of a new identity. To many on the Right, the worst possible scenario had become reality. The powerful German nation-state headed by the Hohenzollern dynasty had allegedly been "stabbed in the back" by politicians and defeatists who supposedly cared more for their own interests than those of the loyal citizen

---

[3]   Ibid., 68.

[4]   The word "völkisch" is nearly impossible to translate properly into English. This German adjective is, therefore, used in this study to convey the Pan-German League's exclusionary nationalism based on a consciously racial definition of German identity. The League often used the term to describe political organizations, movements, or ideas that promoted their specific vision of radical nationalist politics. However, as recent scholarship has suggested, this was a hotly contested term with origins stretching well back in to the nineteenth century. For an outstanding discussion of this concept, the word's origins, and the development of the so-called vökisch movement, see: Puschner, *Völkische Bewegung*, esp. 9–42; and Rüdiger vom Bruch, "Wilhelminismus-Zum Wandel von Milieu und politischer Kultur" and Günter Hartung, "Völkische Ideologie" in Uwe Puschner, Walter Schmitz, and Justus H. Ulbricht (eds), *Handbuch zur Völkischen Bewegung 1871–1918* (Munich, 1999), 3–41.

and the undefeated soldier on the front.[5] Although the end of the war and the revolutionary upheaval that quickly followed destroyed or radically altered most other right-wing political organizations, the Pan-German League survived. The League met again in February 1919 for the first time since the end of the war to chart a new course for itself and the new nation. Much had transpired, however, in the roughly four months which had passed since its last wartime gathering in October 1918.

Throughout the five-month period from October 1918 to February 1919, the Pan-German League's very existence was not completely assured. A number of the League's regional and local organizations had either temporarily disbanded or were unable to get clear direction from League headquarters in Berlin.[6] Many of the smaller regional chapters that disbanded existed in areas that the League assumed would be occupied by the Allies, overwhelmingly in the West.[7] Even the League's chairman Heinrich Claß was tipped off by several people that he was at the top of a French list of possible candidates for Allied war-crimes trials.[8] Although none of these suspicions concerning Allied retribution directed against the Pan-German League or its members were ever realized, the possibility was enough to cause considerable internal confusion and disorganization for the League during these initial post-war months.

Furthermore, during this same period the country as a whole faced the very real prospect of outright revolution. Starting with an uprising by soldiers and sailors in the northern port cities of Wilhelmshaven and Kiel in early November 1918, the revolutionary wave reached other parts of Germany in a matter of days. By 8 November, workers' and soldiers' councils appeared in major cities like Hamburg, Bremen, Cologne, Leipzig, Frankfurt, and Munich. By 9 November

---

[5]   For more on Germany's defeat in World War I and impact see: Ulrich Heinemann, *Die verdrängte Niederlage: Politische Öffentlichkeit und Kriegsschuldfrage in der Weimarer Republik* (Göttingen, 1983).

[6]   SGA, 16–17 February 1919, BARCH R8048/123, 25–27.

[7]   Ibid., 26. Some of the most prominent of these chapters were: Bonn, Koblenz, Cologne, and Wiesbaden. Because of the League's radical pro-war, annexationist stance, some members of the Pan-German League in areas open to Allied occupation were concerned that they might be singled out for prosecution or legal action by the occupying powers, particularly France.

[8]   Heinrich Claß, *Wider den Strom, vol. II* (hereafter "Claß, *WdS v. II*") unpublished manuscript, N2368 Nachlass Heinrich Claß/3, Bundesarchiv-Koblenz (hereafter "BA-Koblenz"), 432–434. Claß actually returned home to Mainz from Berlin in the second half of November 1918 to check on his ailing wife and his property. He left Mainz shortly thereafter on 8 December for Würzburg largely because he was concerned that he was in danger of capture by French troops. In fact, only two weeks later, on Christmas Eve, French troops and military police appeared at Claß's house in Mainz to question him and search for possible incriminating evidence. He had already left, and the French authorities did not follow up on their investigation.

the revolution reached Berlin.[9] Faced with the threat of radical political upheaval, the national government under Friedrich Ebert allied with the army and newly created *Freikorps* ("Free Corps") paramilitary units to suppress the revolutionaries violently in the name of restoring order to the country. This momentous decision, and the revolution's subsequent collapse, would cast a long shadow over the history of the Weimar Republic.[10] For the Pan-German League in the short term, however, the revolutionary threat only reinforced the importance of their organization in a time of national upheaval.

The Pan-German leadership's main goal throughout this tenuous period was simple. The League had to hold together with a clear sense of purpose at all costs. On 15 November 1918, shortly before he left his home in Mainz to travel to Würzburg, Heinrich Claß drafted and distributed a statement to all League members.[11] It asked his fellow Pan-Germans to remain loyal to the League and outlined the group's most pressing tasks. Members were expected to recruit the greatest number of reliable, truly patriotic Germans who believed unflinchingly in Germany's rebirth and would work tirelessly for it. The League and its allies would continue to support all patriotic Germans, particularly those in areas which might be occupied or even annexed by the victorious Allied powers. Finally, League members should be prepared to support all actions that maintained law and order in Germany and prevented the forces of socialism and revolution from tearing the country apart.[12]

Although Claß's statement provided a rough guideline for League members to follow in the chaos that followed Germany's collapse at the end of 1918, it did not offer any specific, long-term agenda for the future. However, it quickly became clear that precisely such an agenda would be necessary for the League's continued existence. Without a clear position concerning the Pan-German League's role in post-war politics, the League's membership could not be expected to hold on indefinitely. So, shortly after his arrival in Würzburg in December 1918, Heinrich Claß began to compose what would become the Pan-German League's post-war manifesto.[13]

---

[9]   Eberhard Kolb, *The Weimar Republic* (London, 1988), 7.

[10]   For valuable overviews of the revolution and the broader significance of its ultimate collapse see: Hans Mommsen, *The Rise and Fall of Weimar Democracy*, trans. Elborg Forster and Larry Eugene Jones (Chapel Hill, 1996), 20–50; and Heinrich August Winkler, *Weimar 1918–1933. Die Geschichte der ersten deutschen Demokratie* (Munich, 1998), 27–68.

[11]   Ibid., 434–435. This statement was published a week later in the Pan-German League's paper the *Alldeutsche Blätter* on 23 November 1918. See: *Alldeutsche Blätter*, 23 November 1918, 32.

[12]   Claß, *WdS v. II*, 434–435.

[13]   Ibid., 449.

From December 1918 until February 1919 Claß made a series of trips from Würzburg to Nürnberg and Berlin, the League's headquarters, to discuss and revise this important document with a close circle of Pan-German confidants. Claß benefited from these direct discussions, as well as from his extensive correspondence with many of the League's local leaders and members.[14] One overarching concept influenced Claß as he rushed to complete the League's manifesto. He wrote in his memoirs:

> It became clear to me that the Pan-German League was the only national organization to survive the November upheaval intact ... The only way for it to be strengthened was ... to present publicly and with convincing force the League's position regarding the current state of our Fatherland as well as a plan to rebuild Germany and save its people.[15]

This goal dominated the Pan-German League's February 1919 gathering in Bamberg in Northern Bavaria.

The Bamberg meeting, the League's first in the post-war period, lasted for two days from 16 to 17 February. All attendees had already been notified that the Bamberg meeting would produce the League's first official public statement regarding the new German state. Members were also well aware that an immediate Pan-German proclamation would come at a delicate time for Germany's transitional government. The National Assembly had been meeting in Weimar since 6 February and on 11 February it had elected the Republic's first president, Friedrich Ebert.[16] In this sense, Germany's first true democracy was already taking shape at the same time that the most influential members of the Pan-German League—an organization overtly opposed to democracy in all forms—were arriving in Bamberg.

From its inception in Imperial Germany, the Pan-German League had always considered itself as a non-party force of the loyal "national opposition."[17] The

---

[14]   The actual volume of letters and suggestions for the future goals of the League from all quarters is immense. In this regard see: BARCH R8048/204 (esp. 692–695, 707–708, 715, 730–731, and 740–741); and BARCH R8048/205 (esp. 1–29, 51–61, 95–109, 135–151, and 159–164).

[15]   Claß, *WdS v. II*, 449.

[16]   For more detailed information on the National Assembly see: Kolb, *Weimar Republic*, 16–22.

[17]   On the League's earlier policies and its role in the "national opposition" in Imperial Germany see: Chickering, *We Men Who Feel Most German*; Geoff Eley, *Reshaping the German Right: Radical Nationalism and Political Change after Bismarck* (2nd edn, Ann Arbor, 1991); and more recently Hering, *Konstruierte Nation*.

League normally directed its criticism at individuals such as former Chancellor Theobald von Bethmann-Hollweg, or at specific foreign or domestic policies of German national or state governments. The League never went so far as to challenge the basic authority of the state itself or the legitimacy of the House of Hohenzollern, even though it was often critical of Kaiser Wilhelm II's individual decisions.[18] Germany's defeat in World War I, the November Revolution, and the abdication of the kaiser and the Hohenzollern dynasty changed the Pan-German position dramatically. The establishment of a new democratic government would transform the Pan-German League's formally loyal opposition into a complete rejection of the fledgling Weimar Republic. This shift was clearly evident in a document that soon came to be known as the Bamberg Declaration.

Before the League's members began formal debate on the document itself, the League's top leadership felt it necessary on the first day of the Bamberg gathering to provide some historical background to the radical declaration that would define the organization's post-war stance. This task was left to the chairman, Heinrich Claß, and his opening presentation clearly summarized the rationale for the Pan-German League's early, radical stance against the Weimar system.[19] Claß blamed Prince Max von Baden and his allies for abandoning the German cause at the end of the war.[20] He claimed that Max von Baden's short-lived chancellorship sealed Germany's fate and left the country in the hands of those who no longer believed in victory or wanted it. Even worse, all of this had happened against the will of the German Military High Command who, in Claß's words, "still believed in a defensive battle that could continue for months."[21] Further perpetuating the "stab-in-the-back" myth, Claß argued that the war had not been lost in the final months on the front, but in Germany itself. Although Germany's army had stood fast on the Western Front, the navy in the North began to come apart. Claß still seemed to believe that Admirals Scheer and Hipper had worked out a "sure-fire" plan of attack against the British navy that would have broken the blockade against Germany and turned the tide of

---

[18]   Uwe Lohalm, *Völkischer Radikalismus. Die Geschichte des Deutschvölkischen Schutz- und Trutz-Bundes 1919–1923* (Hamburg, 1970), 16.

[19]   Ibid., 16–17.

[20]   For Claß's complete statement, see: SGA, 16–17 February 1919, BARCH R8048/123, 10–17.

[21]   In reality, this assertion was far from accurate. Already on 29 September 1918 General Ludendorff, facing a nervous breakdown, informed the German government that an immediate armistice was absolutely necessary to avoid a complete military collapse. Max von Baden was not appointed chancellor until 3 October 1918. See: Mommsen, *Rise and Fall of Weimar Democracy*, 10–16.

the war. Instead, the cowardly sailors rebelled against their leaders when decisive action was most urgently needed.[22]

Claß also chastised segments of the German population. Many who had previously supported the war were partially guilty for their "cowardliness and lack of character" as the socialist revolution broke out over Germany. Claß blamed some, but not all, members of the aristocracy—although he still clearly supported the institution itself—for failing to go to the front at the decisive moment and sacrifice their lives for the monarchy. Instead, too many Germans simply resigned themselves to the coming revolution as a fait accompli and thereby cleared the way for a "regime of destructiveness." Too few of Germany's citizens were willing to join together and fight to preserve the Imperial German state. Instead, large segments of the bourgeoisie and aristocracy hid behind Max von Baden's government hoping to prevent the worst excesses of what many considered to be a "second French Revolution" in Germany.[23] Claß's message was clear: this sort of cowardice would not be tolerated in the League's upcoming struggle against the new state.

Claß continued that Jews, especially war profiteers and the "Jewish-liberal press," were also directly responsible for Germany's defeat. Claß concluded that "without the role of Jewry, it would have been impossible for the war to end the way it did."[24] Claß's unpublished memoirs also reflect the importance that he and other Pan-German leaders placed on the "Jewish Question" as a focus for the Bamberg meeting. He noted that the meeting should produce the first clear "declaration of war" against the new Republic as well as "a new campaign against Jewry."[25]

Claß summarized his presentation with a clear message to the meeting's assembled members. The Pan-Germans and their allies would oppose the new republic at all costs. Germany lost the war because of an unfortunate combination of "un-German" influences, not because the authoritarian, monarchical system itself was flawed. In effect, the National Assembly then meeting in Weimar would surely produce "an un-German government forced upon them by the victorious Allies."[26] Claß concluded that the League could "never recognize a government so overburdened with cowardliness and criminality, a regime which is merely a child of mutiny in the face of the enemy."[27] In this spirit, the Pan-German League

---

[22]   SGA, 16–17 February 1919, BARCH R8048/123, 11.

[23]   Ibid., 13.

[24]   Ibid., 13–14.

[25]   Claß, *WdS v. II*, 450.

[26]   SGA, 16–17 February 1919, BARCH R8048/123, 13.

[27]   Ibid., 14.

declared its unequivocal opposition to the new republican system by approving the "Bamberg Declaration" on 17 February 1919.

The Declaration was to serve several major purposes. First, it would defend the Pan-German League against critics who accused it of war-mongering and fanatical annexationism by "objectively" explaining the League's position. Secondly, the statement would demonstrate to the League's foreign and domestic enemies, and to other disparate elements of the German Right, that the Pan-Germans had survived the war and were prepared to fight the new order. Finally, it would serve as the guiding program for the League's future work.[28] By no means, however, was the Declaration thought of as a guide exclusively for the League's members. Indeed, the Pan-German leaders hoped to expose broad segments of the German population to their message, especially middle- and upper-middle class citizens shocked by Germany's defeat and eager to channel their anger through new membership in an organization like the Pan-German League.[29]

Although the original version of the Bamberg Declaration appeared on the front page of the Pan-German League's newspaper the *Alldeutsche Blätter* on 1 March 1919, its ultimate distribution was far more extensive.[30] In the months following the Bamberg meeting, the League's leadership corresponded extensively with editors from a wide range of national, regional, and special-interest newspapers. As a result of these negotiations, the League ultimately distributed almost 700,000 copies of the Bamberg Declaration in the first half of 1919 to be used as inserts, supplements, or special editions.[31] This extensive distribution throughout Germany ensured that hundreds of thousands of Germany's citizens would be exposed to the Pan-German League's attack on the Weimar state.

---

[28]   Ibid., 16.

[29]   Ibid., 21.

[30]   The Pan-German League's *Alldeutsche Blätter* first issued the Bamberg Declaration was on 1 March 1919. It has also been reprinted in its entirety in: Werner Jochmann, *Nationalsozialismus und Revolution: Ursprung und Geschichte der NSDAP in Hamburg, 1922–1933, Dokumente* (Frankfurt am Main, 1963), 10–24.

[31]   BARCH R8048/603, 1–43. Over 50 different publications carried the Bamberg Declaration (number of copies in parentheses). They ranged from small, special interest newspapers/ journals like the *Deutsche Richterzeitung-Organ des deutschen Richterbundes*, Hannover (11,500) or the *Wirte Zeitung für Magdeburg und die Provinz Sachsen – Alleiniges Organ von über 50 Gastwirtsvereinen* (7,500), to major national newspapers/journals like the *Allgemeiner Anzeiger*, Braunschweig (55,000), *Deutsche Tageszeitung*, Berlin (65,000), *Deutschlands Erneuerung* (J.F. Lehmann's journal) Munich (8,000), *Hamburger Nachrichten* (35,000), or the *Süddeutsche Zeitung*, Stuttgart (20,000). The largest request came from the *Leipziger Neuste Nachrichten* which ordered 135,000 copies for its local edition and another 50,000 for its foreign edition.

The Declaration's content warrants attention insofar as it establishes the general principles that influenced the Pan-German League's action throughout the Weimar period. Three major issues stand out in this regard. First, the Pan-German League sought to refute unequivocally the accusation that it drove Germany into World War I and unnecessarily prolonged the war once it seemed clear that Germany had lost. The League demanded that Germany and the Allies open their foreign office archives to expose the "truth" behind the outbreak of World War I. This act would, the Declaration stated, prove conclusively that the responsibility for the war lay with the Allies, not Germany or the Pan-German League.[32] Additionally, the statement carried in bold letters the wholly unfounded assertion that "even the Social Democrat [Karl] Kautsky who, during the revolutionary upheavals, gained access to the foreign office archive ... found nothing in the files which presented the Pan-Germans as the instigators of the war."[33]

Secondly, in spite of the nation's complete breakdown, the Pan-German League still believed that the German people themselves could be saved. Toward this end, the League vowed to work tirelessly to awaken in the German people a renewed sense of "national consciousness." Germans needed to be "inoculated" with the will to overcome the shame of defeat so that they could again be worthy of their name. This new-found pride would in turn become the driving force of "völkisch re-birth."[34] The Declaration argued that the German people were simply not suited to a democratic form of government, but rather needed to trust strong leadership represented by a monarchy. On this point the League affirmed that "we remain particularly strongly attached to the monarchical ideal and we trust that this concept will retain the age-old efficacy with which it has proven itself repeatedly in our history."[35]

The third and most significant point for those gathered at the Bamberg meeting was the League's policy regarding the so-called Jewish Question. In fact, the Pan-German League's anti-Semitic agenda stemmed directly from their larger attempt to renew national consciousness among all true Germans. The Declaration stated "The power-political demands of national rebirth find their direct counterpart in the necessity to curb Jewish influence in domestic-political, moral, and cultural matters."[36] To effect this change, the League pledged to support all measures which "calmly and firmly insure that Germany belongs to the Germans and that all its domestic, foreign, cultural,

---

[32] *Alldeutsche Blätter*, 1 March 1919, 1.

[33] Ibid.

[34] Ibid.

[35] Ibid.

[36] Ibid.

and economic decisions will be guided by this principle."[37] This essential policy was based on the "indisputable fact" that the Jews constitute a "foreign element" of the national population and that "the rejection of their claims to power has absolutely nothing to do with questions of faith."[38] German statecraft could therefore only be conducted, comprehended, and supported by men who are raised and who feel truly "German."

The Declaration closed by reaffirming the Pan-German League's commitment to Germany's rebirth. Throughout the past 30 years the League's warnings were supposedly too often ignored even though later events proved that its advice had been sound. Even if others gave up hope, the Pan-Germans would continue to trumpet Germany's greatness and would remain true to its people. "We look back on the past with a clean conscience, and with a clean conscience we now begin our work ... may our greatest glory be that others see in us the shock troops of the völkisch cause. Praise to the German Volk!"[39] Within three and a half months of the proclamation of the new republic, the Pan-German League had declared its undying hatred toward it.

First Steps

The Bamberg Declaration and the League's calls to action that preceded it clarified several important issues for the organization's leadership and members. Indeed, in the months following the Declaration's publication, many League members began to promote the Pan-German cause with increased commitment. This activity was evident throughout the country as many of the League's local and regional chapters began active recruitment programs and initiated contact with other groups on the Right to spread the Pan-German message. An examination of the League's local group (*Ortsgruppe*) in Dresden provides a clear example of attempts by local Pan-German members to fulfill the major goals put forth at Bamberg.

One of the Dresden chapter's first major actions was to provide members and financial support for the Saxon citizen councils (*Bürgerrate*).[40] In the

---

[37]   Ibid.

[38]   Ibid.

[39]   Ibid.

[40]   Allgemeine Schriftwechsel (hereafter "AgS"), Stadtarchiv Dresden, Alldeutscher Verband-Ortsgruppe Dresden und Oberelbgau (hereafter "StADresden ADV-OD") 1919/2, 243. The local chapter (*Ortsgruppe*) in Dresden was one of the largest and most active local groups in Germany. The group's archive includes over 100 folders with extensive correspondence, flyers, and situation reports covering all aspects of right-wing politics in Dresden and eastern Saxony.

November Revolution's aftermath, many Saxon burghers organized so-called citizen defense leagues in Dresden and other major cities.[41] These leagues also appeared in many other parts of Germany from the end of 1918 through the spring and summer of 1919.[42] The Saxon citizen leagues intended to counter the socialist workers' councils that effectively ran municipal government in the state starting in mid-November 1918. These groups promised to defend bourgeois civil-rights and uphold the basic tenets of a free-market economy. In addition to the formal reorganization of the Saxon bourgeois party structure to compete with the SPD and the USPD, these citizen leagues played an important role in organizing opposition to the workers' councils and in mobilizing large segments of the Saxon *Bürgertum* for future political action against the Left.[43]

In the period immediately following the Bamberg Declaration's publication, the Pan-German League's Dresden chapter also significantly increased its public speeches and discussion evenings with the goal of attracting new members to their cause.[44] Their speeches became more frequent through the first half of 1920 and touched on a wide range of issues essential to the League's new campaign for German rebirth. The speeches bore titles like: "The German Spirit in National Reconstruction"; "Socialism's Current Direction"; "The Jewish Danger"; "Völkisch Life in the German Home"; and "Bismarck's Heritage for Our Times."[45] These presentations by prominent local and national right-wing speakers lent additional prestige to the League's cause and served as important public venues for disseminating Pan-German propaganda.

Furthermore, the Dresden chapter began a city-wide campaign to found an adult evening school (*Volkshochschule*) to promote a wide range of nationalist topics.[46] This school was to "encourage a strong völkisch, national consciousness" for a wide range of Dresden's citizenry.[47] A prominent member of the League's local chapter, Bruno Tanzmann, headed the school campaign. Starting on 15 July 1919 and running every Sunday for the following 15 weeks, Tanzmann presented a series of lectures under the general title "Fifteen Speeches on German Ideas" that were intended to increase popular support for the founding

---

[41] For more detailed information on the activities and history of the *Bürgerräte* in Saxony see: Benjamin Lapp, *Revolution from the Right: Politics, Class, and the Rise of Nazism in Saxony, 1919–1933* (Atlantic Highlands, 1997), esp. 29–36.

[42] See, for example, Peter Fritzsche, *Rehearsals for Fascism: Populism and Political Mobilization in Weimar Germany* (Oxford, 1990), 28–32, 71–75.

[43] Lapp, *Revolution from the Right*, 29.

[44] *Jahresbericht* 1918/1919, StADresden ADV-OD/50, 129–139.

[45] Ibid., 130–131. See also: *Jahresbericht* 1919/1920, StADresden ADV-OD/50, 140–141.

[46] *Jahresbericht* 1918/1919, StADresden ADV-OD/50, 133–134.

[47] Ibid., 133.

of the *Volkshochschule*. The school, christened the *Bismarckhochschule*, officially opened on 27 October 1919 with a four-evening series of lectures.[48]

The Dresden chapter, like the national organization itself, also emphasized the crucial importance of the "Jewish Question" for Germany's future. As the chapter's official yearly report stated in 1919:

> To this point, one spoke of a 'Jewish Question.' It is no longer a 'question.' It has grown into an obvious Jewish threat through the further encroachment of the corrosive Jewish influence in public life, through the disgraceful agitation of the Pan-Jewish press during the war, and through the now crystal-clear responsibility of this group for Germany's collapse. This danger must be combated by all means.[49]

To further this general campaign against Jewish influence, several of the Dresden chapter's most prominent leaders helped organize the "Working Group for the Promotion of Germanic Character" in the first half of 1919.[50] The group was to serve as an umbrella organization for all völkisch groups in Dresden and the surrounding area. The organization would coordinate the activities and propaganda of individual right-wing groups so that time and effort were not duplicated or wasted, especially in the campaign to educate Dresden's citizenry on the gravity of the Jewish problem.[51] This Dresden organization was tied to a larger, recently created national organization in Berlin called the "Central Office of Patriotic Leagues" (Zentralstelle vaterländischer Verbände).[52] On a smaller scale, this early effort prefigured the founding of the much more extensive and influential United Patriotic Leagues of Germany (Vereinigte vaterländische

---

[48]   *Jahresbericht* 1919/1920, StADresden ADV-OD/50, 142. The Dresden chapter continued to support the school financially and in its advertisements. In 1920 and again in 1921, the chapter paid out 500 Marks directly to the school and several prominent local Pan-Germans remained on the board of directors. See: *Jahresbericht* 1920/1921, StADresden ADV-OD/50, 145.

[49]   *Jahresbericht* 1918/1919, StADresden ADV-OD/50, 134.

[50]   Ibid., 134–135.

[51]   For example see the three-page draft letter circulated by this group dated 24 September 1919 in: AgS 1919, StADresden ADV-OD/2, 116–118.

[52]   The Dresden chapter made a special financial contribution to the creation of this national organization in Berlin. *Jahresbericht* 1919/1920, StADresden ADV-OD/50, 142. For more information on these early patriotic umbrella organizations see: Kurt Finker, "Vereinigte vaterländische Verbände Deutschlands (VvVD) 1922–1933/34," in Dieter Fricke (ed.), *Lexikon zur Parteiengeschichte: Die bürgerlichen und kleinbürgerlichen Parteien und Verbände in Deutschland (1789–1945)* (Köln and Leipzig, 1986), vol. 4, 314–321. See also: James Diehl, "Von der 'Vaterlandspartei' zur 'Nationalen Revolution', die 'Vereinigten vaterländischen Verbände Deutschlands' (VvVD) 1922–1932," *Vierteljahrshefte für Zeitgeschichte*, 33, 1985, 617–639.

Verbände Deutschlands) in Berlin on 20 January 1923.[53] To support the Dresden chapter's initial efforts, the Pan-German League sponsored two major evening lectures. The first talk on 31 May 1919, titled "The Battle of the German Press," was given by the nationally recognized editor of the Pan-German-controlled *Deutsche Zeitung*, Reinhold Wulle. On 5 July 1919, Alfred Jacobsen, a prominent Hamburg lawyer, national Pan-German leader and DNVP member, gave a speech on the "Jewish Threat."[54]

All of this activity paid off in the years immediately following the end of World War I. The League's Dresden chapter grew dramatically from a low point immediately following the war of 519 active members to the highest total in its history roughly two years later with 690 at the end of 1922.[55] This pattern mirrored the League's success at the national level. After losing members in the immediate aftermath of the war and the November Revolution, the Pan-German League gained members regularly until the end of 1922, when inflation began to force some members out because they were unable to pay dues. At the end of 1922, however, the Pan-German League had attained its highest membership total with roughly 38,000 active members.[56] At the local, regional, and national level, the League's message as presented by the Bamberg Declaration not only ensured the League's survival but also helped the Pan-Germans set new membership records.

Events at the national level also indicated that the Bamberg Declaration was an important step in the League's attempt to translate its words into meaningful action. Of all of the issues with which the Bamberg Declaration dealt, the League's leadership and the majority of its members felt that the so-called Jewish problem deserved greatest emphasis. It provided a clear, concrete starting point from which the Pan-German League could begin its campaign to restore Germany's greatness more generally. In this sense, the Bamberg meeting accomplished one more very important thing: it established a new, mass organization with the express purpose of combating presumed Jewish influence in all areas of German

---

[53] The Pan-German League was heavily involved in the founding and overall leadership of this organization at both the national and regional level. Finker, "VvVD," 316–321, and Diehl, "Von der 'Vaterlandspartei," 618–626. For a contemporary perspective on the formation of the VvVD, see: Gen. Major a.D. Graf v.d. Goltz, "Die vaterländischen Verbande," in Bernhard Harms (ed.), *Volk und Reich der Deutschen*, vol. II (Berlin, 1929), esp. 173–177.

[54] Wulle and Jacobsen were in high demand as speakers for the Pan-German League, the DNVP, as well as other major right-wing organizations. Their appearance in Dresden certainly lent credibility to the League's efforts there. See: *Jahresbericht* 1918/1919, StADresden ADV-OD/50, 135.

[55] See pages from the following *Jahresberichte*: 1918/1919, 138; 1919/1920, 143; 1920/1921, 145; 1921/1922, 148.

[56] SGA, 1–2 December 1928, BARCH R8048/156, 55–56.

life. This organization soon became known as the German Völkisch Offensive and Defensive Alliance (*Deutschvölkischer Schutz- und Trutzbund*—hereafter "SuTB").

In reality, the Pan-German League's business management committee meeting in September 1918 already laid the groundwork for SuTB's founding. At this meeting the Pan-German League clarified its stance on the "Jewish Question" and the anti-Semitic movement in Germany as a whole.[57] To address this specific issue, the members voted to create a special "Jewish Committee." Directed by the League's assistant chairmen Leopold von Vietinghoff-Scheel and General Konstantin von Gebsattel, this special committee would develop a systematic approach to the Jewish Question and report to the membership at the next meeting on its progress. Included on this panel were some of the Pan-German League's most prominent members: Theodor Fritsch and Alfred Roth from the Reichshammerbund; Professor Paul Langhans from the Deutschbund; and Professor Adolf Bartels, the well-known anti-Semitic literary historian.[58]

At the League's next meeting in Berlin in October 1918, Leopold von Vietinghoff-Scheel opened a general discussion about the League's stance on the Jewish Question. All those in attendance expressed the strong commitment to deal directly and publicly with the threat that the "Jewish influence" posed to Germany. The League's chairman Heinrich Claß argued that this issue had to be dealt with not only economically and politically, but also in a more practical fashion. Claß explained that even the casual reader of "Jewish-controlled" newspapers like the *Frankfurter Zeitung* could clearly see the Jewish agenda for Germany's destruction.[59] Furthermore, he argued, the Jews now dictatorially controlled large segments of Germany, especially Berlin.

Other prominent members agreed wholeheartedly with Claß. One member, Professor Gebhard, argued that "the importance of the Jewish Question cannot

---

[57]   Lohalm, *Völkischer Radikalismus*, 19–20.

[58]   Ibid., 19.

[59]   SGA, 19–20 February, BARCH R8048/121, 75. Claß and the Pan-German League repeatedly came under fire in the Center/Left press. The *Frankfurter Zeitung* wasted little time in continuing its criticism of the Pan-Germans in the post-war period. For example, on 2 September 1919 the newspaper reported: "The Reaction is on the March! ... after only a brief period of silence following the revolution, the Pan-Germans are rearing their head again more boldly than ever before ... After poisoning the German people and dividing them during the war, they [the Pan-Germans] now hope to harvest the fruits of their subversive activities." *Frankfurter Zeitung*, 2 September 1919, 2. The USPD's official paper *Die Freiheit* also blasted the Pan-Germans and warned of their increasing influence in German public life: "It was proven already during the war that, with the significant help of their financial backers, they [the Pan-Germans]secured a wide-ranging influence ... and it is to be feared that they may now succeed in making inroads ... among the bourgeoisie again." *Die Freiheit*, 2 September 1919, 2.

be overstated." Indeed, he continued, Germany's defeat in the war could be directly attributed to the destructive influence of the Jews in all areas of German life. Agreeing with Heinrich Claß's earlier assertion, Gebhard stated that "the Jewish Question cannot be handled piecemeal, or simply from an economic perspective. It must be dealt with directly and in the broadest sense as an ideological battle."[60] As with many other members in attendance, Gebhard argued emphatically that the Pan-German League take the lead on this issue. The general desire for a direct response to the Jewish Question, as well as the behind-the-scenes work of the "Jewish Committee," came to rapid fruition at the League's Bamberg meeting in February 1919.

As Heinrich Claß recalled in his memoirs, there was widespread interest within the Pan-German League and among its close allies for some clear, decisive action to be taken to fight the Jews' "pernicious influence" in Germany. The question of means was, however, open to debate. After the League's members unanimously approved the Bamberg Declaration's final draft, they turned to the Jewish Question and the possible ways it could be effectively addressed. The members favored the creation of a new organization with the express purpose of combating Jewish influence in Germany.[61] The Pan-German leadership felt that the League was already so overloaded with work in its broader attempt to recruit new members and create a unified anti-government right-wing movement, that it alone would be unable to devote the necessary resources and single-minded focus to such a task. The proposed campaign against the Jews was of such major importance that it would require the undivided attention of a separate organization. With this in mind, those gathered at Bamberg voted to create a new group charged with the direct responsibility to "protect German culture from the threat of Jews ... and to make this threat clear by any means necessary to the broadest possible audience, especially in the masses of the working-class."[62]

The SuTB's founding committee remained in Bamberg for several weeks following the formal end of the League's meeting. These men, including Heinrich Claß and Konstantin von Gebsattel, the former leader of the League's "Jewish Committee," sat down to draft the major guidelines for the new organization.[63] By the beginning of March they had completed the SuTB's by-laws. Despite some minor changes in October 1920, these by-laws remained intact throughout the SuTB's existence. A three-man managing committee composed of leading Pan-Germans headed the new organization. The committee's leader was the decorated war veteran Captain Alfred Roth from Hamburg. The other two

---

[60]   SGA, 19–20 October 1918, BARCH R8048/121, 75.

[61]   SGA, 16–17 February 1919, BARCH R8048/123, 22.

[62]   Ibid.

[63]   Claß, *WdS v. II*, 453–455.

members were Alfred Jacobsen and General von Gebsattel. With these three men firmly in control of the organization, the Pan-German League could be sure that its influence on the SuTB would remain decisive. Indeed, control of this organization was purposely concentrated in this three-man committee.[64] The managing committee made all major decisions regarding financing, propaganda, formation of local chapters, and the dates and location of the SuTB's "German Day" (the annual national gathering) after consultation with a broader advisory committee composed of prominent local group leaders.

The SuTB made an immediate impact and attracted unexpectedly large numbers of committed members. By the end of 1919, the group could count slightly over 30,000 members. In May 1920, that number had reached 70,000, and by the end of 1920 the group had attracted almost 110,000 members. Ultimately, the SuTB reached its high-point in early 1922 with almost 170,000 members.[65] This child of the Pan-German League had become very successful in a relatively short period of time. However, its open and direct anti-Semitic agitation also proved to be its undoing.

The Weimar government kept very close tabs on the SuTB and when, in June 1922, the Jewish government minister Walther Rathenau was assassinated, the SuTB and the Pan-German League came under immediate suspicion. Although a federal court later ruled that the SuTB played no direct role in Rathenau's assassination, the Weimar government first temporarily outlawed and then formally dissolved the group in January 1923 under the "Law for the Protection of the Republic."[66] The high court that upheld the dissolution ruled that the SuTB had created an environment in which anti-Semitic actions, even violent ones, could become acceptable. Even though the group's leaders did not actually murder Rathenau, the court maintained that they contributed to the climate in which such an act against a government minister could take place and, therefore, the group had supported an attack on the Weimar state itself.[67]

Ultimately, the Pan-German League's creation of the SuTB is significant for three major reasons. First, it marked the earliest attempt by any major right-wing

---

[64]   Ibid., 454–455. For a more detailed analysis of the organization and structure, see: Lohalm, *Völkischer Radikalismus*, 88–121.

[65]   BARCH R8048/253, 108–109, and Lohalm, *Völkischer Radikalismus*, 89–90.

[66]   On the SuTB's dissolution see: Lohalm, *Völkischer Radikalismus*, 210–272. For the Law for the Protection of the Republic and its impact see: Gotthard Jasper, *Der Schutz der Republik. Studien zur staatlichen Sicherung der Demokratie in der Weimarer Republik 1922–1930* (Tübingen, 1963).

[67]   For a superb study of the Rathenau assassination and its broader implications see: Martin Sabrow, *Die Verdrängte Verschwörung. Der Rathenaumord und die deutsche Gegenrevolution* (Frankfurt am Main, 1999).

group to build a broad-based mass organization that openly espoused an anti-Semitic and anti-democratic agenda in the Weimar period.[68] Secondly, it provides a clear example of the League's broader Weimar strategy of gaining influence over other right-wing groups through a network of personal political connections without necessarily exposing the Pan-German League itself to direct attention. Finally, the SuTB's ultimate collapse also illustrates the limitations of the Pan-German approach to political power. While the SuTB enjoyed remarkable early success, it could not sustain its dynamic growth and failed to translate its early popularity into more tangible political influence. In spite of Pan-German efforts to undermine the Weimar Republic with an extra-parliamentary radical nationalist organization like the SuTB, the League's leaders also realized that they could not simply ignore the realm of party politics. Ultimately, it was in that realm that the Pan-German League would have its greatest influence on the development of the German Right during the Weimar period.

Political Parties and the New System

The Pan-German League's relationship to organized political parties and party politics was ambiguous from the League's founding. In one sense, the Pan-Germans supported a vague, organic notion of politics in which the elite, guided by a strong monarchy, would paternalistically enforce policy for the rest of society. Therefore, many Pan-Germans considered the development of formal party politics in Imperial Germany to be divisive and destructive to the overall life of the people. However, with the formalization of political parties and their growing importance to the political process, the Pan-Germans were forced to develop a coherent stance on the importance of certain parties and leaders.

In the pre-1914 period, the Pan-German League claimed to support any political party that furthered the nationalist cause. In reality, this meant a complete rejection of the Social Democrats, the Center Party, and the Progressives.[69] Throughout World War I, the League's earlier ties to the National Liberals broke down. The National Liberal Party had ceased to be a dominant force in many areas already before the war and the Pan-Germans felt that most liberals were generally moving too far to the Left. By contrast, the League began to improve its relationship with the German Conservative Party because of growing frustration with the allegedly weak policies promoted by

---

[68]   On earlier unsuccessful attempts to develop specifically anti-Semitic political parties in the Second Reich, see: Richard S. Levy, *The Downfall of the Anti-Semitic Political Parties in Imperial Germany* (New Haven and London, 1975).

[69]   Chickering, *We Men Who Feel Most German*, 203.

Chancellor Bethman Hollweg.[70] In conjunction with a younger, more aggressive generation of conservative politicians, the Pan-Germans gradually came to play a significant role within the Conservative Party. The Conservatives ultimately supported many of the Pan-German League's most extreme war-aims and backed the German war effort to the bitter end. The end of World War I and the re-formation of the political party system solidified the relationship between key Pan-Germans and the new conservative German National People's Party (*Deutschnationale Volkspartei*—hereafter "DNVP").[71]

The League articulated its stance on the new party system and its support for the DNVP very early in the Weimar Republic. One of the most prominent representatives of the new Pan-German/DNVP alliance was the Breslau professor Dr. Axel Freiherr von Freytagh-Loringhoven. He was a key member of the Pan-German League's executive committee, a prominent member of the DNVP's constitutional committee, and one of the party's most visible speakers. In a lengthy speech presented to a nationalist audience in Breslau on 3 January 1919, Freytagh-Loringhoven detailed the Pan-German position on politics and the party system in the Weimar period.[72] He began with a background discussion of the development of liberal and conservative strains within the bourgeois political context.

Freytagh-Loringhoven identified two major strands in what he referred to as the German bourgeois worldview: liberalism and conservatism. Both emerged from the turmoil of the French Revolution. The notions of freedom and equality promoted by the French and imposed on large parts of Germany by Napoleon's military successes led to the glorification of individualism. Freedom and equality in the sense of the French Revolution meant the destruction of the old order in Prussia and elsewhere in Germany. It created a "completely atomized mush in which individualism ran its course without the least consideration for the

---

[70]   On the League's growing ties to the Conservative and Free-Conservative parties in the years leading up to World War I see: Eley, *Reshaping the German Right*, esp. 316–334; Chickering, *We Men Who Feel Most German*, esp. 278–283; Abraham Peck, *Radicals and Reactionaries: The Crisis of Conservatism in Wilhelmine Germany* (Washington, DC, 1978), esp. 107–111 and 128–150; and James N. Retallack, *Notables of the Right: The Conservative Party and Political Mobilization in Germany, 1876–1918* (Boston, 1988), esp. 210–221.

[71]   The German National People's Party emerged in late November 1918. It represented overwhelmingly elements of the pre-war Free-Conservative and Conservative parties. Until the Nazi party's rapid expansion in 1929–1930, the DNVP consistently proved to be the largest right-wing party during the Weimar Republic. For the party's founding and early history see: Werner Liebe, *Die Deutschnationale Volkspartei 1918–1924* (Düsseldorf, 1956).

[72]   Axel Freiherr von Freytagh-Loringhoven, *Bügerliche und sozialistische Weltanschauung*. Published in the series of lectures and pamphlets by the *Deutschnationale Volkspartei-Landesverband Schlesien* (Breslau, 1919).

good of the whole society."[73] This individualistic "mush," according to Freytagh-Loringhoven, represented liberalism's most basic form.

German conservatism emerged as an essential counterweight to this onslaught. Conservatism fought liberalism's destructive effects by establishing itself as the true protector of society's well-being as a whole. Freytagh-Loringhoven explained that while liberalism sought to elevate the individual and his concerns above the common needs of society and the state, conservatives preserved the common good by reinforcing the state's power and authority. This did not mean, however, a simplistic reactionary response to preserve the power structures of the Old Order. As Freytagh-Loringhoven concluded:

> For those who fought this battle [against liberalism and individualism], their emphasis was not merely on the stuffy rejection of the new for its own sake ... but rather on the preservation of the interest of the whole, the State ... Therefore, simply holding on to medieval constitutional forms could not be conservatism's goal. The key was the protection of the state's interests against the boundless individualism that the liberal message preached.[74]

With the rapid pace of industrialization later in the nineteenth century, liberalism sought to form a tactical alliance with socialism. According to Freytagh-Loringhoven, the key to this alliance was both groups' common hatred of bourgeois government. On the one hand, liberals sought to minimize the influence and the power of the state over the rights of the individual. Since their creation, socialists had worked for a complete overthrow of any bourgeois anti-worker state. In forging this alliance, however, liberalism gradually began to take on more and more socialist elements. In their desire to reduce the role of the state, liberals had ironically sacrificed their basic notion of individualism to the mass-based socialist movement. Freytagh-Loringhoven argued that liberalism gradually moved further away from its original goal of individual freedom, and was swept up in the "socialist stream." The final result, particularly evident in the last years before World War I, was that liberalism had surrendered its independence. Although "liberal" parties still existed in name, they were in reality no more than "socialist pawns."[75]

From this argument, Freytagh-Loringhoven deduced several specific tactics. With this long-term development and the consequent rise of socialism, conservatism was now the only true force left to uphold the state and

---

[73] Ibid., 12.

[74] Ibid., 12–13.

[75] Ibid., 24–26.

promote the bourgeois worldview. Those liberals who rejected the alliance with socialism—especially those on the right of the National Liberal Party—had simply moved further to embrace conservatism. Therefore, according to Freytagh-Loringhoven's curious analysis, the basic political choice in 1919 was conservatism or socialism. Conservatism stood for a strong monarchical state, an efficient military, and an aggressive foreign policy. It supported the Christian church and school, the sanctity of marriage, private property, and the rule of law (the *Rechtsstaat*). Ultimately, Freytagh-Loringhoven assured the crowd that the battle between these two worldviews could not be resolved by cowardly compromise or concessions. Only a victorious conclusion to this battle would prove that "the German bourgeoisie is suited for, and deserving of, its continued existence."[76]

While this narrative highlighted the general conceptual background of the League's movement toward a strong alliance with conservatism, Freytagh-Loringhoven did not articulate the Pan-German attitude toward specific parties in the Weimar system. Although ideally the Pan-German League preferred an authoritarian monarchy with a non-socialist party system offering plebiscitary support, even the most radical members of the League realized that the Weimar party system would not be a temporary arrangement. Therefore, the League was forced to evaluate seriously the party system and focus its efforts on those political parties that seemed to best represent Pan-German goals. Although publicly the League continued to claim that it stood "above-the-parties," the Pan-Germans would in fact become deeply embroiled in party politics. Their main party political ally would be the DNVP.

From the Pan-German view, the DNVP remained the only party to hold true to the basic principles of a strong German state:

> If you want a strong, united Germany which stands in honor before the whole world, which protects domestic peace and order, and in which German devotion and German morality are dominant, then you belong under the black-white-red banner of the *Deutschnationale Volkspartei*.[77]

Although Pan-German support for the DNVP vacillated at times between 1919 and 1933, the League's relationship with Germany's dominant conservative

---

[76]   Ibid., 34.

[77]   Excerpt taken from a published collection of five speeches given by Freytagh-Loringhoven in April 1919. Axel Freiherr von Freytagh-Loringhoven, *Politik: Eine Einführung in Gegenwartsfragen* (Munich, 1919), 88.

party was never in serious doubt.[78] As this study will demonstrate, the Pan-German League's influence on the DNVP would ultimately prove to be of immense importance for the development of the German Right and the fate of the Weimar Republic more broadly.

The Kapp Putsch

In spite of its prominent position within the post-war German Right, the Pan-German League was by no means the only disaffected radical nationalist group that sought to destabilize or even overthrow the new government. In fact, the League's early anti-democratic efforts often led it into negotiations with other similarly-minded organizations and individuals. Such was the case in the short-lived relationship between the Pan-German League and the political circle surrounding Wolfgang Kapp.[79]

Wolfgang Kapp's first formal contact with the Pan-German League came the day after the founding of the German Fatherland Party (*Deutsche Vaterlandspartei*) on 1 September 1917. Disparate nationalist groups formed the party to counteract the growing peace movement and the increasing war-weariness of large segments of the German population. The party brought together large segments of the pre-war nationalist bloc including elements of the Conservative and Free-Conservative parties and a variety of non-party political interest groups. This new political force formally supported the most extreme right-wing annexationist goals and demanded that the government continue to fight the war until a decisive German victory was achieved.[80]

Kapp asked Claß to join on 2 September 1917, and after he became a member Claß and other Pan-Germans played a major role in the organization and propaganda of the party. Toward the end of the war, however, Claß became disillusioned with Kapp's leadership of the organization. Claß felt that Kapp was unable to see the larger picture and questioned his basic commitment to the organization. The Fatherland Party did not survive beyond Germany's defeat

---

[78] The most common concern about the DNVP was the existence within its ranks of weak "compromise" politicians. Already in early 1919, the Pan-German League made clear that it supported the DNVP for its strong, uncompromisingly nationalistic goals. For more on this discussion see: SGA, 16–17 February 1919, BARCH R8048/123, 13–14.

[79] Kapp was a prominent figure of the German right during and after the war and was instrumental in the founding and direction of the German Fatherland Party during World War I. For a useful biographical sketch of Kapp see: Hagenlücke, *Deutsche Vaterlandspartei*, 109–142.

[80] On the Fatherland Party's platform and major goals see: ibid., 192–215.

in World War I and Claß and Kapp maintained only irregular contact in the immediate post-war period.[81]

The next major step in Kapp's relationship to the Pan-German League came at the end of 1919 in Berlin. Kapp attended a meeting of the League's Berlin chapter where Claß's close personal friend and economics expert Paul Bang spoke on the relationship between statecraft and the economy.[82] Kapp spoke with both Bang and Claß afterward and explained how deeply impressed he was with Bang's presentation. Several days after the meeting, Kapp contacted Bang and invited him to join his counterrevolutionary circle. Bang had developed a deep hatred of the new German government and he believed Kapp's plans for an overthrow seemed promising.

Indeed, Kapp's group had initially devoted a great deal of time and effort to its plan for the overthrow of the German government. Toward the end of October Kapp's organization founded the "National Association" (*Nationale Vereinigung*—hereafter "NV") as an umbrella organization designed to unify various paramilitary forces already in Germany, and to recruit forces returning from the East. This organization clearly represented the rabidly anti-government sentiment of Kapp and his associates.[83] In practical terms, the most significant member of the NV was its general-secretary Waldemar Pabst. He was a highly decorated veteran of World War I and had previously served in the elite *Garde-Kavallerie-Schützen-Division* until he was discovered in July 1919 to be planning a Putsch attempt of his own against the government.[84]

During the winter of 1919–1920 Pabst had some success in fomenting significant discontent and anti-government feeling within many of the paramilitary units. With his extensive military background, Pabst found it relatively easy to establish contacts with a number of prominent paramilitary leaders, and he initiated extensive propaganda efforts to increase or maintain

---

[81]   For Claß's role in the Fatherland Party and his early relationship with Wolfgang Kapp, see: Claß, *WdS v. II*, 208–227. On the Pan-German League's relationship to the Fatherland Party, see: Hagenlücke, *Deutsche Vaterlandspartei*, 352–362.

[82]   Claß, *WdS v. II*, 531. The speaker, Paul Bang, was one of Heinrich Claß's closest friends and advisors. He was also one of the Pan-German League's experts on economics and financial issues. On the Claß-Bang relationship, see: Claß, *WdS v. II*, 486–490.

[83]   For a more detailed examination of the composition and history of the *Nationale Vereinigung* see: Johannes Erger, *Der Kapp-Lüttwitz-Putsch: Ein Beitrag zur deutschen Innenpolitik, 1919/1920* (Düsseldorf, 1967), esp. 85–107.

[84]   James M. Diehl, *Paramilitary Politics in Weimar Germany* (Bloomington, 1977), 67, and Erger, *Kapp-Lüttwitz Putsch*, 89. For Pabst's own version of the Kapp Putsch and the events leading to it, see: Waldemar Pabst, "Das Kapp-Unternehmen," in Wulf Bley (ed.), *Revolutionen der Weltgeschichte* (Munich, 1933).

the anti-government leanings among angry Free Corps (*Freikorps*) units.[85] Pabst placed special emphasis on influencing returning Baltic Free Corps members, and the newly created "Civil Guard" (*Einwohnerwehren*) units in Germany.[86] He also gained support for the NV's plans among these various paramilitary units, and he tentatively settled on Hermann Erhardt's brigade to lead the assault on Berlin.[87] When Pabst secured the support of General Walther von Lüttwitz, a high-ranking wartime general with extensive connections to the current army's general staff, it seemed as if the military plans were set.[88] Indeed, when Kapp informed Paul Bang about these preparations, everything appeared to be well under control.

However, when Bang informed Claß and other Pan-German leaders of his involvement with Kapp's Putsch preparations, they were highly skeptical.[89] Claß recounted his negative experience with Kapp in the Fatherland Party. That organization also seemed to hold great promise, but ultimately disintegrated because of a lack of organization and communication. Claß felt that Kapp was, without doubt, a "brave and independent individual, but seriously lacking in his knowledge and assessment of people and unclear in his goals."[90] Nevertheless, Claß grudgingly supported Bang in his decision and agreed that Bang should declare himself ready to associate with the Kapp group and to keep the Pan-German League apprised of any major developments.[91] The League was kept

---

[85] Diehl, *Paramilitary Politics*, 67–68, and Erger, *Kapp-Lüttwitz Putsch*, 90–97.

[86] The *Einwohnerwehren* were regional, ad hoc, civilian militia units. Their staying power and reliability varied greatly from unit to unit. In December 1918 in Berlin, for example, hundreds of small Civil Guard organizations sprung up in the wealthy conservative, middle-class districts and suburbs to protect banks and other buildings from robbery and looting. See: Diehl, *Paramilitary Politics*, 32–38.

[87] Ehrhardt was a prominent *Freikorps* leader. His unit, the "Ehrhardt Brigade," was the best organized and trained of all the *Freikorps* units. The Brigade itself had already seen extensive action in defeating the short-lived revolution in Munich in April 1919 and fighting Polish insurgents in Upper Silesia in August 1919. The unit swelled with new troops returning from the Baltic in the second half of 1919. On Erhardt's role in the preparation for, and execution of, the Kapp Putsch see: Diehl, *Paramilitary Politics*, 67–77; and Erger, *Kapp-Lüttwitz Putsch*, 112–115, 120–152, and 210–216.

[88] Diehl, *Paramilitary Politics*, 68. General von Lüttwitz was brought on board in the hope that his presence in the Kapp government might secure the support of the Republican Army (*Reichswehr*), when the crucial moment came during the Putsch. At the very least, Kapp and others felt that he might ensure *Reichswehr* neutrality that would allow the Putsch time to consolidate control.

[89] Claß, *WdS v. II*, 531.

[90] Ibid., 532–533.

[91] Ibid., 533.

abreast of the preparations in Kapp's camp and Claß soon discovered that General Erich Ludendorff was also a leading member of Kapp's organization.[92] Although several other high-ranking Pan-Germans attempted to bring Claß closer to Kapp's group, Claß remained distant. He firmly believed that the entire enterprise had little chance of success. In particular, he thought that Kapp's political leadership was hopelessly flawed and chronically indecisive.[93]

During the winter of 1919–1920, a series of events occurred that seemed to support Claß's position regarding Wolfgang Kapp's organization. Through their ties to Kapp's group, Claß and other Pan-German leaders were informed that the Ehrhardt Brigade had officially been given the assignment to lead the assault on Berlin. Ehrhardt's forces were to occupy certain crucial strongholds in the city, particularly the key buildings in the government sector, and then capture the Reich president and the leading government ministers. Although Claß had respect for Ehrhardt's unit, he felt that Kapp and Ludendorff had prepared things so haphazardly and with such little attention to secrecy, that most of Germany already knew something of Kapp's intentions. It was, Claß noted, truly amazing that Kapp's group had not already been arrested.[94]

In fact, Claß's worst fears were realized a short time later. Sick in bed with the flu, the Pan-German League's chairman picked up the morning newspaper on 12 March to read that the government had issued an arrest warrant for Kapp and his co-conspirators.[95] Around six o'clock that evening, Bang paid a visit to Claß to inform him of the day's events. Even after the arrest warrant's announcement, Kapp had walked over to the Pan-German League's headquarters near the main government district in Berlin in broad daylight to inform Bang that the time had come for the Putsch to be launched. Kapp explained that his ability to walk the streets freely in spite of a pending arrest warrant only further demonstrated the national government's complete incompetence.[96] At that point, Bang began to have his first serious reservations regarding Kapp's sincerity. Although Bang had tentatively promised to serve in Kapp's new government as finance minister, he was now reconsidering the offer.

---

[92]   After serving with General Paul von Hindenburg as the leader of the German military's High Command during World War I, General Ludendorff became a major right-wing politician. On Ludendorff's political career and the "circle" of acquaintances which surrounded him in the early years of the Weimar Republic see: Bruno Thoß, *Der Ludendorff-Kreis 1919–1923. München als Zentrum der mitteleuropäischen Gegenrevolution zwischen Revolution und Hitler-Putsch* (Munich, 1978).

[93]   Claß, *WdS v. II*, 533.

[94]   Ibid., 534–535.

[95]   Ibid., 534.

[96]   Ibid.

Kapp assured Bang that everything was in order and that all of the ministers-to-be, including Ludendorff, were scheduled to meet at the Brandenburg Gate in the heart of the government sector at seven o'clock the following morning.[97] As Bang explained to Claß, he was not prepared to break his promise to Kapp and gain a reputation as a coward, but he was no longer convinced that the enterprise had any real chance of success. Claß warned Bang for the last time that he should think seriously about whether or not to follow through on his promise to Kapp. Ultimately, however, Bang reluctantly agreed to appear the following morning and take up his position in Kapp's new government cabinet.

On the morning of 13 March, Bang arrived at the Brandenburg gate at precisely seven o'clock. Only some of the Putsch planners including Kapp, the former Berlin police president Traugott von Jagow, and Ludendorff's personal adjutant Colonel Max Bauer joined him. Ludendorff was conspicuously absent from the crowd of conspirators. Bang and the others moved over to the government buildings, took up office, and reported two hours later for the first scheduled cabinet meeting. However, Kapp was forced to cancel the session when his main political advisor Georg Wilhelm Schiele failed to show up with the necessary draft proclamations for the new government.[98]

As these events transpired, Ehrhardt's brigade descended on the other government buildings. Ehrhardt had been slow in bringing his troops into the government quarter and, as a result, President Ebert and his cabinet ministers were able to escape the city and flee first to Dresden and then later to Stuttgart. From Stuttgart, Ebert issued a call for a general strike to which almost the entire country, led by the trade unions, gave support. This strike, combined with ongoing civil service resistance to carry out Kapp's orders, brought the Putsch to an ignominious end within 24 hours.[99] Bang and the other ministers fled the city to escape arrest. Surprisingly however, Bang was never bothered by the authorities or directly implicated in the Putsch itself. The only member of the entire organization to be tried and convicted of treason was the former police minister Traugott von Jagow.[100]

---

[97]   Ibid., 535–536.

[98]   Ibid., 538–539.

[99]   For a detailed account of the Putsch and the government's response see: Erger, *Kapp-Lüttwitz Putsch*, esp. 108–272. Historian Hagen Schulze argues that the Putsch had largely unraveled by the time the strike began because of the fundamental lack of support from the civil service and government bureaucracy for Kapp and his associates. See: Hagen Schulze, *Weimar. Deutschland 1917–1933* (Berlin, 1982), 211–221.

[100]   Ibid., 42 and 295. After initially fleeing to Sweden, Kapp returned to Germany. He died of cancer in June 1922 before his trial could begin.

The Pan-German League criticized the entire endeavor publicly and privately. A front-page article entitled "The 100-Hour Reign" appeared in the Pan-German-controlled daily newspaper the *Deutsche Zeitung* just after the attempted Putsch. The article blasted Kapp for attempting his "counterrevolution" with such ridiculously inadequate means and preparation. "One can only scratch one's head," the article continued, "at the fact that [Kapp] would have seriously had a hand in such a charade."[101] The article clearly separated the Pan-German League from any involvement in the affair and ignored Bang's role. "We know from the Pan-German leadership that there has been no relationship between Mr. Kapp and the Pan-German League for years." The author continued that this "fact" would not, of course, prevent the so-called "truth seekers" on the Left from "reeling out the same old lies and stubbornly spreading them into public life."[102] The Pan-German League was prepared, the article claimed, to fight these charges. It had survived such "storms of lies" in the past and the League would always "stay true to its political path."[103]

Later that summer at the Pan-German League's Berlin meeting on 19–20 June 1920, Claß again criticized the entire enterprise as riddled with "limitless thoughtlessness."[104] He explained that one of the major reasons for the Putsch's overall failure was Kapp's decision to accept Jews and Social Democrats in an attempt to broaden the cabinet's political authority. Clearly, Claß argued, any right-wing movement that was willing to "sell-out" so quickly in this fashion was doomed to failure.[105] Claß asserted that world history "will never again see such a serious issue seized upon with so little understanding, carried out with such cowardliness and lack of commitment."[106]

Ultimately, the Kapp Putsch's failure temporarily crushed any serious hopes that the Pan-German League might have held for an outright overthrow of the government during the Weimar Republic's earliest years. The League had already made clear its fundamental opposition to the democratic system in its Bamberg Declaration, yet it now seemed that a forceful overthrow of the government would be almost impossible in the near future. The failure of Kapp's poorly planned and executed Putsch greatly increased the national spotlight on all potentially dangerous anti-government, right-wing paramilitary activity.

---

[101]   *Deutsche Zeitung*, 24 March 1920, 1. The League's own bi-weekly newspaper the *Alldeutsche Blätter* also sharply attacked Kapp for his lack of planning and preparation. *Alldeutsche Blätter*, 27 March 1920, 1.

[102]   Ibid.

[103]   Ibid.

[104]   SGA, 19–20 June 1920, BARCH R8048/128, 8.

[105]   Ibid.

[106]   Ibid.

In fact, the Pan-German League itself came under increased surveillance by government security forces, and League members were forced to become more careful about their association with other illegal groups.[107] Furthermore, the embarrassing fallout from Kapp's failed Putsch dealt a serious blow to the Pan-German League's hopes for uniting all radical nationalist organizations against the Weimar Republic. As the next chapter will demonstrate, the Pan-Germans soon faced another major threat to their goal of a unified German Right in the League's conflict with Reinhold Wulle, Albrecht von Graefe-Goldebee, General Erich Ludendorff, and the newly founded German Völkisch Freedom Party.

---

[107] The government's focus on the Pan-German League's activities in the period following the Kapp Putsch became very clear when at least three local and regional League chapters (Thuringia, Hamburg, Schaumberg-Lippe) were temporarily banned in the summer of 1922. According to official sources, the government suspected these chapters of various anti-government, right-wing activities and of a possible connection to Walther Rathenau's recent assassination. The government later lifted these bans when it failed to produce sufficient evidence to support the allegations. For the government's charges and the League's response see: BARCH R8048/671, 94b–94d. On the government's response to the German Right in the wake of the Rathenau murder generally see: Mommsen, *Rise and Fall of Weimar Democracy*, 126–128; and Sabrow, *Die Verdrängte Verschwörung*.

Chapter 2
The Völkisch Malaise, 1919–1924

The poor planning, execution, and ultimate failure of the Kapp Putsch dealt the first serious blow to the Pan-German League's plans for greater coordination of the radical Right in the immediate post-war period. However, an even more destructive political conflict lay directly ahead. By 1923, Heinrich Claß and the League had become embroiled in a very public, acrimonious, and bizarre feud with the German Völkisch Freedom Party (*Deutschvölkische Freiheitspartei*—hereafter DVFP), a new political party founded by Reinhold Wulle, Albrecht von Graefe-Goldebee, Wilhelm Henning, Erich Ludendorff, and several other prominent right-wing leaders. As Claß would later comment, the full destructiveness of this split in the völkisch movement became clear only after it was too late to prevent it.

The origin of this intense right-wing political conflict goes back to 1918 and an initially isolated personnel decision in the offices of the Pan-German League's leading daily newspaper. Early that year, Heinrich Claß was forced to replace the chief editor of the *Deutsche Zeitung*.[1] At a time when Germans were suffering from the extreme privations of World War I and the army was preparing to launch its last great offensive in the spring, this decision seemed relatively insignificant. The new candidate, Reinhold Wulle, was a young, energetic member of the Pan-German League's Essen chapter and he had served as the editor-in-chief of the conservative *Rheinisch-Westfälischen Zeitung*. Wulle was well respected in right-wing circles as a writer and editor and Alfred Hugenberg also seriously considered him to take over the recently founded *Telegraphen-Union* news service. Claß became impressed with Wulle's "impartiality" because the young editor refused to support a vicious attack on Claß and the League in the *Rheinisch-Westfälischen Zeitung* by an ex-Pan-German League member Theodor Reismann-Grone.[2]

---

[1]   The previous editor, Lutz Korodi, suddenly had to step down for personal reasons. On the *Deutsche Zeitung*, its relationship to the Pan-German League, the Hugenberg newspaper empire, and its role in the Weimar Republic, see: Heinz-Dietrich Fischer, *Handbuch der politischen Presse in Deutschland 1480–1980* (Düsseldorf, 1981), esp. 497–503.

[2]   On Wulle's background and his early relation to Heinrich Claß, see: Claß, *WdS v. II*, 603–605. For a short biographical sketch of Wulle see also: Reimer Wulff, *Die Deutschvölkische Freiheitspartei 1922–1928* (PhD Dissertation, Marburg University, 1968), esp. 190 n46. A more

After meeting Claß in Essen, Wulle agreed to assume complete control of the paper as of 1 October 1918. Claß returned to Berlin convinced that the *Deutsche Zeitung* had secured a competent new leader and that the paper would continue to serve successfully as the "impartial mouthpiece" of the German Right. Although Claß and the Pan-German leadership could not have predicted it at the time, this new relationship with Reinhold Wulle actually marked the beginning of a highly fractious period in the history of the German Right. Along with the Kapp Putsch and Hitler's "Beer Hall" Putsch in November 1923, these developments would effectively destroy the Pan-German goal of radical nationalist unity by the end of 1924.

Reinhold Wulle and Heinrich Claß: Personal Differences

The explosive conflict that ultimately broke out between Claß, Wulle, and their respective supporters actually began at the personal level. As agreed, Reinhold Wulle showed up for work on 1 October 1918. Although Germany was in terrible shape by that time, Wulle kept his word and immediately poured himself into his work. As Claß recalled, Wulle performed exceedingly well in the first months of his assignment as the head of the *Deutsche Zeitung*. In spite of the kaiser's abdication and the humiliation of the Versailles treaty terms, Wulle continued to improve the newspaper's content and the circulation.[3] Furthermore, Claß was pleased to learn that on occasion, Wulle had used his considerable rhetorical skills to speak in the evenings at local Pan-German League meetings. In short, as long as Wulle did not become too involved in other activities and continued to run the paper efficiently, Claß had every reason to be pleased with his choice. However, much to Claß's dismay, this state of affairs did not last long.

Although Wulle's first year on the staff of the *Deutsche Zeitung* had been productive, problems between Claß and Wulle began to arise by the beginning of 1920. In January 1920, Claß received word that Wulle planned to stand as a candidate for the DNVP in the upcoming March Reichstag elections. While Claß had been pleased with Wulle's occasional speaking engagements for the Pan-German League outside of his normal duties as editor-in-chief, Wulle's decision to run for formal political office was a different issue altogether. Claß's main concern was certainly not with Wulle's choice of a political party, as the Pan-Germans had supported the DNVP from its inception. Several other

---

detailed but ideologically distorted contemporary biography can be found in: Junius Alter [Franz Sontag], *Nationalisten. Deutschlands nationales Führertum der Nachkriegszeit* (Leipzig, 1930), 57–67.

   [3] Claß, *WdS v. II*, 605.

League members also held important posts in the party and worked tirelessly in the campaign leading up to the March 1920 elections. The main problem that Claß and others had with Wulle's candidacy was the negative impact that it would certainly have on his services to the *Deutsche Zeitung*. Claß was concerned that Wulle would not be able to live up to clauses in his contract which required him to commit his "entire energy" to the successful administration of the newspaper.[4] Claß was convinced that Wulle's attention to the day-to-day affairs of the newspaper would inevitably wane over the course of a grueling political campaign. Only a year into Wulle's contract, Claß scheduled a meeting to discuss these most recent developments.

In fact, Claß and Wulle met several times in the weeks leading up to the June 1920 elections. Claß explained that Wulle simply could not fulfill his duties to the newspaper because of his choice to run for public office and he would, therefore, have to resign from his post at the newspaper. Wulle assured Claß that he would be able to carry out both jobs simultaneously and that his influence on the paper would in no way be affected. For a time, Claß held off on making the final decision to fire his editor-in-chief, giving Wulle a chance to balance his political and editorial responsibilities. In the run up to the elections, Wulle's work did not seem to be greatly affected. However, after Wulle won the election and assumed his responsibilities in the Reichstag, his attention to the newspaper began to suffer.[5]

One of Claß's closest associates at the *Deutsche Zeitung* informed him that in the few months after Wulle had become a Reichstag deputy, the editor-in-chief had virtually disappeared from the newspaper's offices. Claß quickly became alarmed that the newspaper's popularity was beginning to taper off in spite of the fact that, according to Claß, the Pan-German League's ideas were so crucial to Germany in this "time of crisis." Claß and Wulle exchanged complaints and renewed promises until early fall. Each time that Claß felt Wulle had to leave, Wulle reiterated his commitment to the paper and assured Claß that he would devote more time to his editorial duties.

Despite Wulle's promises, by October 1920 Claß finally decided to remove him. By mid-December, Claß found Wulle's replacement in Max Maurenbrecher, a Lutheran pastor in Dresden. Maurenbrecher was the son of the well-known nationalist historian Professor Wilhelm Maurenbrecher. As a student, Max Maurenbrecher had belonged to the nationalist "Association of German Students" (*Verein Deutscher Studenten*). Before the outbreak of World War I, Maurenbrecher had actually joined the Social Democratic Party, but

---

[4] Ibid., 606.

[5] Ibid., 608–609.

quickly became disillusioned and returned to the nationalist fold during the war. Claß was pleased to find a candidate who had seen the "error of his ways" and had rededicated himself to the "nationalist struggle" after his "horrible error in judgment" with the SPD.[6]

Claß arranged a final meeting at the end of the month to release Wulle from his responsibilities with the *Deutsche Zeitung*.[7] Claß had already met with the newspaper's advisory board and received their support to replace Wulle. Claß offered Wulle a year's salary in cash payment and held out the opportunity for Wulle to continue speaking at various Pan-German functions, as well as the possibility of contributing articles to the *Deutsche Zeitung*. Clearly Claß tried to paper over his differences with Wulle, and he certainly hoped to avoid any public uproar over the affair. After some discussion, Wulle consented to these conditions and agreed to run a lead article in the 1 January 1921 edition that would explain to readers that he had resigned his editor's position in order to fulfill his duties as a member of the DNVP Reichstag delegation. The meeting ended, and Claß and several of his other associates who were present at the meeting agreed that Wulle seemed to accept the decision well and had left the paper on good terms.[8]

When Claß opened his copy of the *Deutsche Zeitung*'s New Year's Eve edition, however, he immediately realized that the Wulle affair was only beginning. In a parting shot at Claß and the newspaper's advisory board, Wulle included a final article announcing his resignation from the paper. Without directly naming Claß and his associates, Wulle implied that he did not want to leave the paper but had, in essence, been forced out. Wulle closed the article in a defiant tone stating: "As always, my friends and enemies will see me on the front lines of the political battle."[9]

By the following morning, Claß and the newspaper's office received a number of angry messages from Wulle supporters demanding an explanation for the editor's dismissal. One of Claß's trusted associates at the paper explained to him that many of the paper's writers and contributors were also upset with

---

[6]　On Maurenbrecher see: Claß, *WdS v. II*, 612–613; and Marlies E. Jansen, *Max Maurenbrecher: der weltanschaulich-politische Weg eines deutschen Nationalisten 1900–1930* (Düsseldorf, 1964).

[7]　Claß, *WdS v. II*, 612–613.

[8]　Ibid., 615.

[9]　*Deutsche Zeitung*, 31 December 1920, 2. See also: Claß to Otto Helmut Hopfen, 8 January 1921, BARCH R8048/392, 829. According to this letter, Wulle also gave a very negative parting address on New Year's Eve to the *Deutsche Zeitung* staff. In addition to the article, Claß felt further betrayed by this behavior and Wulle's alleged misrepresentation of the circumstances surrounding his departure from the paper.

Wulle's alleged mistreatment. Claß immediately called together the newspaper's editors and writers and explained the actual context of Wulle's dismissal. Claß and the newspaper's publishing house, the *Neudeutsche Verlags- und Treuhand-Gesellschaft m.b.H* then published a six-page, single-spaced circular for private distribution to all full Pan-German League members and regular subscribers of the *Deutsche Zeitung.* This document detailed Claß's own version of the account and placed the blame for the uproar squarely on Wulle's shoulders.[10] Although Claß and his associates were able to prevent further dissension within the paper's staff, Wulle's article had already done real damage by exposing what now appeared to be serious problems within the paper's leadership.[11]

As Claß soon discovered, that article was only the beginning of Wulle's campaign against the *Deutsche Zeitung* and the Pan-German League itself. With the help of his close friend and fellow Reichstag deputy Albrecht von Graefe-Goldebee, Wulle and his supporters held numerous meetings in Berlin, distributed mass-mailings to many of the paper's subscribers, and publicly challenged Claß and several of his associates to duels.[12] Claß tried once more to smooth out his differences with Wulle and his associates in light of these new attacks. Claß arranged a meeting with Graefe-Goldebee on 12 January 1921 that ultimately accomplished nothing.[13] Graefe-Goldebee claimed that Claß's decision to fire Wulle was "inexcusable" and that it represented a potential "death blow to the national movement."[14] Graefe-Goldebee concluded his

---

[10]   "Die Vorgänge beim Ausscheiden des Herrn Wulle aus der Schriftleitung der 'Deutsche Zeitung," BARCH R8048/490, 38–40.

[11]   Wulle to Claß, 10 January 1921, BARCH R8048/490, 16–20. In this letter, Wulle outlined his own response to Claß's outrage at the editor's alleged "breach of faith." While Wulle assured Claß that he had no intention of attacking the newspaper or Claß publicly, his assurance stemmed more from his concern about what such a public feud would do to his own career: "It is fairly clear who would gain the upper hand in a public controversy between me and the *Deutsche Zeitung.*" Wulle warned Claß, however, that "if my friends ask me, I must tell them how I view these things." As events unfolded, Wulle clearly overcame his initial fear of openly attacking Claß and the *Deutsche Zeitung.*

[12]   Graefe-Goldebee was one of the DNVP's earliest members and, with Wulle, represented the party's most intransigent, anti-Semitic wing. Graefe-Goldebee was a representative of the German Conservative Party before World War I and during the war he joined the Pan-German League. Claß valued his membership and was deeply impressed by his speaking ability. For more on Graefe's background. See: Claß, *WdS v. II*, 609–610; Wulff, *Deutschvölkische Freiheitspartei*, 190 n45; and Alter, *Nationalisten*, 46–56.

[13]   This meeting came in response to an angry exchange of letters between Claß and Graefe-Goldebee roughly one week before. See: Graefe-Goldebee to Claß, 20 December 1920, BARCH R8048/490, 9–10; and Claß to Graefe-Goldebee, 3 January 1921, BARCH R8048/490, 11.

[14]   Claß, *WdS v. II*, 618–619.

hyperbolic diatribe and promised to "demolish" his "deadly enemies" the Pan-German League and the *Deutsche Zeitung*.[15] Despite earlier assurances to the contrary, Claß now realized that the situation had become far more than an isolated personal feud, even if he could not comprehend Graefe-Goldebee's and Wulle's seemingly irrational behavior.

Ultimately, these attacks did a great deal to divide not only the *Deutsche Zeitung's* immediate supporters, but they also began to raise problems within the nationalist, völkisch oriented public as a whole. Indeed, although the Claß–Wulle split began primarily because of personal issues, the uproar surrounding the affair had very public political ramifications. In fact, while he lamented the impact of the situation personally, Claß was much more concerned about its larger political fallout.

The Growing Völkisch Divide

Although barely a month had passed from the time of Wulle's "New Year's Eve" article, it was already obvious to the Pan-German League's leadership that this new conflict could seriously weaken the völkisch movement in Germany. The Kapp Putsch in March 1920 had been the first major test of radical nationalist unity, and by February 1921 Claß and many of his colleagues feared that the split with Wulle might develop into a larger political struggle that could permanently affect the Right's overall unity. Therefore, the crisis in the völkisch movement was one of the top items on the agenda of the League's business management committee meeting in Berlin on 5–6 February 1921.

All of the members present at the meeting lamented the growing discord within the German Right in the wake of the Kapp Putsch.[16] Furthermore, Claß highlighted the problems that the League now faced in the new public attacks from Wulle and his allies. The Pan-German chairman demanded that "an end must be made of this [affair] and the pests of the völkisch movement must be called to account."[17] However, Claß and his associates were unsure of their next course of action. For the time being, they decided to defend themselves privately and seek a resolution to the situation without airing the growing split to the public at large.

The letters that began to pour into the Pan-German League's headquarters through the late summer of 1921 made a private resolution of the situation

---

[15] Ibid., 619.

[16] SGA, 5–6 February 1921, BARCH R8048/130, 35–40.

[17] Ibid., 37.

impossible. Claß and the League were forced to deal with a wide range of questions, comments, and criticism concerning the political ramifications of Claß's feud with Graefe-Goldebee and Wulle.[18] Many letters explained that since both Claß and Wulle were popular figures on the local and regional right-wing scene, many Pan-German League chapters found themselves torn between the two men. Some groups, like the Pan-German League's Leipzig chapter, voiced serious concern over Wulle's firing and urged both parties to reconcile their differences for the good of the völkisch movement.[19]

The tension between Claß, Wulle, and Graefe-Goldebee continued throughout 1921 and the first half of 1922. Throughout this period, the League's leadership felt compelled to answer complaints and questions about the affair more directly after it became apparent that the situation could no longer be resolved privately.[20] The League's main office also started to receive numerous complaints about the general lack of right-wing unity in many parts of central, and particularly northern, Germany. Even for areas that possessed a relatively large number of right-wing organizations, attempts at unifying these elements almost always failed.[21]

During this same period, Graefe-Goldebee and Wulle founded two new newspapers, one in Graefe-Goldebee's home state of Mecklenburg and another in Berlin. The *Mecklenburger Warte* and the *Deutsche Tageblatt* both began to publish articles that not only discredited Claß and the Pan-German League, but also supported Graefe-Goldebee and Wulle's ideological and political aspirations. In addition to attacks alleging that Claß and the League had destroyed right-wing unity and defamed Wulle's name, the attacks often strayed even further into the realm of political conspiracy. Most notable in this regard

---

[18]   For this complete correspondence see: BARCH R8048/490, esp. 72–220.

[19]   Managing Committee of the *Ortsgruppe* Leipzig to League Headquarters/Berlin, 24 February 1921, BARCH R8048/490, 105. For a detailed report of the proceedings of the spirited Managing Committee meeting that produced this official letter, see: Theodor Weicher to Claß, 20 February 1921, BARCH R8048/490, 83. Similar letters pleading for quick reconciliation for the good of the völkisch cause came in from local and regional groups throughout Germany. See, for example, letters from the *Ortsgruppen* Kassel, Hannover, Frankfurt-am-Main, and Darmstadt, BARCH R8048/490, 72–75.

[20]   For example, see: League Headquarters to *Oberpostrat* Pretsch (Darmstadt), 21 November 1921, BARCH R8048/207, 473–474. Claß also wrote to his close friend Alfred Hugenberg to discuss the possibility of preventing Wulle from gaining control over several right-wing papers to air the dispute more extensively. See: Claß to Alfred Hugenberg, 28 February 1921, BARCH R8048/490, 124.

[21]   This was apparently even the case in Dortmund. See for example: Wilhelm Reith, Chairman of the *Ortsgruppe* Dortmund to Claß, 11 September 1922, BARCH R8048/208, 406–409; and Claß to Reith, 22 September 1922, BARCH R8048/208, 421.

was the Graefe-Goldebee–Wulle camp's apparent obsession with the issue of Freemasonry.

Freemasonry, and its alleged ties to international Jewry, was a surprisingly frequent topic among many right-wing groups in the Weimar Republic.[22] Either as a rhetorical device or out of a genuine, yet totally irrational, conviction, Wulle and Graefe-Goldebee vigorously attacked Claß and many of his closest colleagues for their purported membership in Berlin's Masonic lodges. Wulle and Graefe-Goldebee argued that the Pan-German League and the *Deutsche Zeitung* had fallen under Freemason-Zionist control.[23] According to this far-fetched argument, Claß and the Pan-Germans could never be true defenders of the nationalist cause because of their ties to this "international" conspiracy and its controlling Jewish influence.

Of course the Pan-German League's unequivocally anti-Semitic stance directly contradicted these bizarre charges. Nonetheless, the feud between Claß and his supporters and the Graefe-Goldebee/Wulle group took on an astonishingly irrational tone that allowed these sorts of bizarre rumors to flourish and gain acceptance among a surprising number of right-wing individuals and groups.[24] Indeed, Claß and the League's headquarters received numerous complaints and questions relating directly to this issue.[25] Claß and his associates categorically rejected all claims that they had any ties to Freemasonry. Claß believed simply that Graefe-Goldebee and Wulle had succumbed to the

---

[22]   On Freemasonry and German right wing politics see: Helmut Neuberger, *Freimauerei und Nationalsozialismus: Die Verfolgung der deutschen Freimauerei durch völkische Bewegung und Nationalsozialismus 1918–1945* (Hamburg, 1980), esp. 19–57 for the origins of the Jewish-Freemason "conspiracy theory" as well as the role of Freemasonry as an ideological target in the wake of Germany's defeat after World War I.

[23]   Claß, *WdS v. II*, 620.

[24]   As Helmut Neuberger correctly asserts, actually "proving" the connection to a Freemason "conspiracy" was far less important than the political and propaganda value that such an accusation could have. Neuberger argues that the Freemason charge was seen by many right-wing groups as a sure way of undermining the legitimacy of other competitors regardless of its accuracy. Neuberger, *Freimauerei*, 96.

[25]   For example see: *Sanitätsrat* Dr. Liebe (Waldorf-Elgershausen) to Claß, 3 February 1921, BARCH R8048/207, 68–69; and Claß to Liebe, 14 February 1921, BARCH R8048/207, 91–92. The surprising resonance of this issue in Pan-German circles extended all the way to the last years of the Weimar Republic. See: Wilhelm Schulz (Diesdorf) to Otto Bonhard, Editor of the *Alldeutsche Blätter*, 31 October 1931, BARCH R8048/472, 4; and Schulz to Baron von Vietinghoff-Scheel, 19 November 1931, BARCH R8048/472, 10. Both of these vitriolic, paranoid letters questioned the Pan-German League's true commitment to the "battle" against the Jews because of its ties to Freemasonry. At one point in his first letter, Schulz argued that "As experience has taught us, the Jew utilizes all types of secret organizations to maintain his influence, especially Freemasonry."

stress of the political limelight and were willing to believe almost anything about their assumed enemies.

However, the practical effect of the Freemason/Jewish charges against Claß and the Pan-Germans had some impact in certain right-wing circles. It gave many of Graefe-Goldebee and Wulle's new supporters something to latch onto beyond Wulle's personal feud with Claß. The broader political impact of these Freemasonic accusations upset Claß the most.[26] As a result of these allegations, Graefe-Goldebee and Wulle won over virtually the entire membership of the Mecklenburg Pan-German League by mid-1922.[27] Although Graefe-Goldebee and Wulle now had a firm base of support, they had not yet formed a clear political platform or a distinct organization to promote their agenda. Before they could do this, they needed to develop a more extensive national reputation. They immediately gained a powerful ally for their cause by developing strong ties to one of Germany's World War I heroes, General Erich Ludendorff. Ludendorff's active participation in this affair quickly transformed the dynamics of this surprisingly intense political conflict.

General Erich Ludendorff

Heinrich Claß and Erich Ludendorff had already met on several occasions during World War I, and the Pan-German League's contact with the German General Staff had been fairly regular during the fall of 1917.[28] Claß held Ludendorff in high regard at the end of the war even after the general fled to Sweden.[29] However, as Ludendorff became more prominently involved in extremist right-wing politics in Germany and Austria in the first years of the Weimar Republic, the League's relations with the General became increasingly strained.[30]

Shortly after Ludendorff's return to Berlin from Sweden in February 1919, he contacted Claß to set up a meeting to discuss the general development of

---

[26] Claß, *WdS v. II*, 620.

[27] Ibid., 619.

[28] For more on Claß's visits to the General Staff headquarters and his meetings with Ludendorff and Colonel Max Bauer, see: ibid., 228–262.

[29] Fearful of Allied retribution against him as a war criminal Ludendorff fled Germany first to Denmark, then on to Sweden by November 1918. On Ludendorff's time in Sweden see: D.J. Goodspeed, *Ludendorff: Soldier, Dictator, Revolutionary* (London, 1966), 221–224.

[30] Although by now there are several Ludendorff biographies of varying quality, by far the best account of Ludendorff's political activity in the wake of World War I is: Thoß, *Der Ludendorff-Kreis*.

right-wing politics in his absence.[31] Claß then arranged to meet the General in his temporary residence in the Viktoriastraße. According to Claß their initial meeting went very well and Ludendorff greeted him "warmly and emotionally."[32] Ludendorff told Claß that he had had time in Sweden to determine the true cause of Germany's collapse at the end of the war. Much to Claß's pleasure, Ludendorff announced:

> I have come to the conclusion that the responsibility for our misfortune lay in the fact that the Military High Command and the Pan-German League could not join together ... [This is] all the more reason for us now to work and stand together.[33]

Claß in turn agreed to this proposal without reminding Ludendorff that the League had, in fact, tried to do "everything it could" to produce precisely this sort of cooperation already during the war.

However, Claß made this commitment with the important condition that their future cooperation would be kept secret. The Pan-German leader was concerned about Ludendorff's "political inexperience" and made it clear to the General that their work was so important to the nation that it could not in any way be compromised by one of Ludendorff's potentially untrustworthy associates. Ludendorff assured Claß that all of those present at his house were completely reliable and could be trusted with any secret. Despite these assurances, Claß left this first meeting convinced of the need to deal only with the General and to avoid contact with any of his new political "handlers."[34]

In addition to these concerns, Claß also came away from that first meeting with several lingering doubts about Ludendorff's political acumen. The names of two men in particular, Gustav Stresemann and Georg Heim, came up during their discussion. As Claß saw it, Ludendorff did not seem to demonstrate the proper disgust with these men and their alleged betrayal of the national cause. Since Stresemann's acrimonious departure from the Pan-German League during World War I and his failure to call openly for an overthrow of the Republic, Claß and the League had written him off entirely.[35] Claß was also disdainful of Georg Heim, the leader of the *Bayerische Volkspartei*. Claß criticized his stance toward the Weimar system and questioned his loyalties to the German state because of

---

[31]   On Ludendorff's decision to return from exile in Sweden and his arrival in Berlin see: ibid., 55–60.

[32]   Claß, *WdS v. II*, 738.

[33]   Ibid., 739.

[34]   Ibid., 740.

[35]   The League's later relationship to Stresemann is explored in greater detail later in this study, especially Chapters 4 and 5.

his alleged Bavarian particularism.[36] Ludendorff's seemingly positive comments concerning these men caused Claß to question the General's personal loyalties and overall political judgment.

Nonetheless, Claß was determined to maintain this connection to Ludendorff and, after meeting with him briefly a second time less than a week later, Claß waited for further contact from Ludendorff regarding a specific course of action.[37] Such contact was not forthcoming and Claß even began to hear rumors of Ludendorff's cooperation with Wolfgang Kapp and his associates.[38] By the time Kapp's Putsch had failed, Claß decided to re-establish contact with Ludendorff in Munich, hoping that the general had learned something from his association with the poorly conceived and executed coup d'état.

At the same time that Claß and Ludendorff had resumed contact in the wake of the Kapp Putsch, new problems began to arise between their two camps. While many on the German Right were upset that Claß and the Pan-German League had failed to support the Kapp Putsch actively, the issue of Austrian right-wing nationalism now further complicated matters. The Pan-German League had long been an important factor in Austrian and especially Viennese politics. But after World War I and the destruction of the Austro-Hungarian Empire, the League began to place increased emphasis on the incorporation of German-speaking Austria into the German Reich. In addition to regular correspondence with local chapters in Austria, the Pan-German League also sent special emissaries to negotiate directly with the wide range of right-wing and paramilitary forces in Vienna and Austria to coordinate events in that region.

Claß's main representative in charge of coordinating right-wing Austrian political action was the decorated World War I Austrian General Alfred Krauß.[39] As Claß put it, Krauß's main goal was to bring together under one united leadership "all 'militant' organizations which felt in any way national or völkisch."[40] After the failure of the Kapp Putsch, however, Ludendorff and his associates also began to look to Vienna and Austria as potential new sources of support for their counterrevolutionary plans.[41] Ludendorff sent his own

---

[36]   For more on Heim and the *Bayerische Volkspartei* see: Klaus Schönhoven, *Die Bayerische Volkspartei 1924–1932* (Düsseldorf, 1972).

[37]   Claß, *WdS v. II*, 742.

[38]   On Ludendorff's ties to Kapp's group and other counter-revolutionary forces, as well as their plans for military action to overthrow the national government, see: Thoß, *Ludendorff-Kreis*, 61–75.

[39]   Claß, *WdS v. II*, 743–744.

[40]   Ibid., 744.

[41]   Ludendorff's interest in Austrian right-wing groups is clearly explained in: Thoß, *Ludendorff-Kreis*, 201–216 and 419–430.

representative, Colonel Max Bauer, to establish direct contact with Austria's paramilitary organizations. For reasons which are not entirely clear, Ludendorff either specifically chose not to contact Claß before making this move, or, in spite of the long term Pan-German presence in Austria, decided to try to gain control of the Austrian radical nationalist scene himself. In any case, Bauer arrived in Vienna and boldly demanded that all groups, including those working with Krauß, unite behind Ludendorff's leadership.[42]

The most logical explanation for this rapidly emerging split had in part to do with Krauß's alleged Austrian allegiance. Rumors began to circulate that Krauß had no interest in uniting Austria's right-wing forces to push for union with Germany, but rather sought to restore the Habsburg monarchy. Furthermore, Krauß was alleged to have "tarnished" himself even further by accepting money from the head of the Bavarian Home Guards unit, Dr. Otto Pittinger. He was also rumored to be working against an Austrian-German unification, playing to Wittelsbach loyalists and Bavarian separatists to gain money and support for a Habsburg restoration. The absurdity of these accusations was certainly apparent to Pan-Germans in Germany and Austria who for years had been working on precisely such a unification of the two nations under a Hohenzollern dynasty.[43]

In short, although Bauer attempted to present Ludendorff as the only real German representative in Vienna, the net result of all these machinations was complete failure. Bauer's appearance in Vienna and his spurious attacks on Krauß and the Pan-Germans only divided the Austrian right-wing scene further. Not only did Bauer return from Vienna without significant support, but he also succeeded in destroying much of the work that Krauß had already begun in Vienna and western Austria. This episode again raised a certain ingrained distrust within the Austrian Right about complete subjugation to German control in any form. The fact that two of the most prominent right-wing groups in Germany could not even coordinate their recruiting efforts further reinforced suspicions within the Austrian camp.

The relationship between Ludendorff and Claß soured further as a result of this episode. Ludendorff fell increasingly under the influence of his advisors and was often too ready to accept the judgments of his close associates rather than his own. Ludendorff's close friends only further reinforced the General's political paranoia. Within this world, Ludendorff gradually came to view Heinrich Claß and the Pan-German League as potential threats to his prominence on the German Right. At the very least, according to information he had received from

---

[42]   Claß, *WdS v. II*, 744.

[43]   The Pan-German League already demanded Austria's incorporation into the German Reich in its Bamberg Declaration in 1919. See: Jochmann, *Nationalsozialismus und Revolution*, 18–19.

Bauer and others, Claß and the Pan-Germans had thwarted plans for right-wing German-Austrian unity under Ludendorff's command. Ludendorff seemed to associate Claß with some form of Habsburg or even Wittelsbach loyalties, and began to question the Pan-German leader's political abilities altogether.[44]

In spite of this rather tense situation, neither Claß nor Ludendorff wanted to break ties completely. In fact, even in the last two months of 1922, the two men exchanged letters attempting to rectify the misunderstandings that had developed between them.[45] One of Claß's letters even held out the possibility that the two men could meet in person to discuss these differences and resolve them in order to re-establish the relationship that existed in the early period after the war.[46] Such a series of face-to-face meetings did in fact take place in Berlin from 23 until 25 November 1922.[47] Both sides clarified their own positions and affirmed their desire to unify the völkisch movement in Germany and Austria. The meeting ended with the general agreement that all "productive forces" must join together to secure the "salvation" of the German Reich as well as Austria. Although the promises at this meeting were vague, it seemed as if the two sides had resolved their essential differences.

Even two weeks after this meeting, the new relationship seemed to be holding up. Ludendorff wrote to Claß, obviously still pleased with the nature of their professional relationship.[48] However, his letter contained a disturbing request. Claß had been aware for some time that Ludendorff had been in contact with Reinhold Wulle and Albrecht von Graefe-Goldebee. Both men had put forth a concerted effort to turn Ludendorff against Claß and the Pan-German League but, at least throughout most of 1922, Ludendorff avoided tying himself formally to either group. He did indicate, however, that he tended to view the affair from "a different angle" than Claß.[49]

Now for the first time, Ludendorff included a formal request in his letter that Claß meet with one of Wulle and Graefe-Goldebee's closest colleagues in

---

[44] This conflict continued into 1923 even though it seemed clear by the end of 1922 that there would be no unified command of Austrian völkisch groups. For details see: Max Bauer to Claß, 23 January 1923, BARCH R8048/423, 79–81; Claß to Alfred Krauß, 12 February 1923, BARCH R8048/423, 113–116; Bauer to Claß, 16 February 1923, BARCH R8048/423, 122–123; Krauß to Ludendorff, 18 March 1923, BARCH R8048/423, 141; and Bauer to Claß, 22 March 1923, BARCH R8048/423, 143.

[45] Claß to Ludendorff, 1 November 1922, BARCH R8048/423, 23–26, and Ludendorff to Claß, 2 November 1922, BARCH R8048/423, 30–32.

[46] Claß to Ludendorff, 6 November 1922, BARCH R8048/423, 34.

[47] For a detailed summary of this meeting see: BARCH R8048/423, 39–41.

[48] Ludendorff to Claß, 10 December 1922, BARCH R8048/423, 44.

[49] Ludendorff to Claß, 2 November 1922, BARCH R8048/423, 30.

the DNVP, Ernst Graf von Reventlow, to resolve the deep divide that existed between the two camps. Ludendorff made it clear that "we must all learn to forgive and forget if we hope to work together for the future. Otherwise we won't so easily be able to overcome the past." Ludendorff concluded that "If I had not learned to forgive, I would never have been capable of constructive work ... We have no time to lose."[50] With this subtle hint, it now seemed clear to Claß that Ludendorff was beginning to cooperate more closely with Graefe-Goldebee and Wulle. It would, however, take one more decisive step to solidify the split between Claß and the Pan-German League on the one side, and Graefe-Goldebee, Wulle, and eventually Ludendorff, on the other. The catalyst for this permanent split was the founding of a new right-wing political party later in December 1922.

The Founding of the Deutschvölkische Freiheitspartei

In December 1922, following a major split in the DNVP over the role of anti-Semitism and völkisch politics in general, Albrecht von Graefe-Goldebee, Reinhold Wulle, and their colleague Wilhelm Henning joined with several other prominent right-wing notables, including General Erich Ludendorff, to form the German Völkisch Freedom Party.[51] Concerned that the conservative DNVP had failed to embrace racist anti-Semitism as a prominent political plank, and frustrated with their inability to steer the DNVP toward a more radical position on the so-called Jewish Question, Graefe-Goldebee and Wulle finally decided to go out on their own in search of formal electoral support for their political agenda. The party's first formal statement of goals was as filled with hyperbole as it was devoid of any specific political solution to Germany's problems:

> Away with the dictates of Versailles! Away with unproductive parliamentarianism! Away with Jewish domination and market capitalism! Away with all forms of worker exploitation! Away with Marxism and Bolshevism, with class struggle and the caste spirit![52]

---

[50]   Ludendorff to Claß, 10 December 1922, 44.

[51]   On the DNVP split, the Pan-German League's role, and the departure of Graefe-Goldebee, Wulle, and Henning see Chapter 4, this volume. For a general survey of the DVFP, see: Wulff, *Deutschvölkische Freiheitspartei*.

[52]   The DVFP's temporary program can be found in: Wulff, *Deutschvölkische Freiheitspartei*, 16 and n76.

While this initial statement clearly did not distinguish the party from a range of other right-wing political organizations in its general goals, the party's founding was certainly cause for concern in right-wing circles. The Pan-German League's leaders were already well acquainted with the problems that Wulle and Graefe-Goldebee posed as a political force. From the very beginning of the personal feud between the two groups, Claß's main concern had always been the impact of such a split on the völkisch movement as a whole. The League's formal acknowledgment of the new party's formation, ironically in the *Deutsche Zeitung*, made these reservations clear.[53]

After announcing the leadership of the new party, the article lamented the inevitable "splintering" of the völkisch movement which such a new party represented. The article pointed out that the Pan-German League had always tried, wherever possible, to prevent precisely such splits in the "nationalist parliamentary front." The article closed with a rather stern warning to the DVFP to avoid a new conflict with the DNVP and other right-wing groups in the wake of the split. "What a tragedy it would be," the article stated, "if that age-old German flaw affected this situation as well, so that the closest relatives, much to the delight of their common enemies, fought against each other."[54]

Nor did the *Deutsche Zeitung* waste any time in publishing an additional editorial by Axel Freiherr von Freytagh-Loringhoven concerning the völkisch conflict. Freytagh-Loringhoven was a leading member of both the Pan-German League and the DNVP and had remained in the party after Graefe-Goldebee's and Wulle's split in 1922. Freytagh-Loringhoven's article attacked the DVFP only days after the party was founded.[55]

According to Freytagh-Loringhoven, the League's worst fears had been confirmed by a recent speech by DVFP leader Wilhelm Henning in Halle. In this speech, Henning openly attacked the DNVP, accusing the party of a weak nationalist stance and susceptibility to Jewish influence. Freytagh-Loringhoven deeply lamented the fact that the DVFP's first major appearance on the national stage featured an attack on another right-wing party rather than the threat posed by the Left. He argued further that the völkisch ideal stood above the parties and certainly could not be judged to be superior in one party simply because it included the term in its title. More specifically, even if Henning and his associates had convinced themselves that they now represented the true champions of the völkisch cause, they had no right to defame or denigrate other right-wing groups for their own benefit. If that behavior continued, Freytagh-

---

53　"Deutsch-völkische Freiheitspartei," *Deutsche Zeitung*, 18 December 1922, 1.
54　Ibid.
55　"Völkischer Zwist?" *Deutsche Zeitung*, 4 January 1923, 1–2.

Loringhoven concluded, it could only mean the destruction of the völkisch movement as a whole.[56]

It did not take long for Graefe-Goldebee and his associates to reply to these accusations. On 9 January 1923, Claß received a letter from Graefe-Goldebee attacking Claß, Freytagh-Loringhoven, and the *Deutsche Zeitung* for their "monstrous attack" on Henning and the DVFP.[57] To Graefe-Goldebee, the *Deutsche Zeitung* article represented an "open declaration of war" on Henning and the party, and he demanded a formal apology and dictated terms to Claß and the League. Either they would come together as friends and work in the closest possible partnership, or they must carry on as mortal enemies "to the hilt."[58] The following day, Claß penned a letter to Graefe-Goldebee explaining that Freytagh-Loringhoven's message was not a declaration of war, but simply an attempt to preserve some sort of unity within the radical nationalist movement.[59] Claß also conveyed his intense disappointment with the timing of Graefe-Goldebee's letter. The fact that he and the DVFP would call for a fight to the death against the Pan-German League, precisely at the time that French troops were beginning to pour into the Ruhr was simply beyond belief.[60]

In spite of a further exchange of letters in January, both sides stood by their original position.[61] Although Claß and Graefe-Goldebee expressed their deep regret over the state of affairs between two of Germany's most influential völkisch groups, they failed to reach any kind of settlement to their dispute. It became clear that this originally private matter had now exploded into a decidedly public, political struggle for control over the völkisch movement, particularly in northern Germany. Indeed, primary support for the DVFP came from Mecklenburg and other predominantly Protestant, northern and central German states. Although the DVFP and its representatives quickly moved to establish ties with their south German counterparts like Adolf Hitler, the DVFP had its greatest potential, and conversely posed its greatest threat to the Pan-German League, in northern Germany.[62]

---

[56]   Ibid., 2.

[57]   Graefe-Goldebee to Claß, 8 January 1923, BARCH R8048/226, 6–7.

[58]   Ibid., 7.

[59]   Claß to Graefe-Goldebee, 10 January 1923, BARCH R8048/226, 13–15.

[60]   Ibid., 15, and Claß, *WdS v. II*, 623–624. Claß referred here to the French occupation of the Ruhr in January 1923.

[61]   Graefe-Goldebee to Claß, 13 January 1923, BARCH R8048/226, 55, and Leopold von Vietinghoff-Scheel to Graefe-Goldebee, 17 January 1923, BARCH R8048/226, 56.

[62]   For more on the DVFP's initial contacts with Adolf Hitler and the Bavarian radical nationalist scene see: Wulff, *Deutschvölkische Freiheitspartei*, 20–23. For the Pan-German League's

Claß's relationship with Ludendorff also worsened decisively in the wake of the DVFP's founding. Ludendorff sided with the DVFP and felt that his position on the German Right could only be strengthened by playing a prominent leadership role in the new organization. The Freemason conspiracy theories peddled for some time by Graefe-Goldebee and Wulle reinforced Ludendorff's suspicions concerning Claß's allegedly "un-German" loyalties. Although Ludendorff's most extensive paranoia emerged later in the 1920s, he was still well versed in the venomous conspiracy theories espoused by his new friends in the DVFP.[63] As Claß recounted, Ludendorff completely bought into the bizarre rumors about Claß's ties to harmful "international" organizations, particularly Freemasons and Jews.[64] Yet again, this extensive feud took a further turn toward the irrational.[65]

In March 1923, Claß met Ludendorff for the last time. Apparently Ludendorff made one last attempt to serve as intermediary between Graefe-Goldebee and Claß.[66] The meeting was practically over before it started. Graefe-Goldebee

---

contacts with the Bavarian radical nationalist movement and Hitler during this same period, see Chapter 3, this volume.

[63]   Ludendorff's nascent paranoia concerning Jews, Freemasons, and even the Jesuits, exploded after his second marriage in 1926 to Mathilde Ludendorff. See: Goodspeed, *Ludendorff*, 235–236. Goodspeed asserts that under Mathilde's influence Ludendorff "began to share her vision of a vast international conspiracy, moving nations and statesmen like pawns for their own dark, unTeutonic purposes. He came to believe that the Catholic Church, international Jewry, and the Freemasons were plotting in improbable combination to overcome the chosen Volk."

[64]   Claß, *WdS v. II*, 625. Ludendorff went on to publish two books allegedly exposing the Freemason conspiracy: Erich Ludendorff, *Vernichtung der Freimaurerei durch Enthüllung ihrer Geheimnisse* (Munich, 1928); and *Kriegshetze und Völkermorden in den letzten 150 Jahren* (Munich, 1931).

[65]   It is interesting to note that even though he was writing about a different nation and a different time, Richard Hofstadter's notion of the "paranoid style" in politics is also applicable here to a large extent. See: Richard Hoftadter, *The Paranoid Style in American Politics and Other Essays* (Cambridge, 1996, original edn 1952). Wulle, Graefe-Goldebee, and Ludendorff's Freemason/ Jewish conspiracy fits well with Hoftadter's notion of the use of paranoid conspiracy theories as a powerful political tool. About the practitioners of this type of politics Hofstadter writes: "The clinical paranoid sees the hostile and conspiratorial world in which he feels himself to be living as directed specifically *against him*; whereas the spokesman of the paranoid style finds it directed against a nation, a culture, a way of life whose fate affects not himself alone but millions of others … His sense that his political passions are unselfish and patriotic, in fact, goes far to intensify his feeling of righteousness and his moral indignation." Hofstadter, *Paranoid Style*, 4.

[66]   Claß, *WdS v. II*, 625. Another such attempt at reconciliation took place one year later on 31 March 1924 at the *National Klub* in Berlin. This time, however, Ludendorff was not present. This meeting was as unproductive as Ludendorff's earlier effort. Claß, Reventlow, Vietinghoff-Scheel, and Graefe-Goldebee all attended the private meeting but failed to reach any agreement.

placed his pocket watch in front of him before the discussion even began and rejected all suggestions for compromise that Ludendorff advanced. Ludendorff threw his hands in the air out of complete frustration and the meeting ended in total failure. Even though the guilt for the meeting's failure probably had less to do with Graefe-Goldebee's actual behavior than the long-term antagonisms which had developed between both sides, this episode clearly demonstrates the extent of right-wing division by the spring of 1923. After this, there could be no discussion of further cooperation between the Pan-German League and the DVFP. As Claß concluded in his memoirs:

> Through their machinations, Graefe [-Goldebee] and Wulle, along with their fanatical followers in the *Deutschvölkische Freiheitspartei*, made the rift in the nationalist camp impossible to heal ... they are responsible for the fact that the völkisch movement split into at least two groups. This was, without exaggeration, a terrible fate for the völkisch cause.[67]

During this same tense period, the League's office received letters from various parts of northern and central Germany detailing the broader ramifications of the DVFP/Pan-German split. The first such report came in from Theodor Weicher, the well-known right-wing Leipzig publisher who distributed Heinrich Claß's widely read *Deutsche Geschichte*.[68] Weicher reported that there was considerable uproar in Leipzig's right-wing circles over the DVFP's founding and the Pan-German League's alleged "declaration of war" against the new party. The League's chief secretary Major von Roeder was compelled by this report to write a lengthy return letter. He assured Weicher that, among other things, the League had in no way deliberately attacked the DVFP, but rather had sought to warn the party about the potential damage it could inflict on the völkisch movement.[69] Weicher thanked von Roeder for his detailed clarification and offered his continued support for the Pan-Germans while criticizing the League's detractors as "hot heads."[70]

Unfortunately for Claß and his associates, other reports were not so easily or successfully resolved. One letter from a Mecklenburg Pan-German was

---

The divide between the two groups was just as pronounced in 1924 as it had been one year earlier. For a detailed report of the meeting, see: BARCH R8048/658, 8–11.

   [67]   Claß, *WdS v. II*, 625.
   [68]   Weicher to Claß, 9 January 1923, BARCH R8048/226, 12. By 1923, Claß's *Deutsche Geschichte*, published under the pseudonym "Einhart," was in its 11th edition and was a top seller for the publisher Theodor Weicher. Einhart, *Deutsche Geschiche* (Leipzig, 1921).
   [69]   Roeder to Weichert, 11 January 1923, BARCH R8048/226, 16–18.
   [70]   Weichert to Roeder, 13 January 1923, BARCH R8048/226, 22.

particularly disturbing to Claß and the rest of the League's leadership.[71] Head Forester Harms, a long-time Pan-German League member and a leader of the group's Mecklenburg local branch, recounted the widespread enthusiasm for the founding of the DVFP in his area and the sense of excitement the new party brought to the right-wing scene in Mecklenburg. Harms explained that within his circle of associates, the DVFP was by no means seen simply as a "splinter group" from the DNVP. Rather, they viewed the DVFP as "a great reservoir into which ... all Germans with a nationalist conscience can, should, and will flow."[72] Harms explained that it was, therefore, all the more disappointing to hear directly from Graefe-Goldebee and Wulle at an assembly in Rostock that the Pan-German League had refused to support the new party. Harms closed by pleading not only for an explanation from the League, but also a clear course of action.

The League's head office responded in detail.[73] In addition to reiterating the same basic explanations for the "misunderstanding" between the Pan-Germans and the DVFP, the League also forwarded copies of the correspondence between Claß, Graefe-Goldebee, and Wulle to support their position in the entire conflict. The League's head business manager Baron von Vietinghoff-Scheel closed the letter with the hope that something could still be done to save the independence of the Pan-German League's Mecklenburg chapter. By this point, however, it appears that the League's head office held out little hope of keeping the Mecklenburg Pan-Germans from falling in completely with the DVFP.[74] Harms wrote back once more claiming that Claß simply had not done enough to set things right to prevent a great split in the radical nationalist movement.[75] Harms explained that a very serious divide had in fact developed within the völkisch community in Mecklenburg. In order to rectify this situation, Claß would have to yield to the DVFP and promise to support the new völkisch party

---

[71]   Harms to Claß, 12 January 1923, BARCH R8048/226, 19.

[72]   Ibid.

[73]   Leopold von Vietinghoff-Scheel to Harms, 15 January 1923, BARCH R8048/226, 26–30.

[74]   Vietinghoff-Scheel to Local Group Leaders in Mecklenburg, 15 January 1923, BARCH R8048/226, 23. The League's head office in Berlin sent this letter on the same day to the leaders of all of the local Pan-German League chapters in Mecklenburg to schedule an emergency meeting on 21 January 1923 to discuss the crisis. Although this detailed letter makes a strong case for maintaining the autonomy of the local chapters, there is no evidence that the requested meeting ever took place. In any event, these local chapters eventually folded themselves into the DVFP party structure, breaking their ties to the Pan-German League altogether.

[75]   Harms to Vietinghoff-Scheel, 17 January 1923, BARCH R8048/226, 32.

in the *Deutsche Zeitung*. Without this sort of commitment, Harms concluded, the League faced a serious problem.

A sort of middle ground was also discernible in responses from local groups outside of Mecklenburg to the growing conflict. Artur Dinter, one of Claß's associates and author of the vulgar novel *Die Sünde wider das Blut* (*The Sins Against the Blood*), wrote a detailed letter about the DVFP's founding in Thuringia and its effect on the Pan-German/DVFP split in that area.[76] Dinter expressed his excitement and support for the new party. While he lamented the DVFP's turn against the DNVP, he conceded that the DNVP had become soft on the Jewish issue. In Thuringia, there was some confusion about the Pan-German League's stance concerning the DVFP, but this was not something that had seriously dampened the enthusiasm for the party's founding in principle.

After reviewing copies of the correspondence between Graefe-Goldebee and Claß, Dinter could understand Claß's concerns about the personal attacks from certain DVFP leaders. Nonetheless, Dinter continued, the new party itself was bigger than these personal differences and it would certainly succeed as a true representative of the völkisch cause. Dinter closed by assuring Claß that he would continue to work for the new party, but not in any conflict with the League or the DNVP. In turn, Dinter expressed his confidence that Claß and the *Deutsche Zeitung* would support the new party when they realized that "it was the only party that fights ... with the völkisch cause ... as the cornerstone of its practical politics."[77]

Of course, this sort of cooperation would not be forthcoming. Instead, the conflict between these two groups intensified further during the remainder of 1923. To a certain extent, the conflict played itself out in the press. Reinhold Wulle's newly founded *Mecklenburger Warte*, and later the *Großdeutsche Warte*, played a key role in perpetuating the conspiracy theories concerning Claß and the Pan-Germans. In a series of articles and editorials, Graefe-Goldebee, Wulle, and their associates attacked Claß and the Pan-German League for all manner of "secretive" or destructive behavior that allegedly contradicted their true mission.[78] Initially, Claß and the Pan-Germans were surprisingly reserved and published little that directly attacked Graefe-Goldebee, Wulle, or the DVFP. At first, as Claß put it: "We replied ... only when we felt we truly had to."[79]

---

[76]   Artur Dinter to Claß, 22 January 1923, BARCH R8048/226, 63–66. See also: Artur Dinter, *Die Sünde wider das Blut: Ein Zeitroman* (4th/5th edn, Leipzig, 1919).

[77]   Artur Dinter to Claß, 22 January 1923, BARCH R8048/226, 66.

[78]   See: "Deutscher Kampf oder Geheimbündelei?" *Mecklenburger Warte*, 25 July 1923, 1; "Preßhebräisches!" *Mecklenburger Warte*, 18 October 1923, 2; and "Der ewig wiederkehrende Dolchstoß," *Großdeutsche Warte*, 13 January 1924, 1.

[79]   Claß, *WdS v. II*, 626.

As the conflict worsened throughout the remainder of 1923, however, the League began to consider far more seriously the possibility of defending itself more rigorously in public against DVFP charges.[80] In August 1923, Claß received a detailed letter from Axel Freiherr von Freytagh-Loringhoven expressing complete disgust with the DVFP's behavior and his exasperation with the pettiness and fanaticism of Claß's opponents.[81] The DVFP's actions were so destructive, according to Freytagh-Loringhoven, that everything had to be done to "put an end to things" with the DVFP. "How deeply disturbing it is to see little 'Wulles' ... springing up throughout the nation and, in brilliant incompetence, destroying all positive ... efforts with intrigue and agitation."[82] Freytagh-Loringhoven demanded that the League begin a concerted campaign through speeches, personal contacts, and the press to discredit and undermine the DVFP.

League headquarters quickly responded to Freytagh-Loringhoven's letter and made it clear that the League planned to take steps against the DVFP. In the letter, Baron von Vietinghoff-Scheel included a copy of Wulle's own published version of the entire affair, including his split from the *Deutsche Zeitung*, the founding of the DVFP, and his feud with Claß and the Pan-German League.[83] Vietinghoff-Scheel made it clear that after reading the document, which was nothing more than "a string of lies pieced together in the style of a trashy novel," Freytagh-Loringhoven would understand the League's current plans to have Wulle's Reichstag immunity lifted in order to begin legal proceedings against him for slander. The League also planned to bring similar proceedings against the *Mecklenburger Warte* and the *Deutsche Tageblatt*.

Two other major issues that further divided the German Right influenced the Pan-German League's increased propaganda against the DVFP in late 1923 and early 1924. The first of these developments was Adolf Hitler's failed "Beer Hall Putsch" in November 1923. As we will see in the following chapter, Claß and the Pan-German League had been in contact with the upstart radical nationalist since 1920. Yet since Claß and the DVFP were still at each other's throats even as they courted Hitler and his Bavarian allies through 1923, the failure of Hitler's coup d'état only further heightened the tensions between the two leading north German völkisch groups. The DVFP in particular quickly sought to blame the

---

[80]   To this end, Claß certainly appreciated the numerous letters he received from various local and regional chapters of the Pan-German League offering support in his conflict with the DVFP. For example: *Ortsgruppe* Hannover to Claß, 21 August 1923, BARCH R8048/491, 20.

[81]   Freytagh-Loringhoven to Claß, 6 August 1923, BARCH R8048/209, 177.

[82]   Ibid.

[83]   For a complete copy of this pamphlet, entitled "Die Vorgänge bei meinem Ausscheiden aus der *Deutschen Zeitung*," see: BARCH R8048/491, 44–49.

Pan-German League for undermining Hitler's "patriotic" effort. The League, of course, maintained its innocence and emphatically refuted the DVFP's claims.

The second major issue was the League's growing relationship with the DNVP. While the Pan-Germans had supported the DNVP from the outset, their interest in the DNVP as a viable political platform for their own radical goals increased significantly after the DVFP's founding. Claß and the League sided with the DNVP in the wake of the so-called "völkisch secession" of 1922. From that point on, the League's increasing criticism of Graefe-Goldebee/Wulle/Ludendorff and the other DVFP leaders served two very crucial functions. On the one hand, the League preserved its own integrity and reputation within the right-wing scene by defending itself against the DVFP's "unfounded" accusations. However, precisely because the League singled out the DVFP as the destroyer of German right-wing unity, the League also strengthened its ties to influential circles within the DNVP that mistrusted the DVFP's intentions.

Nonetheless, this was certainly not what Heinrich Claß and the Pan-German League had envisioned at the beginning of the Weimar Republic. The League had dedicated itself to leading a united radical nationalist movement against the fledgling Weimar Republic. None of this, however, came to pass. In fact, primarily because of the bizarre personal and political feud between the Pan-Germans and the DVFP there would be no unity of the völkisch movement or the German Right in a broader sense.

Neither side was blameless in this affair. Certainly, Graefe-Goldebee and Wulle's paranoid conspiracy theories and Claß's own uncompromising attitude both contributed to such an outcome. These traits were indeed representative of a widespread right-wing paranoia exacerbated by the extreme conditions of Germany's defeat and the November Revolution. In this tense climate, even isolated, initially personal, incidents could be interpreted as affronts that were also sometimes perceived as symptoms of some deeper, menacing conspiracy. This environment, combined with a generally deep-seated self-righteousness on the part of both the Pan-German League and the DVFP, ultimately produced an open split in the German radical nationalist movement that would never truly be repaired. As bizarre and irrational as the circumstances surrounding the split may appear, this divide had a very real and lasting impact on the development of right-wing politics in the Weimar Republic. As the rest of this study demonstrates, almost all of the Pan-German League's subsequent decisions and political commitments were shaped by the deep divisions that developed in the völkisch movement in the first post-war years. Indeed, it is this surprising disunity that emerges as the hallmark of most German right-wing activity until 1924 and beyond.

Chapter 3

Early Contacts: Adolf Hitler and National Socialism, 1920–1924

In addition to their attempts to forge political alliances in northern and central Germany in the immediate post-war years, the Pan-Germans were also keenly interested in improving their ties to potential new allies in the south. In large part, this search led them to Bavaria and a range of right-wing groups that had emerged there following the violent defeat of the short-lived Bavarian Soviet in late-spring 1919.[1] The Pan-German League already possessed several strong contacts in Munich through prominent Pan-German members like the right-wing publisher J.F. Lehmann and Otto Helmut Hopfen, and also through the League's association with members of the Escherich Organization (*Organisation Escherich*) and, later, the Bavarian Order Block (*Bayerischer Ordnungsblock*).[2] Through these sources, Heinrich Claß and Pan-German leaders became aware of a small but growing force called the German Workers' Party (*Deutsche Arbeiterpartei*). This movement would soon become the National Socialist German Workers' Party (*National Sozialistische Deutsche Arbeiterpartei*— hereafter "Nazi Party" or "NSDAP") under the leadership of the political upstart Adolf Hitler.[3]

The NSDAP was only one part of a complex right-wing milieu in post-war Munich. Since the defeat of the Munich Soviet in 1919, Bavaria, and Munich specifically, had become a haven for a wide range of counterrevolutionary forces.[4]

---

[1]   On this issue see: Allan Mitchell, *Revolution in Bavaria, 1918–1919: The Eisner Regime and the Soviet Republic* (Princeton, 1965).

[2]   Both groups served as umbrella organizations for a range of right-radical and paramilitary groups. See: Harold Gordon, *Hitler and the Beer Hall Putsch* (Princeton, 1972), 43, 92, and 118.

[3]   For a detailed account of the chaotic political scene in post-World War I Munich see: Gordon, *Hitler and the Beer Hall Putsch*, esp. 3–184. For an intriguing look at the ties between cultural and political developments in Munich in this period see also: David Clay Large, *Where Ghosts Walked: Munich's Road to the Third Reich* (New York and London, 1997). The *Deutsche Arbeiterpartei* was changed under Hitler's leadership to the *Nationalsozialistische Deutsche Arbeiterpartei* at some point in the first half of 1920. For more on the party's early history and Hitler's decisive involvement in it, see: Dietrich Orlow, *The History of the Nazi Party, 1919–1933* (Pittsburgh, 1969), esp. 1–45.

[4]   Mommsen, *Rise and Fall of Weimar Democracy*, 153.

Bavaria's Minister President Gustav von Kahr was a career civil servant and a dedicated monarchist whose power base was located as much in the various citizens' militias and paramilitary groups as it was in the Bavarian Landtag.[5] Kahr's attitude toward the many paramilitary organizations and right-wing parties was representative of many of Bavaria's other conservative leaders. Kahr once remarked that:

> If there were no Left-oriented antinational radicalism, there would also be no Right-oriented nationalism. The one is the result of the other, and the moral responsibility for the latter and its deeds can therefore be placed with far more justice on antinational radicalism than on the government.[6]

The Bavarian Soviet and the relatively slim threat which it had posed of a permanent communist government in Germany nonetheless left a lasting impression on many of Bavaria's moderate and conservative leaders. As a result, a large number of right-wing organizations were allowed to emerge and flourish in this climate. However, for Heinrich Claß and other Pan-German leaders, Adolf Hitler and the nascent Nazi movement seemed to stand out from the wide spectrum of right-wing and monarchist organizations. Very early in 1920, this initial interest quickly developed into active negotiations between the Pan-German League and Nazi Party. In the burgeoning relationship between the Pan-German League and the NSDAP, the specific personal connection between Heinrich Claß and Adolf Hitler proved to be of particular importance.

Forging the Relationship

In late January 1920 in Munich, Heinrich Claß met Adolf Hitler for the first time. Their meeting lasted a little over two hours. As Claß recalled, it was not really a "discussion" but rather a two-hour session of Hitler's lectures and rants embellished with fanatical gesticulations. Claß seemed at once shocked and impressed with Hitler's raw political skill and fanatical devotion to the fatherland:

> This man was a political savage ... [nonetheless] every word that he spoke was absolutely sincere and accurate. This young man had learned well and his powers of perception were solidly grounded in a national, even völkisch, worldview. Any problems I might

---

5   Ibid.
6   Kahr quoted by Joseph Graf Pestalozza in: Gordon, *Hitler and the Beer Hall Putsch*, 31.

have had with his ideas had primarily to do with the influence of his upbringing and background. On the whole, he represented something totally new in the political life of our volk, and someone from whom we might expect some success in loosening the ties of the working class to the Communist Party.[7]

However, two issues bothered Claß after his first meeting with the Nazi leader. First, Hitler boldly stated that if he were able to gain a significant foothold among the masses, he would be willing to give up on the basic tenets of his political program later on if necessary. This tactical flexibility shocked Claß's more traditional political sensibilities. As Claß put it "Are the ends meant to justify the means?"[8] Secondly, Claß was disturbed by Hitler's unshakable belief in his own powers of persuasion and the way in which he presented himself. Already after the first 15 minutes of their meeting, Claß became convinced that he was dealing with an absolute hysteric.[9] While it was entirely possible that this "hysterical eloquence" could have a great impact on the masses, Claß questioned whether or not Hitler really possessed the inherent abilities required of a true statesman.[10]

After their first face-to-face meeting, Heinrich Claß and Adolf Hitler remained in fairly regular contact throughout 1923. Specifically, Claß asked fellow Munich Pan-German Dr. Otto Helmut Hopfen to keep him apprised of Hitler's activity. Aside from direct conversations, Claß also received periodic letters with reports and information concerning the Nazi movement. In the second week of August 1920, Claß received a detailed letter from Helmut Hopfen regarding Hitler.[11]

Hopfen had already heard a number of Hitler's speeches in Munich and found the Nazi leader quite promising. Hitler's demands for universal conscription and his strong anti-French proclamations led Hopfen to suggest that Hitler might be a good addition to any number of Pan-German meetings or programs. Hopfen also approached Hitler about a possible speaking arrangement for the

---

[7]   Heinrich Claß, Unpublished Memoirs-*Wider den Strom volume II-addendum* (hereafter "*WdS v. II-addendum*"), N2368/3, Bundesarchiv Koblenz 8–9. This section of Claß's memoirs is a unique source of information concerning his personal contact with Hitler and the early Nazi movement. The section specifically devoted to the Claß–Hitler relationship is located in an addendum at the end of the Claß memoirs. This source, along with numerous documents in the Pan-German League's main archival holdings, provides a detailed picture of the relationship between the growing Nazi movement and the Pan-German League.

[8]   Claß, *WdS v. II-addendum*, 9.

[9]   Ibid.

[10]   Ibid.

[11]   Hopfen to Claß, 10 August 1920, BARCH R8048/392, 134–135.

Pan-German League. Hitler politely declined, stating that "such an appearance could be easily misinterpreted by my followers."[12] This was a clear reference to Hitler's desire to maintain the independence of the Nazi movement and to avoid the appearance that he was simply a tool of the Pan-German League. Yet Hitler still hoped for some level of cooperation in the form of financial support from the coffers of the Pan-German newspaper the *Deutsche Zeitung*. As Hopfen recounted to Claß, Hitler requested 1,000 Marks for a proposed 14-day speaking trip to Austria in advance of upcoming elections. In a letter dated 18 August 1920, Claß informed Hopfen that the 1,000 Marks would be made available for Hitler's Austria trip.[13]

On his next trip to Munich, Claß again met with Hitler. This time the two men spoke in a side room of the Sterneckerbräu, which doubled at the time as the business office of the Nazi Party. Claß congratulated Hitler on his early successes in Munich and Bavaria, and asked if he felt that workers were attending his speeches in any numbers. Hitler replied that even though the other parties did everything they could to keep the workers away, the Nazis were making some inroads.[14] The meeting closed with general agreement to Claß's proposal that Helmut Hopfen would cover Hitler and the activities of the Nazi Party more closely in the pages of the Pan-German-controlled *Deutsche Zeitung*.

By January 1921, Claß believed that Hitler was prepared to expand the Nazi movement to northern Germany with significant Pan-German support. This idea was inspired by a meeting between Claß and Hitler at the end of 1920.[15] Perhaps to reassure Claß of his credentials, Hitler brought with him to this meeting a letter of recommendation from Dr. Ernst Pöhner. Pöhner was the Bavarian police director, a staunch supporter of right-wing groups, and one of Claß's trusted acquaintances. Pöhner wrote:

> The bearer of this letter, Herr Hitler, is already known to you from your visit to Munich. I have personally had several long discussions with Hitler and I am convinced that he is an exceptionally bright and capable defender of our common goal. He is an organizational and agitational force of the highest order and is known throughout Bavaria as the best speaker for the National Socialist German Workers' Party ... If the necessary financial support can be arranged, Herr Hitler, as he has made clear to me, is prepared to involve himself in northern Germany as well. I

---

[12]   Ibid.

[13]   Claß to Hopfen, 18 August 1920, BARCH R8048/392, 142.

[14]   Claß, *WdS v. II-addendum*, 10.

[15]   The records do not indicate whether this December 1920 meeting took place in Berlin or Munich.

wish to recommend Herr Hitler with best regards, and I am confident that he will provide you excellent service.[16]

Pöhner's letter led Claß to believe that Hitler was now prepared to expand his movement into northern Germany. As the de facto head of the northern German völkisch movement, Claß could have expected to benefit by combining his established political credentials with Hitler's populist speaking style and charismatic leadership.

In late January 1921, Claß wrote a detailed letter to Dr. Otto Gertung in Nürnberg.[17] Gertung was a member of the board of directors at the MAN works (Maschinenwerke Augsburg-Nürnberg). Claß praised the Nazi movement's successes in Munich and southern Bavaria, particularly its alleged progress in fighting the "Red Terror." Nazi successes were so great, Claß continued, that he had "come to an agreement" with the leaders of the movement to open a new political front in northern Germany. Claß clearly believed at this point that Hitler was sincere in his desire to break out of Bavaria and expand to Berlin.[18]

In late spring 1921, Claß pressed Hitler to begin making appearances in Berlin and to establish a formal party office in the nation's capital. In conjunction with these requests, Claß again traveled to Munich and met directly with the Nazi leader. Hitler indicated that he was still prepared, in principle, to attempt the move north. But the costs—Hitler suggested a sum of about 60,000 Marks—would have to be covered in advance.[19] Claß assured Hitler that he would make every effort to raise the money.

This loose agreement did not hold up for long, however. Only weeks later, Hitler returned to Berlin and informed Claß that, after very careful consideration, he would not be able to make the move north after all. Hitler explained that it would make no sense for him to hold one or more major rallies in Berlin as it would require him to be away from Munich for three weeks or a month in order to start a viable party organization there. He felt he could not

---

[16]   Ernst Pöhner to Claß, 11 December 1920, BARCH R8048/258, 198. In the typewritten text of the letter, an extra handwritten "t" was added to Hitler's name.

[17]   Claß to Dr. Otto Gertung, 29 January 1921, BARCH R8048/258, 238.

[18]   Claß's correspondence with Otto Gertung also covered financial support for Hitler's proposed move north and for the *Völkischer Beobachter*, the recently purchased Nazi newspaper. Hitler's representatives had pressed the Pan-German League for money and Claß, in turn, asked Gertung if he or his company could provide any assistance. In spite of these requests, there is no record of any financial assistance from Gertung or MAN through Claß and his associates for Hitler and the Nazi movement. See: Gertung to Claß, 27 February 1921, BARCH R8048/258, 239; Claß to Dr. Paul Tafel, 1 March 1921, BARCH R8048/258, 240; and Claß to Dr. Paul Tafel, 8 June 1921, BARCH R8048/258, 243.

[19]   Claß, *WdS v. II-addendum*, 10.

afford the time away from Munich because he needed to be there to supervise everything personally. Claß ultimately conceded that their earlier plan could not be carried out, but he expressed hope that the Nazi movement would be able to expand to the capital in the very near future.[20]

In light of broader developments in the Nazi Party in the summer of 1921, Hitler's seemingly abrupt decision to break off negotiations over a move to northern Germany becomes much clearer. First, it is entirely possible that Hitler never had any intention of expanding the Nazi movement out from Munich so early on in its development. It is also possible that he led Claß to believe that this was a possibility primarily to keep all of his options open, including financial ones, in connection with the Pan-Germans.

Secondly, and perhaps more plausibly, if Hitler ever sincerely considered expansion to northern Germany, that plan would have been put off as a result of the Nazi Party leadership crisis that developed in the summer of 1921.[21] Although successful in fending off merger proposals between the NSDAP and the smaller DSP (*Deutschsozialistische Partei* or "German-Socialist Party"), Hitler still feared challenges to his control of the party. After furiously resigning on 11 July, he officially rejoined the party on 26 July after party members confirmed his status as undisputed leader of the NSDAP. Although Hitler emerged from this intra-party conflict as a clear victor, it cost valuable time and effort and distracted him from other important party business. This clearly included his negotiations with the Pan-German League.

The relationship between Heinrich Claß and Adolf Hitler after July 1921 was never the same. Claß's memoirs indicate that after the summer of 1921 until the summer of 1928, he and Hitler only met directly again twice, once in May 1922 and again in May 1923. In the meantime, one of Hitler's associates came to Berlin in early 1922 to beg Claß yet again for financial assistance for the *Völkischer Beobachter*.[22] Claß's memoirs indicate that he was able to collect about 30,000 Marks for the *Völkischer Beobachter* from funds controlled by the Pan-German *Deutsche Zeitung*.[23] However, Claß expressed his growing frustration with the Nazi movement's never-ending demands when he observed: "Never once did we receive a single word [of thanks] for our assistance either from the publisher or from the [Nazi] party."[24]

---

[20]   Ibid., 11.

[21]   For this intra-party power struggle and its outcome see: Orlow, *History of the Nazi Party*, 25–45; and Ian Kershaw, *Hitler 1889–1936: Hubris* (New York, 1999), 160–165.

[22]   Claß, *WdS v. II-addendum*, 11. Claß does not supply the name of Hitler's associate.

[23]   Ibid.

[24]   Ibid., 12.

In spite of this increasingly turbulent relationship with Hitler and the Nazi movement, Claß and the Pan-German leadership were not yet ready to distance themselves entirely from Hitler. The Nazi leader's growing stature and potential for the anti-Weimar effort were simply too much to ignore. In May 1922, after learning that Hitler intended to make another visit to Berlin, Claß wrote the Nazi leader and suggested that they should meet again during Hitler's upcoming stay in the capital.[25] Claß even offered to pay for Hitler's round-trip train-fare so that they could meet "with a small group trusted friends to discuss certain issues of utmost importance."[26] This meeting took place at the end of May in connection with Hitler's speech before the Berlin chapter of the highly exclusive "National Club of 1919," a radical right-wing discussion group of which Claß and several other prominent Pan-Germans were charter members.

Although Claß's memoirs do not recount any of the details from this meeting, it is likely that it involved the old issue of financial support for the Nazi Party. Only six weeks after Hitler's May visit to Berlin, Dr. Emil Gansser, a Nazi supporter and fundraiser, contacted Heinrich Claß concerning money that the Pan-German League had allegedly promised to the Nazi movement but had not yet delivered.[27] According to Gansser's letter, Claß had promised to wire 50,000 Marks to Munich. Whether this money was to come solely from the Pan-German League's coffers or from other sources is unclear. After some confusion regarding the actual status of the funds, the Pan-German League's headquarters sent a letter confirming that the money had been transferred to contacts in the Bavarian Order Block.[28]

It is very clear from Gansser's correspondence with Claß that Hitler sought funds from the Pan-German League to support the Nazi movement generally, but also more specifically for an increased propaganda campaign to begin in the summer of 1922.[29] However, there is no record of how, if ever, this money reached the Nazi Party from the Bavarian Order Block. Furthermore, there is no evidence of any direct Nazi response acknowledging final receipt of the funds. As in Claß's previous dealings with Hitler and the Nazi Party, it is likely that even this substantial contribution did not warrant a formal statement of thanks from the Nazi Party leadership. Hitler's desire to maintain the appearance of his movement's strict independence from all other right-wing groups probably ensured this result. In effect, the Pan-German League and its allies were good

---

[25]   Claß to Hittler [*sic*], 11 May 1922, BARCH R8048/208, 221.

[26]   Ibid.

[27]   Emil Gansser to Claß, 21 July 1922, BARCH R8048/208, 316.

[28]   League's Leadership Committee to Emil Gansser, 26 July 1922, BARCH R8048/208, 405.

[29]   Ibid.

enough to provide whatever financial assistance they could muster, but not significant enough to secure any sort of political or personal loyalty from Hitler in return. From this point on there would be no further Pan-German financial assistance for Hitler and the Nazi movement.

Historians stressing continuity between the Pan-German League and National Socialism have emphasized this early financial relationship as evidence of strong continuity between the established Right and Hitler's new movement.[30] However, as a closer examination of the evidence makes clear, Pan-German funding for Hitler was actually sporadic and largely ineffective in securing closer cooperation between the two groups. In reality, the limited Pan-German financial assistance to Hitler's movement was motivated by the League's desire to gain greater control over the Nazi Party as part of a larger Pan-German attempt to destabilize the Republic. Hitler's repeated lack of gratitude for Pan-German assistance and his unwillingness to cooperate with his elders in the radical nationalist movement further divided the Pan-German leadership from the Nazi Party. As Hitler's desire to remain independent from the Pan-German League became completely clear, the political connection between the two organizations became increasingly strained.

Claß, Pöhner, Kahr, and Bavarian Politics

At roughly the same time that Heinrich Claß's negotiations with Hitler and the Nazi Party began to intensify, the Pan-German leader also cultivated two other important contacts on the Bavarian political scene. Again through his ties to the Bavarian Order Block, Claß established a working relationship with the Minister President of Bavaria Gustav von Kahr, and the Munich Police Chief Dr. Ernst Pöhner. In the Weimar Republic's early years, these men were among the most powerful leaders in Bavaria. Pöhner had already played a direct role in Claß's relationship with Hitler through the letter of recommendation that he wrote for Hitler in December 1920.[31]

In the fall of 1920, Claß traveled to meet with Pöhner personally at police headquarters in Munich.[32] Claß had been informed by many of his Bavarian contacts that Pöhner was favorably predisposed toward groups that worked to undermine the Weimar Republic. Claß was intrigued by this information and thought he might find in Pöhner a valuable ally in the Pan-German League's

---

[30]   The two best examples of this interpretation are: Chamberlin, *The Enemy on the Right*; and Petzold, "Claß und Hitler."

[31]   Ernst Pöhner to Claß, 11 December 1920, BARCH R8048/258, 198.

[32]   Claß, *WdS v. II-addendum*, 13.

attack on the Weimar system. Along with the two leaders of the Bavarian Order Block, Paul Tafel and Erwin Pixis, Claß talked for some time with Pöhner about the possibility of cooperation and coordination of their anti-Weimar campaigns. Pöhner even stated that, in his opinion, nothing should be attempted in Bavaria before Claß and others in the north were completely prepared. Claß and Pöhner closed their meeting by agreeing to share all information regarding planning and organization between Berlin and Munich.[33]

Pöhner also strongly suggested that Claß pay a visit to Gustav von Kahr. Pöhner described the Minister President as "a brave ... man who felt the way they did, but lacking in resolution and often in need of some ... political tutoring."[34] Claß in fact met with Kahr and was impressed. Kahr agreed that the only way to accomplish any meaningful political change in Germany would be to coordinate northern and southern German radical nationalist forces. Kahr clearly articulated his support for, and asked to be kept informed of, the developments between Claß and Pöhner. Claß returned to Munich several times in 1921 and 1922 to discuss with Pöhner a variety of options for action against the Weimar Republic. None of these initial negotiations produced any specific action, however. It would take a major new development in January 1923 for Claß and Pöhner's plans to take on a real sense of urgency.

On 11 January 1923 French and Belgian troops occupied the Ruhr, ostensibly to enforce German reparations payments by taking over control of the rich coal and steel producing industries in that region. While the French were in fact concerned about reparations payments, the move also represented a larger attempt by the French government under Raymond Poincaré to weaken Germany by separating the country from its most significant industrial region.[35]

Most Germans viewed the French move into the Ruhr with outrage. Heinrich Claß and his colleagues believed firmly that the French had to be driven out with military force. The initial lack of decisive action and the subsequent policy of passive resistance on the part of the Weimar government only further convinced Claß and his associates that the Republic was incapable of protecting Germany's world standing. Claß, Pöhner, and Kahr all felt that the time had come to create an independent army to drive the French out of the Ruhr. In theory, this success

---

[33]   Ibid.

[34]   Ibid.

[35]   On the history of the Ruhr occupation and its impact see: Mommsen, *Rise and Fall of Weimar Democracy*, 129–136; and Kolb, *Weimar Republic*, 45–48. For the most recent scholarship on the international dimensions of the Ruhr crisis see: Gerd Krumeich and Joachim Schröder (eds), *Der Schatten des Weltkrieges. Der Ruhrbesetzung 1923* (Essen, 2004); and Anna-Monika Lauter, *Sicherheit und Reparation. Die französische Öffentlichkeit, der Rhein und die Ruhr 1919–1923* (Essen, 2006).

might also gain them sufficient public support to attack the "weak" republican system itself. This might clear the way for a transitional military dictatorship, with Pöhner leading a civilian dictatorship in Bavaria.[36]

To discuss this operation in greater detail, Claß traveled to Munich on several occasions during the first months of 1923. Pöhner was in complete agreement with the Pan-German leader that the time to act was at hand. Pöhner explained to Claß that many of the right-wing groups in Munich were already arming themselves already and that a great deal of money was at hand to support their preparations. From his previous discussions with major industrialists like Fritz and Heinrich Thyssen, Claß already realized that, particularly among those industrialists most acutely affected by the French move into the Ruhr, demands for a private army financed by industrial funds was growing daily.[37] However, the accelerating inflation complicated the task of financing a private military effort against the French.

Claß and his colleague Dr. Paul Bang traveled to Munich again in the spring of 1923. On this trip, Pöhner made it clear that Hitler would have to be included in their plans so that the Nazi Party would support the move. Pöhner reasoned that "without Hitler I can accomplish nothing in Bavaria."[38] However, Claß explained that Hitler wanted nothing to do with the Pan-German League or its associates because Hitler had broken off connections months ago. Claß further questioned whether, in light of Hitler's apparent need for complete independence, it would be a good idea even to bring him into the secret discussions. Pöhner assured everyone that he was in "continuous contact" with Hitler and that there was no question that Hitler would participate if he were invited. Pöhner promised that he would arrange for Hitler to travel to Berlin to meet personally with Claß. As Pöhner promised, Hitler arrived in Berlin on 20 May to talk directly with Claß.[39] This would be the last face-to-face meeting between the two leaders until the final years of the Weimar Republic.

---

[36]   Claß, *WdS v. II-addendum*, 15. Claß initially hoped to convince General Hans von Seeckt to head such a military dictatorship. Claß met with Seeckt on several occasions in early 1923. However, Claß quickly discovered that the General would not even entertain the idea of a military dictatorship with him, the Pan-German League, or anyone else until it seemed certain that Germany could actually wage a successful campaign against the French in the Ruhr and perhaps even defend against Polish incursions in the East. Claß broke off discussions with Seeckt judging him to be a great disappointment to the nationalist cause. For more detail on the Claß-Seeckt negotiations see: Claß, *WdS v. II*, 639–718. For Seeckt's position see: Friedrich von Rabenau, *Seeckt. Aus seinem Leben* (Leipzig, 1941), 387–388.

[37]   Claß, *WdS v. II*, esp. 650–674.

[38]   Claß, *WdS v. II-addendum*, 15.

[39]   Ibid., 16.

Without revisiting any of their previous difficulties, Claß explained that his "trusted contacts" in all parts of Germany reported the same sense of frustration with the government response to the French occupation. These feelings had risen to such a level that an "act of salvation" was expected almost everywhere and indeed many people simply could not believe that some decisive action had not been taken already. Claß asserted that both the national and the Prussian governments had failed so miserably because of the influence of the Social Democrats and the "treasonous behavior of the Marxists" in all military issues.

Hitler, in turn, informed Claß about the difficulties he had experienced in an earlier meeting with General von Seeckt.[40] According to Hitler, Seeckt had requested a meeting to ask the Nazi party to "submit itself" to a coordinated military effort against the French if the time were right. Hitler flatly told Seeckt that the Nazi movement would not be tied to any broader coalition and that, after hearing this, the General replied that he would therefore have to regard Hitler as an enemy. Although this was similar to the complex negotiations that Claß had earlier with Seeckt, Hitler's description of Seeckt's belligerence confirmed Claß's belief that the Army Chief of Staff could not be relied on to head any sort of military or civilian dictatorship.[41]

It is clear from Claß's account of this discussion that Hitler had argued for some sort of armed action to drive the French out of the Ruhr and perhaps even move against the national government. However, the specific details of such a plan remained extremely vague. Both men had heard wild rumors that paramilitary forces and volunteer armies stood ready for a move against the French in the Ruhr and against government forces in Berlin.[42] Hitler claimed to share Claß's belief that if such a military strike succeeded, veterans and other German nationalists would join the cause and help establish some sort of military dictatorship. A permanent civilian dictatorship might then follow this action. Claß expressed concern about the gravity of the solution which they were proposing, but if the "November traitors' government of hypocrisy" were to be ended once and for all, he argued, extreme measures would be necessary.[43] In light of Hitler's apparent consent, the two leaders agreed to meet again to develop more specific plans on 22 May in Claß's hotel room in Munich.[44]

---

[40] This meeting took place on 11 March 1923. On the background and context of this meeting, see: Gordon, *Hitler and the Beer Hall Putsch*, 145–147 and 635.

[41] Claß, *WdS v. II-addendum*, 17.

[42] Ibid., 14. Claß had heard rumors of a large "workers army" of roughly 42,000 men ready to strike in the Ruhr. This rumor, like many others circulating at the time of the French occupation, turned out to be utterly false.

[43] Ibid., 18.

[44] Ibid.

Accordingly, Claß and Paul Bang traveled to Munich on Monday evening 21 May. The following morning they entered the meeting room attached to Claß's hotel room and found Ernst Pöhner already speaking with Wilhelm Frick, the new chief of the Munich criminal police division, and both leaders of the Bavarian Order Block.[45] A man unknown to Claß stood in the back of the room. It was clear that Hitler had not come to the meeting. After Claß quickly related to Pöhner the story of his recent meeting with Hitler, Pöhner explained that the unknown man in the room was in fact Hermann Göring. Göring claimed to be standing in for Hitler because the Nazi leader had not yet returned to Munich. Pöhner hesitated to discuss the political aspects of their plans in front of Göring, because Göring was not responsible for the Nazi Party's political negotiations. After being asked to leave and return again on Thursday when the military aspects of the plan were to be discussed, Göring left in a huff.[46]

After Göring's departure, Pöhner and Claß expressed their outrage that Hitler had not attended the meeting. Although Pöhner had by this point been replaced as Bavarian Police Commissioner, he still had contacts in the office. Pöhner then asked one of his contacts to determine personally if Hitler was indeed in Munich. Later that day the news reached the group that Hitler was indeed in the city but had simply not showed up. Hitler explained to Pöhner's investigator that "something" from northern Germany had forced him to break his promise to Claß.[47] The discussions went forward in spite of Hitler's absence. After the first two days of discussion, the attendees were sufficiently satisfied with the plan's political dimension. The military aspect remained, however, very much undecided.

On Thursday, 24 May, Göring was invited back to discuss plans for a military intervention in the Ruhr and a move against the Weimar government. Göring arrived and again claimed to speak for Hitler because the Nazi leader had not yet arrived in Munich. As soon as the meeting began, Göring asked to speak. Before he could make any meaningful contribution to the discussion, he demanded to be informed of the political plans for the operation in spite of the fact that he had been excluded earlier. Claß replied that it was very difficult for him to

---

[45]   On Wilhelm Frick's career see: Günter Neliba, *Wilhelm Frick: der Legalist eines Unrechtstaates: eine politische Biographie* (Paderborn, 1992).

[46]   Claß, *WdS v. II-addendum*, 18.

[47]   Ibid., 20. This is most likely a reference to Hitler's growing connection to the leaders of the north German *Deutschvölkische Freiheitspartei*. As Chapter 2 made clear, Reinhold Wulle, Albrecht von Graefe-Goldebee, and Erich Ludendorff had become Claß's bitter enemies during 1921–1922. As Hitler's relationship to Claß and the Pan-German League waned, his relationship to Wulle, Graefe-Goldebee, and Ludendorff grew. It is very likely that these men advised Hitler against any further cooperation with the Claß–Pöhner group.

believe that Göring, as Hitler's designated representative, knew nothing of these plans. After all, Claß had only recently discussed these very issues with the Nazi leader in Berlin. To this Göring replied only that he would inform Hitler of Claß's decision not to divulge any information regarding the plan's political aspects. After this exchange, Göring refused to participate and the meeting ended abruptly.

Without Hitler's full cooperation, Pöhner was not convinced the operation could proceed at all. Although Pöhner talked with Paul Bang and Claß after the meeting and expressed his outrage at Hitler's behavior, he realized that there was little he could do to convince Hitler to join the group. Claß and Bang returned to Berlin with little hope for their operation's success. Claß speculated that Reinhold Wulle and Albrecht von Graefe-Goldebee had probably dissuaded Hitler from further cooperation. Whatever the true reasons were, Claß felt that Hitler had once again turned his back on the Pan-German League and cemented his reputation as a completely unreliable part of any future unified right-wing movement.

In reality, the Claß–Pöhner strategy to include Hitler in their plans was probably doomed from the start. As historian Harold Gordon points out, even after the French occupation of the Ruhr, Hitler and the Nazi Party remained highly skeptical of any cooperation with other forces.[48] As early as 14 January, Hitler expressed his disdain for the underwhelmingly "nationalist" nature of the resistance forming against the French. On that day, a crowd of about 100,000 gathered at a "National Day of Mourning" rally sponsored by the United Patriotic Leagues of Munich. At this meeting, however, one of the leading speakers was a prominent Jesuit named Rupert Mayer.[49] Hitler was convinced that his movement could never be allied with such "un-German" forces, especially the republican forces in the Ruhr (the SPD, Center Party, and trade unions) who were leading the resistance effort. Indeed, Hitler's main focus remained on his plan to overthrow the Weimar government in Berlin first before any other plans could be made to move against the French or any other foreign power.[50]

Nonetheless, the Nazi leader's decision to withdraw his movement came as a real surprise to many in the right-wing camp including Claß and the Pan-Germans. Publicly, Hitler explained to his critics that the NSDAP simply could

---

[48]   Gordon, *Hitler and the Beer Hall Putsch*, 185–186.

[49]   Ibid.

[50]   For a clear statement of Hitler's true intentions and his contacts with the French over the Ruhr crisis see: George-Henri Soutou, "Vom Rhein zur Ruhr: Absichten und Planungen der französischen Regierung," in Krumeich and Schröder, *Der Schatten des Weltkrieges*, 63–83. For a comprehensive analysis of this crisis and its domestic and foreign policy implications for Germany see: Conan Fischer, *The Ruhr Crisis, 1923–1924* (Oxford, 2003).

not allow itself to join with other bourgeois organizations.[51] He also continued to point out that the real enemy remained the republican government itself:

> As long as a nation does not drive out the murderers within its own borders ... success in dealing with other countries remains impossible. While spoken and written protests are hurled against the French, the real enemy of the German people lurks within its gates.[52]

Again only two weeks after his 11 March 1923 meeting with Seeckt, Hitler bluntly repeated this assertion directly to a high-ranking representative of Chancellor Cuno: "Not down with France, but down with the traitors to the Fatherland, down with the November criminals; that must be our slogan!"[53]

Yet again, Hitler's strict desire to work only on his terms, and his unwillingness to surrender his movement's autonomy seriously undermined other right-wing efforts, including those of the Claß–Pöhner group, to bring military force to bear against the French. In spite of Hitler's numerous promises to Claß, the Nazi leader never had any real intention of going along with a plan that contradicted his own both in terms of execution and overall goals. Ultimately, Hitler's actions poisoned any future working relationship with Claß and the Pan-Germans, while also creating a serious split in Munich's right-wing camp.[54] As Hitler would soon discover, his unpredictable and erratic behavior in the first part of 1923 would come back to haunt him in his own attempt to overthrow the Munich government on 8–9 November 1923.[55]

The "Beer Hall" Putsch and its Aftermath

By September 1923 the Pan-German League's relationship with Hitler and the Nazi Party seemed beyond repair. After Claß's 20 May 1923 meeting with Hitler

---

[51]   For more on Hitler's role in these events see: Kershaw, *Hitler*, 191–200, and Joachim Fest, *Hitler* (New York, 1974), 163–166.

[52]   Hitler quoted in: Fest, *Hitler*, 164.

[53]   Ibid.

[54]   For more specific information on the underlying tensions within the nationalist camp in Munich, as well as Hitler's relationship to other right-wing groups, see: Editor-in-chief of the *München-Augsburger Abendzeitung* to the Dresden Pan-German League chairman Georg Beutel, 18 April 1923, StADresden ADV-OD/5, 126–129. See also: Gordon, *Hitler and the Beer Hall Putsch*, esp. 185–211.

[55]   For more detail on right-wing Putschism generally in this period see: Raffael Scheck, *Alfred von Tirptiz and Right-Wing Politics, 1914–1930* (Atlantic Highlands, 1998), esp. 95–113.

in Berlin, the Pan-German leader had no further direct contact with Hitler again until 1929.[56] There is also no evidence that Heinrich Claß, Paul Bang, or any other leading Pan-Germans were involved in the planning or execution of Hitler's so-called "Beer Hall" Putsch on 8–9 November 1923. As Hitler had already demonstrated through his actions, he was determined to produce Germany's "rebirth" on his own terms and his own schedule. Therefore, Claß was caught somewhat off guard when the first news reached him of Hitler's assault on the Bavarian government.

Between 3:00 and 4:00 a.m. on 9 November, Heinrich Claß awoke to news of Hitler's actions in the Bürgerbräukeller. The Nazi leader and his co-conspirators had kidnapped Gustav von Kahr, Ernst Pöhner, and the Commander in Chief of the Bavarian army Otto von Lossow, while proclaiming a national dictatorship under Erich Ludendorff.[57] That same morning, Claß called a meeting of his closest advisors and associates. It quickly became clear that no one had any real idea of the true nature of Hitler's action or whether or not it had any chance of success. While the meeting was still in session, Claß received the latest copy of the *Deutsche Zeitung*, relating news of the violent end of Hitler's Putsch. Claß immediately decided to travel to Munich that evening, accompanied by fellow Pan-German Paul Bang.[58]

A martial scene greeted the Pan-German leaders upon their arrival in Munich the following morning. Artillery and machine guns had been set up at the train station and a number of infantry and cavalry columns were visible. Claß arrived at his hotel and was greeted by Hermann Ehrhardt's lieutenant Eberhard Kautter.[59] Kautter invited Claß and Bang to a meeting with Ehrhardt. All three men met briefly in Ehrhardt's room at the Ring Hotel and agreed that Hitler's poorly planned and coordinated attempt was doomed to fail.[60] After this brief meeting, Claß, Bang, and Kautter traveled to the Munich military barracks to meet with Kahr, Lossow, and others in charge of the anti-Putsch forces.

Both Kahr and Lossow were furious with Hitler. After Hitler's "holdup" at the *Bürgerbräukeller*, Kahr had no other choice but to put down the Putsch and

---

[56] According to Claß's memoirs, Paul Bang occasionally saw Hitler in social gatherings with common acquaintances in Berlin between 1923 and 1929. See: Claß, *WdS v. II-addendum*, 33–34.

[57] Ibid., 27.

[58] Ibid.

[59] Ibid. Claß and the Pan-German League maintained contact with Herrmann Ehrhardt in the period following the Kapp Putsch. Ehrhardt often kept Claß up-to-date on events in Munich and the surrounding area.

[60] Ibid., 28.

prevent any further misfortune.[61] Kahr explained that his conscience was clean and he felt no responsibility for the deaths at the Odeonsplatz earlier that day. Indeed, the responsibility belonged with those who began the "propaganda march" in the first place, with full knowledge that Kahr and his ministers had withdrawn their support and would be forced to stop the demonstration.

Considering the negative light that these events cast on Kahr and all of the Bavarian Right, Claß at first suggested a general amnesty for all parties involved to defuse the situation. Kahr responded angrily that anyone who had been privy to the "monstrous breach of law" on the evening of 8 November could never even consider protecting these men from punishment. At this point, Claß thanked Kahr for the information and wished him luck in restoring order. For his part, Kahr requested that Claß and Bang make it perfectly clear to their associates in the north that he was forced to act against the Putsch.[62]

Claß's meeting with Lossow and Kahr only confirmed to the Pan-German leader the futility of a Putsch without sufficient preparation or broader right-wing unity. In Claß's mind, Hitler bore significant responsibility for this disastrous failure. Publicly, Claß and the Pan-German leadership reluctantly backed Gustav von Kahr and his suppression of the Putsch. The League's leaders concluded that the issue simply came down to the maintenance of state authority over total chaos.[63] Perhaps most importantly, the Pan-German League's leadership determined that "the salvation of the German Reich can never come out of Bavaria ... it can and will only be possible from here [Berlin/Prussia]."[64]

---

[61]   Ibid, 29. Already on 26 September 1923, in the face of growing rumors of a Putsch or some sort of military action, the Bavarian Prime Minister Eugen von Knilling declared a state of emergency and appointed Gustav von Kahr as state commissioner with dictatorial powers. It was in this capacity that Kahr and his ministers General Otto von Lossow and Hans von Seisser met on the night of 8 November in the Bürgerbräukeller. Hitler knew that for his Putsch plans to succeed, he would require the formal backing of Kahr and his ministers. That evening, accompanied by the *SA*, Hitler stormed into the Hall, fired one shot into the ceiling, and declared the beginning of the "national revolution." After much cajoling, in part at gunpoint, Hitler secured the grudging support of Kahr, Lossow, Seisser, and later General Ludendorff. Kahr, therefore, in some initial reports, was characterized as one of the Putsch leaders. In reality, as soon as Hitler left the building that evening, Kahr issued a proclamation retracting his support for Hitler, explaining that he had been forced into it at gunpoint. General von Lossow, in charge of the Bavarian Reichswehr forces, also backed away from his "pledge" to Hitler. With the support of the Reichswehr, Kahr set up headquarters in the Munich army barracks and proceeded to combat the Putsch. See: Fest, *Hitler*, 173–175 and 182–189, and Kershaw, *Hitler*, 206–211.

[62]   Claß, *WdS v. II-addendum*, 30.

[63]   Graf von Reventlow to Hermann Meyer (Leipzig), 22 November 1923, BARCH R8048/209, 283–284.

[64]   Ibid., 284.

The League's press spared little in its immediate response to the Munich fiasco. On 10 November 1923 the *Deutsche Zeitung* ran a lead article titled simply: "Adolf Hitler."[65] The article declared that Hitler was "finished" as a politician. But unlike others involved in the Putsch, Hitler's failure was ultimately traceable to a fundamental character flaw. Hitler "lacked the steel-hard strength" to protect him from the pitfalls of the very career he had selected for himself. Without question, the article continued, Hitler was an honorable man driven by the "holiest passion" for his country. Forced to endure the shame and suffering of his beloved fatherland, Hitler had chosen a career in politics as a platform for his message of renewal and "awakening." The Nazi leader had done much in his early career to earn the respect and enthusiastic support of his fellow nationalists. In the wake of the lost war and the devastating revolution, Hitler seemed to offer genuine hope for creating a real "workers' nationalism" that might have one day destroyed the power base of socialism and communism once and for all in Germany.[66]

According to the article, Hitler's hubris proved to be his undoing. As the crowds increased at his speeches, and the ranks of his movement swelled, Hitler lost touch with his "humble" beginnings. He no longer saw himself as the simple but successful agitator and quickly became accustomed to the titles "master" and "Führer" as his followers stoked his ever-increasing ambition. Soon, he found himself caught up in an event that quickly slipped beyond his control. Whatever his motivation to act as he did on 8–9 November, the dreadful outcome of the Putsch attempt had destroyed him as a politician. However, in spite of Hitler's failure, the article concluded that the core ideas that drove his movement had to be preserved at any cost:

> It is still true that [Hitler] gave new life and faith to communist workers who had been led astray. He imbued Germany's post-war youth with a new sense of idealism. He was the first to declare ... the end of the Marxist age, and to introduce to the masses the fundamental concepts of a new cultural epoch. And this creation must not end with the individual ... One spokesman might have failed ... but hundreds of others will take his place ... and the völkisch ideal will still triumph.[67]

Behind the Pan-German League's somewhat hyperbolic public stance, however, there was genuine private concern about the ramifications of the Beer Hall

---

[65] *Deutsche Zeitung*, 10 November 1923, 1–2.

[66] Ibid., 1.

[67] Ibid., 2. The Pan-German League frequently stated that the Nazi movement's basic ideals would survive even after Hitler's personal failure. See: "Hitler und wir," *Deutsche Zeitung*, 12 November 1923, 2.

Putsch for the progress of Germany's radical nationalist movement as a whole. One the League's leaders, Ernst zu Reventlow, expressed the League's serious reservations about the future of the radical nationalist movement in a letter to a prominent Pan-German member in Augsburg.[68] He claimed that Hitler's ill-conceived action had seriously damaged the völkisch cause and had rendered it useless for a major undertaking for some time. Nothing more could be expected from Ludendorff either. The entire affair made it clear that there were no "real leaders" in Bavaria and as a result, echoing an earlier theme, Reventlow stated that Germany's salvation would have to come from Berlin/Prussia. The Pan-German League would continue to work for the goal of a truly völkisch Germany but the path ahead would not be easy.

The Pan-German League's official stance supporting Kahr and opposing Hitler in the wake of the Putsch caused some disturbances within the Pan-German League's rank and file membership. Already by 1923, some Pan-German members had also joined the Nazi Party. To these members, the League's harsh public stance against the Nazis caused a great deal of concern and even led, in a few cases, to the loss of members. The most prominent example of this phenomenon involved the case of a long-time Pan-German member in Esslingen.

In the middle of December, the League's Berlin headquarters received a copy of a long letter from the local chapter in Esslingen to its district leadership explaining that one of Esslingen's most highly respected Pan-Germans had resigned his membership.[69] The letter recounted how Wilhelm Murr, who also served on the executive committee of the local NSDAP, resigned from the Ortsgruppe because of the *Deutsche Zeitung*'s treatment of Hitler's role in the Putsch. According to the letter, however, Murr's resignation was symptomatic of a deeper division that had recently developed in the radical nationalist camp in Esslingen.

Some of the local Pan-Germans felt that the League headquarters had not given them enough information on the League's relationship to the NSDAP at the national level. It even appeared to some members that the League had no clear policy regarding the Nazi movement and that each local and regional organization was simply left to work out its own policy, even if that route caused considerable dissension. In addition, when news of the failed Beer Hall Putsch reached local groups, many members could not understand the League's criticism of Hitler's behavior. Moreover, the League seemed to defend Kahr's

---

[68]   Graf von Reventlow to Baron von Haller-Hallerstein (Augsburg), 3 January 1924, BARCH R8048/210, 18–18a.

[69]   *Ortsgruppe* Esslingen to Heinrich Calmbach (*Gauvorstand-Cannstatt*), 14 December 1923, BARCH R8048/209, 289–290.

actions to the hilt, even though Hitler had already proven himself as a man of action who had at least attempted to rectify Germany's pitiful condition. The letter concluded that "Hitler, who at least understood the necessity of speaking to the masses, was now crippled, and other völkisch forces did not seem overly upset about it."[70]

These accusations clearly disturbed the League's leadership. In a long and detailed response, Ernst zu Reventlow, writing for the executive committee, dealt with the major points of the *Ortsgruppe* Esslingen's report.[71] The letter began in a very conciliatory fashion. Reventlow contended that the League always felt that both Kahr and Hitler had Germany's "best interest" at heart. In hindsight, one might even question the wisdom of Kahr's decision to use violence to suppress the uprising. As the League had also made clear on other occasions, they did not really consider Kahr to be the truly great statesman that Germany required to lead it out of its suffering. In this regard, Reventlow even criticized Kahr for his failure to act more decisively to establish his own dictatorship in the wake of the Hitler Putsch. Nonetheless, he argued, Kahr was a far lesser evil than those who might replace him and pursue a reckless program of "unbounded international, ultramontane politics."[72]

Most importantly, however, Reventlow believed that Hitler's plan simply never could have worked. Hitler's strategy would have first required wresting complete control of Bavaria away from Kahr and his associates. Even if that phase had been temporarily successful, Reventlow argued, Hitler's plan to then drive north to Berlin and take control of the rest of Germany would have been out of the question. After battling Kahr for control of Bavaria, it would have been impossible to put together a force strong enough and unified enough to launch any serious assault on the nation's capital. Moreover, Reventlow claimed, it was certainly questionable whether Hitler, "with his educational background," could ever have succeeded as Germany's leader.[73]

In general, Reventlow's response was consistent with the League leadership's earlier private appraisals of Hitler and the Nazi movement. In the early Weimar period, the Pan-German League had strong connections to virtually all elements of the German Right. Within this context, Heinrich Claß sought to establish a working relationship with Hitler. Claß always remained convinced, however, that only he and his Pan-German associates had the proper background, training, and education to successfully lead any anti-government effort. Claß's arrogance

---

[70] Ibid., 290.

[71] Graf von Reventlow to *Ortsgruppe* Esslingen, 15 January 1924, BARCH R8048/210, 21a–21c.

[72] Ibid., 21b.

[73] Ibid., 21a.

concerning Hitler's own background constantly led him to assume that Hitler would remain content with his role as an agitator and a mass speaker. Claß and the Pan-German leadership assumed that Hitler would do his duty and gladly place his movement and his skills at the service of those men who, like Claß, were best suited for serious political decisions.

This strategy left Claß and the Pan-German League in an extremely awkward position when Hitler actually began to step beyond the boundaries his elders in the völkisch movement thought they had imposed on him. When Hitler actually had the audacity to attempt a major assault on the government by himself, it seemed destined to fail. Reventlow's letter to the *Ortsgruppe* Esslingen perfectly summarized the League's real reaction to the Putsch and its aftermath. Although in the League's opinion, Hitler's failure seemed to vindicate the Pan-German assessment of his shortcomings as a German statesman, that vindication was truly cold comfort.

The failure of the Beer Hall Putsch and the subsequent crackdown on many right-wing organizations crippled any unity that might have remained within the right-wing camp in Bavaria and other parts of Germany. Claß and the Pan-German leadership clearly realized that their own plans for an assault on the French forces in the Ruhr, or even the German government itself, were no longer feasible. In addition, the League's treatment of Hitler's actions alienated some Pan-German members who also held the Nazi movement and its leader in high regard. Although it seemed clear to the League's leadership at the time that Hitler was finished, the League was still faced with the challenge of damage control in the aftermath of the Putsch.

This task became infinitely more complicated by Hitler's trial which lasted from February through April 1924. Hitler fully intended to use the courtroom as a political forum. As far as Claß and the Pan-German League were concerned, the trial itself only further reinforced the League's deep-seated mistrust of the Nazi leader. Hitler used the trial for his own purposes and turned the proceedings into a trial of the "November Criminals." He justified his actions on 8–9 November with the assertion that the Weimar government possessed neither the vision nor the resolve to do away with the destructive forces within and outside of Germany that were tearing the Reich apart.[74]

However, Hitler did not direct his rage only at the Weimar government or its supporters. During the course of the trial, Hitler argued that if what he had committed was high treason, then members of the Pan-German League should be tried themselves, as they were already planning a similar undertaking in the

---

[74]   For Hitler's speeches at the trial see: Eberhard Jäckel and Axel Kuhn (eds), *Hitler: Sämtliche Aufzeichnungen 1905–1924* (Stuttgart, 1980), 1061–1226. For an analysis of Hitler's use of the trial, see: Kershaw, *Hitler*, 213–216.

summer of 1923. Heinrich Claß had, Hitler asserted, approached him earlier that summer about plans for a directory with Kahr and Pöhner. Hitler claimed that his own move against the government was done primarily out of concern that Claß, Kahr, and his associates were going to strike first. Most importantly, Hitler implied that Claß actually traveled to Munich immediately before the Putsch, and convinced Kahr to crush the Nazi leader's effort. Claß did this, according to Hitler's argument, because the Pan-German League leader did not wish to see Hitler's attempt succeed and thereby spoil the League's own plans for military action in which Hitler had refused to participate. Although Claß was never called to testify, he wired the court and published an open letter refuting Hitler's charges.[75] In response, Hitler reiterated his accusation that Claß was creating a "directory" which the Pan-German leader planned to head.[76]

Hitler's accusations stung Claß and other leading Pan-Germans. What was most disappointing, Claß recalled, was not the fact that Hitler publicly accused him of high treason, but rather the fact that Hitler blamed him for undermining the Hitler Putsch itself. After all, Claß argued, Hitler's actions were the only issue on trial. Hitler knew that Claß was not in Munich on 8 November to influence Kahr's decision. The only possible rationale for Hitler's defense was to divert attention away from his own decision to act by placing it within a supposedly larger context of right-wing plots against the government. Claß felt that Hitler's decision to bring up hearsay evidence of earlier rightist plots did not help Hitler's defense at all and only succeeded in tarnishing the Pan-German League's reputation.[77]

Shortly after the trial's conclusion, Claß published in the *Alldeutsche Blätter* his final commentary on the entire affair.[78] Claß repeated his denial that he had anything to do with the failure of the Hitler Putsch or Kahr's decision to act against it. Claß pointed out that the last time that he and Hitler spoke about any plans for action against the French and the German government was on 20 May 1923. He did not meet again with Hitler that summer, as the Nazi leader claimed during the trial. Moreover, Hitler knew full well what Claß intended to do from that May meeting. Claß argued that he had always intended to

[75]   Claß's open letter appeared as: "Justizrat Claß und der Münchener Prozeß: Ein Brief an den Vorsitzenden des Volksgerichts," *Deutsche Zeitung*, 23 March 1924, 1. Claß denied that he had ever given his word to Kahr for a planned move against the government. Taking a legalistic approach, however, the Pan-German leader never gave the court or the public any indication of the extent to which he had indeed discussed and planned the feasibility of such an operation.

[76]   Jäckel and Kuhn, *Aufzeichnungen*, 1195.

[77]   Claß, *WdS v. II-addendum*, 33.

[78]   "In eigener Sache. Nachwort zum Münchener Hochverrats-Prozeß," *Alldeutsche Blätter*, 19 April 1924, 18–19.

take on the French in the Ruhr first, perhaps in cooperation with other right-wing groups. Only after removing the French could the issue of the Weimar government even be considered.

Hitler was also clearly lying at the trial, Claß continued, when he asserted that the Pan-German leader had approached him about the creation of a "directory." Hitler would have known from their 20 May meeting that Claß never planned to institute anything else but a dictatorship. A directory, Claß argued, would never be decisive enough and always required a majority decision to act. Claß's only faith was in a dictatorship, where the decision-making and the responsibility lay with one man alone. Moreover, Hitler's assertion that Claß sought to head either a directory or a dictatorship was completely false. Anyone that knew the Pan-German leader, the article stated, would realize immediately that Claß never sought the leading role for himself, but always sought to work behind the scenes to insure that the "best man" got the job.[79]

Conscious of the difficult position in which the Pan-German League found itself throughout the entire affair, Claß closed his article by stating that: "The curtain has fallen on the Munich trial. Let us hope that overwrought emotions subside and that, as a result, those accusations with no basis in fact will cease."[80] By April 1924, however, the damage had already been done. The Putsch and subsequent trial dashed Pan-German hopes for Hitler as a völkisch agitator and mass speaker.[81] More importantly, the unity of the völkisch movement for which the Pan-German League had worked since the beginning of the Weimar Republic now seemed out of reach.

After the Putsch trial, Pan-German connections with Hitler's movement virtually ceased. The League's headquarters occasionally received letters during the Weimar Republic's middle years from individual members who tried to encourage the League to resurrect its ties to the Nazi Party. However, these requests produced no substantial change in the League's approach. One example of these failed attempts can be found in the correspondence between Marie Gareis of Nuremburg and the Pan-German/Nazi leadership. Gareis wrote several times directly to Hitler, requesting that he meet once more with Claß to resolve their differences. As a result, Claß received a rather coolly worded letter from Rudolf Hess explaining that Hitler was unable to meet with Claß and, in any case, would certainly not rely on "some woman in Nuremberg" to arrange

---

[79]   Ibid., 19.

[80]   Ibid.

[81]   Claß's low opinion of Hitler's political skills certainly did not improve with the publication of *Mein Kampf*. After reading Hitler's book, Claß remarked that "anyone who has read this book and is still not convinced of Hitler's political incompetence is beyond help." SGA, 4 September 1925, BARCH R8048/144, 19.

his political affairs. The League in turn requested that Gareis cease her efforts to unite the two leaders.[82] This episode accurately reflected the deteriorating relationship between the Pan-Germans and the Nazi movement in the Weimar Republic's middle years.

The League was now faced with the harsh reality that a new course of action was necessary to maintain its influence on the German Right. A decisive new phase in the League's entire approach to political action was about to begin. In the wake of the Hitler trial and the complete break with Wulle, Graefe-Goldebee, Ludendorff, and the DVFP, the League would soon shift its focus on the field of mainstream party politics. As Chapter 4 will demonstrate, the chosen partner for this new strategy would be the German National People's Party or DNVP.

---

[82] This correspondence between Gareis and League Headquarters stretched from April to June 1925. See: BARCH R8048/211, 146–152, 158–161, 165, 173–179, and 204; Hess to Claß, 9 June 1925, BARCH R8048/211, 185; and League Headquarters to Gareis, 24 June 1925, BARCH R8048/211, 204.

Chapter 4
The Demands of Party Politics, 1919–1925

By 1924, the fallout from the Pan-German League's public conflict with the German Völkisch Freedom Party (DVFP) and the disastrous impact of Hitler's failed Beer Hall Putsch and subsequent trial left the League in search of a new political strategy. The anti-Weimar extremist Right was in shambles, split apart by fractious infighting and paranoid struggles over leadership of the radical nationalist movement. The temporary merger of Hitler's followers with the DVFP in 1924 in the National Socialist Freedom Movement (*Nationalsozialistische Freiheitsbewegung* or "NSFB"), as well as the Nazi Party's re-founding in February 1925, explicitly excluded the Pan-German League.[1] These events confirmed to the League's leadership that the unity of Germany's radical nationalist movement would likely never be accomplished. The Pan-Germans were still firmly committed to establishing a völkisch authoritarian state, but in the wake of Adolf Hitler's spectacular failure it seemed clear that the means to that end clearly did not lie with a coup d'état.[2]

The League's main post-war goal had always been to exercise influence through other organizations rather than drawing public attention to itself. However, the Pan-German attempt to coordinate the radical right-wing campaign in the Weimar Republic's first years had not produced the desired results. Consequently, throughout 1924 the League developed a new approach in response to the rapid fragmentation of the extremist right-wing milieu. Even though significant challenges remained for the Weimar system, the government had successfully weathered multiple attacks from the Left and Right, the disastrous hyper-inflation, and a broader struggle for political legitimacy in the wake of the Versailles Treaty. By 1924 the Weimar Republic had begun to stabilize, and mainstream party politics gained greater influence at the local,

---

[1] On the negotiations leading to the relatively shaky merger of these two forces, see: Kershaw, *Hitler*, 224–234. For more detail about the Nazi Party in the period immediately following the Hitler Putsch, see: David Jablonsky, *The Nazi Party In Dissolution: Hitler and the Verbotszeit 1923–25* (London and Totowa, 1989).

[2] Pan-German League headquarters to Freiherr von Haller-Hallerstein (Augsburg), 3 January 1924, BARCH R8048/210, 18–18a.

regional, and national level throughout Germany in advance of the May 1924 Reichstag elections.[3] The Pan-German League was fully aware of this shift.

By this time, the League's leadership also recognized another stark reality. In addition to the political infighting and intrigue in which the Pan-Germans were constantly embroiled between 1919 and 1924, the League also faced a declining membership total. After reaching its highest numbers in League history in 1922 at roughly 38,000 members, the League fell into a steady decline. By December 1928, the League counted only about 16,000 members.[4] The Pan-German leadership attributed this decline to two primary factors. First, the terrible inflation of 1922–1923 prevented many members from paying regular dues and also forced the League's offices to reduce their workload significantly. Second, the League blamed the infighting in the radical nationalist movement as an important cause of membership loss.[5] While both political and economic instability contributed to this decline, the Pan-Germans faced an uncertain future already in 1924.

In response, the League's leadership began to shift its primary focus away from the hopelessly fractious world of groups like the DVFP, Hitler, Ludendorff, and the paramilitary Right. Instead, from 1924 on the Pan-Germans focused primarily on conventional party politics and especially on the DNVP. In accordance with this shift in strategy, the League devoted its remaining resources and political influence to a campaign they hoped would force Germany's largest conservative political party away from participation in coalition politics, and toward an intransigent stance of permanent opposition to the Weimar Republic.[6] While the League had failed to unite Germany's extremist Right during the Republic's first years, it now hoped to have greater success shaping the course of Germany's largest and most influential conservative party.

The party that the Pan-Germans now targeted was a formidable political force. The DNVP was the dominant conservative party in Weimar Germany. Between 1924 and 1928 it was the largest single non-socialist party overall. Despite its size and influence, however, it was never truly united. In fact, for much of the party's history it was divided between two major factions. On one side stood the more moderate majority that grudgingly came to terms with the realities of Weimar politics. This moderate group eventually involved the DNVP in two national coalition governments in 1925 and again in 1927. These party

---

[3]   Mommsen, *Rise and Fall of Weimar Democracy*, 172.

[4]   For a detailed discussion of the League's Weimar-era membership from 1918 to 1928 see: SGA, 1/2 December 1928, BARCH R8048/156, 55–56.

[5]   Ibid.

[6]   Heinrich Claß directly identified this shift in Pan-German strategy in his memoirs. See: Claß, *WdS v. II*, 843.

moderates were opposed by a smaller but influential radical minority that worked tirelessly to drive the party away from any political compromise or acceptance of the Weimar system, regardless of the cost. These party radicals hoped to use the DNVP as a lynchpin for a future right-wing nationalist government that would stand up unequivocally to Germany's enemies abroad and dismantle the democratic system at home.

The Pan-German League and its close circle of party allies stood at the heart of this radical group. Using internal party leadership connections, its public press coverage, and its influence with the DNVP's regional and local groups, the League constantly attacked party moderates and worked tirelessly to drive the party away from any further accommodation with the Weimar Republic. While the Pan-Germans were not always immediately successful in their efforts, ultimately their strategy bore fruit with the election of Alfred Hugenberg as party leader in October 1928. The Pan-German League and its party allies played a significant role in Hugenberg's election and the subsequent departure of remaining party moderates between 1928 and 1930. While the Pan-German campaign intensified between 1924 and 1928, the groundwork had in fact already been established in the Weimar Republic's first years. Therefore, it is necessary to turn first to the early history of the Pan-German League's involvement with the DNVP.

The DNVP's Early History and the "Völkisch Secession" of 1922

Founded in November 1918, the DNVP encompassed a relatively diverse collection of right-wing parties and organizations stunned by Germany's defeat and openly opposed to the new political changes precipitated by the founding of the Weimar Republic. The new party united influential pre-1918 political parties including rightist elements of the National Liberals, the Free Conservatives, the German Conservative Party, Christian Socialists, and a number of extremist völkisch organizations.[7] With the Emperor and the old restrictive Wilhelmine political system now gone, these groups now faced a fundamentally different situation in the post-1918 period. Party leaders and members hoped that the DNVP would present an effective political platform with broad public appeal and significant influence in the emerging post-war political system.[8]

---

[7] For the history of pre-war German Conservatism see: Retallack, *Notables of the Right*.

[8] D.P. Walker, "The German Nationalist Peoples' Party: The Conservative Dilemma in the Weimar Republic," *Journal of Contemporary History*, 14, 1979, 627. For other general surveys of the DNVP's early development see: Lewis Hertzman, *DNVP: Right-Wing Opposition in the*

However, the party never fully resolved its basic position regarding the newly created Weimar Republic. Many conservatives simply viewed the government as a child born out of wartime defeat and a constant reminder of the monarchy's collapse. Yet in spite of these considerable ideological hurdles, many DNVP members also realized that they needed effective political representation on crucial economic, social, and foreign policy issues. Furthermore, many German conservatives took seriously their responsibility to uphold the state and its institutions. Hans von Lindeiner-Wildau, the party's general secretary after 1919, best summarized the party's moderate majority view on this issue:

> The fundamental rejection of an illegitimate state dictated a clear stance of opposition, but the feeling of personal involvement with the fate of the state, which is the essence of conservative thought, encouraged constructive cooperation.[9]

Even though Lindeiner and many of his moderate DNVP colleagues were deeply disturbed by the Hohenzollern dynasty's collapse and the establishment of the Weimar Republic, they gradually acknowledged that their responsibility as conservatives lay in support of the state regardless of which governmental form it adopted.

Axel Freiherr von Freytagh-Loringhoven, representing the party's intransigent Pan-German wing, approached the question much differently. He argued that the state—an organic entity which transcended the formal institutions of government power—and the actual government leaders or the political system itself were not always synonymous. Freytagh-Loringhoven argued that "a clear conceptual distinction remains between them [national leaders] and the state as a complete entity." Therefore, he concluded that:

> With a clear separation of these terms ... it is entirely possible that the individual, as well as a party, could ... hold true to his convictions which support and preserve the state, while at the same time oppose the holders of state power because they [in fact] do not support or preserve the state itself.[10]

Weimar Republic, 1918–1924 (Lincoln, 1963); Liebe, *Deutschnationale Volkspartei*; and Thimme, *Flucht in den Mythos*.

[9]   Lindeiner-Wildau quoted in: Walker, "Conservative Dilemma," 627.

[10]   Axel Freiherr von Freytagh-Loringhoven, *Deutschnationale Volkspartei* (Berlin, 1931), 11.

Freytagh-Loringhoven's stance was the cornerstone of the Pan-German League's policy regarding the DNVP's political goals.[11]

Despite these fundamental differences, both constituencies recognized that outright political violence or a Putsch were not effective political weapons. This position developed early on in response to a party crisis regarding the participation of several DNVP members without party sanction in the March 1920 Kapp Putsch. Although only a handful of members, like the radical pastor Dr. Gottfried Traub, took part in this action, the party condemned the Putsch and distanced itself from the perpetrators.[12] And even though the DNVP was highly critical of Matthias Erzberger and Walther Rathenau, the party never sanctioned their murders, and in fact disapproved of political assassination as harmful to the proper functioning of the state.[13]

Despite agreement on the general rejection of political violence, significant differences concerning the DNVP's stance toward the Weimar Republic still represented a significant fault line within the party. Initially, these differences did not seriously impede the party's early success. Outrage over the Versailles Treaty and the alleged incompetence of Germany's leaders fueled the party's propaganda campaign in the run up to the first national Reichstag elections scheduled for 6 June 1920.

In these elections the DNVP gained a respectable 15 percent of the total vote and 71 seats.[14] Many members felt that the party had weathered the initial storms of the November Revolution and forged a broadly based representative platform for a wide variety of conservative interests. As Albrecht Philipp, a prominent Saxon DNVP politician, observed, the newly elected Reichstag delegates "constituted a colorful mixture of representatives of all groups, ages, and regions, just as one would expect from a 'Volkspartei.'"[15] Philipp's overly optimistic assessment belied the substantial differences that would ultimately divide the party in the coming years.

In fact, the party did not have long to wait until it faced the first major challenge to its early solidarity. The DNVP had been successful early on as a protest party that pledged to address all manner of troubles supposedly connected to the new republican system. Nonetheless, one specific issue, anti-

---

[11] See also: Manfred Dörr, *Die Deutschnationale Volkspartei 1925 bis 1928* (Diss. Phil., Marburg/Lahn, 1964), 53.

[12] For the DNVP's stance on the Kapp Putsch, as well as the involvement of individual members, see: Liebe, *Deutschnationale Volkspartei*, 51–61.

[13] Hertzman, *DNVP*, 132–133.

[14] Kolb, *Weimar Republic*, 194.

[15] "Albrecht Philipp Memoirs," SHStA Dresden, NL Albrecht Philipp (hereafter "NL Philipp")/4, 91.

Semitism, began to pose problems for the party's leadership and rank and file members. While most members shared general personal prejudices against Jews, their attitudes regarding the specific political use of anti-Semitism were widely divergent. Some DNVP politicians made extensive and blatant use of anti-Semitic rhetoric, while others found it much less effective.[16] So even as the party enjoyed its first national electoral victory in 1920, the issue of anti-Semitism was already coming to a head. In the ensuing political struggle over this issue, the Pan-German League became involved for the first time in the DNVP's internal politics.

Already at the DNVP's first party congress in July 1919, the extreme racist right-wing, led by Albrecht von Graefe-Goldebee, pushed to include an explicitly anti-Semitic plank in the party's platform. In spite of a spirited debate that extended beyond the party congress, Graefe-Goldebee and his allies introduced a vaguely worded anti-Semitic statement in the party program beginning in 1920. It argued that the DNVP, as a representative of the German people, would fight all "destructive, un-German elements" either from Jewish or other circles. Specifically, the clause stated that "[The DNVP] particularly opposes Jewish domination which has become increasingly disastrous since the revolution in government and public life."[17]

However, the party's leadership and some rank and file members did not fully support this anti-Semitic statement and certain members were uncomfortable with, or even confused by, the party's official stance. Was this clause aimed at preventing Jewish membership or "influence" within the party itself, or was it intended as a broader commentary on German society? Furthermore, what determined a person's Jewish status? Was this to be a fundamentally racial anti-Semitism that would influence specific policy decisions, or would the issue remain largely rhetorical based on established religious and cultural anti-Semitic themes?

The party's leadership sought to clarify this confusion. In November 1921 members of the executive committee and regional party representatives passed a motion proposed by Karl Helfferich, one of the party's most prominent members. Helfferich argued that there was no need to exclude Jews from formal party membership, but that the party itself would continue to fight for conservative goals in German society.[18] This could mean the use of anti-Semitic themes in party propaganda as the situation required. Helfferich's compromise proposal was aimed at maintaining party unity without entirely backing away

---

[16]   Liebe, *Deutschnationale Volkspartei*, 64–65.

[17]   Quoted in: ibid., 65.

[18]   Hertzman, *DNVP*, 137–138.

from the political potential of anti-Semitism. In spite of this effort, the leading right-wing extremists in the party, including Albrecht von Graefe-Goldebee, Reinhold Wulle, and Wilhelm Henning, found this policy unacceptable.

From mid-1921 until fall 1922, the party's leadership focused a good deal of attention on these party extremists. As the party's leadership cracked down and tried to maintain unity, the Graefe-Goldebee/Wulle/Henning group became even more determined to assert its own radical position within the party. They pushed even more forcefully for a racially purified, openly anti-Semitic DNVP. To pursue this goal, the men formed a separate organization called the German Völkisch Cooperative Group (*Deutschvölkische Arbeitsgemeinschaft*) in September 1922.[19]

Although Graefe-Goldebee, Wulle, and their colleagues initially intended this new organization to support the DNVP and deal explicitly with racial issues, the party's leadership viewed the Cooperative Group as a potential "party-within-the-party" and as a direct threat to the DNVP's overall unity. In the weeks leading up to the Görlitz party congress scheduled for 26–28 October 1922, the racial issue and broader concerns about party organization came to a head. The DNVP's moderate Christian Social wing had already denounced the radical anti-Semitic goals of the racists, and a growing number of party moderates were concerned that such an openly radical stance might hurt the DNVP's chances for future government participation.[20]

In spite of mediation attempts between the party's leadership and the radicals, no compromise seemed possible. Although the Görlitz congress did not directly expel Graefe-Goldebee, Wulle, or Henning from the party, it effectively destroyed any chance the men had to maintain their unique position within the DNVP. Indeed, the majority of the party representatives supported the leadership's policies and opposed the disruptive radicals. To blunt the troubling agitation of Graefe-Goldebee, Wulle, and Henning, the DNVP sanctioned the creation of a National Völkisch Committee (*Völkischer Reichsausschuß*) within the party. In the wake of the Görlitz congress Graefe-Goldebee, Wulle, and Henning all resigned from the party and on 17 December 1922 they publicly announced the formation of the new German Völkisch Freedom Party (*Deutschvölkische Freiheitspartei* or DVFP).[21] The DNVP and the DVFP quickly turned on each

---

[19] Liebe, *Deutschnationale Volkspartei*, 65–66. For the radical view of the growing divide within the DNVP see: Reinhold Wulle, "Die Vorgänge in der deutschnationalen Volkspartei," July 1922, Nachlaß Westarp-Gärtringen (hereafter "NL Westarp")/87, np.

[20] Liebe, *Deutschnationale Volkspartei*, ibid., 67–68.

[21] Many DNVP members expressed deep regret at the radicals' departure from the party and the founding of the DVFP. For example, the party's Osnabrück chapter issued a statement referring to the creation of the new party as an event that would "only bring fragmentation in

other in a conflict characterized by harsh propaganda and paranoid personal attacks.[22] As we will see, the Pan-German League came to play an important role in this conflict, as the League already had experience dealing with the newly departed DNVP radicals.

As Chapter 2 explained, Reinhold Wulle and Albrecht von Graefe-Goldebee both became Pan-German League members during World War I. In fact, Reinhold Wulle was an active member of the League's Essen chapter and later became chairman Heinrich Claß's handpicked appointee as editor-in-chief of the Pan-German *Deutsche Zeitung* in October 1918. Wulle's apparent commitment to the League and his initial handling of the *Deutsche Zeitung* encouraged Claß and other Pan-German leaders. Albrecht von Graefe-Goldebee also joined the Pan-German League in Mecklenburg during the course of World War I. Claß was deeply impressed with Graefe-Goldebee's political skill and speaking abilities.[23]

However, this amicable relationship quickly deteriorated as Wulle and Graefe-Goldebee broke free from their exclusive commitment to the Pan-German League. The League's struggle with Wulle and Graefe-Goldebee over control of the radical nationalist movement completely alienated the former allies by 1921. As was often the case on the German extremist Right in the early post-war period, the desire for political control became more important than a general ideological commitment to anti-Semitism and an authoritarian state. Once these personal conflicts became public, they were nearly impossible to resolve.

As the feud between Claß, Graefe-Goldebee, and Wulle exploded publicly in 1921, the Pan-German League began to seek out new allies. This search led them to the DNVP in part because of the party's own conflict with Wulle, Graefe-Goldebee, and Henning. While the Pan-Germans backed the DNVP's leadership from the start and openly lamented the DVFP's founding, the League also realized that it had discovered a new opportunity to strengthen its ties to German conservative politics.

---

our nationalist camp. We ask our members, as always, to stay true to German Nationalist People's Party." Niedersächsisches Staatsarchiv Osnabrück (hereafter "NsäStA-Osnabrück"), C1 "DNVP Osnabrück" (hereafter "C1")/7, 48.

[22]   The extensive files of the Westarp Nachlaß provide a good sense of the intensity of the feud that developed between the DNVP and the DVFP. Westarp and other DNVP party leaders received hundreds of letters from regional and local DNVP chapters and individual members concerning the split and its broader impact on the political fortunes of the German Right, especially from 1922 to 1924. See especially: NL Westarp, folders 25, 29, 35, 37, 86–89, and 122.

[23]   Claß, *WdS v. II*, esp. 603–628.

From the beginning of the Weimar period, the Pan-German League's connection to the DNVP was stronger than with any other party.[24] Many leading Pan-Germans belonged to the DNVP and even represented the party in the Reichstag. Along with Alfred Hugenberg, a co-founder of the Pan-German League, this list included men like Axel Freiherr von Freytagh-Loringhoven, Walther Graef (Thüringen), Leopold von Vietinghoff-Scheel, Paul Bang, Karl Lohmann, and Carl Gottfried Gok, the prominent head of the Blohm and Voß shipbuilders in Hamburg. As the crisis in the DNVP and in the Pan-German League's relationship to the Graefe-Goldebee–Wulle group worsened simultaneously, these members resolutely backed both the League and the DNVP's leadership.

For Freytagh-Loringhoven and his pro-DNVP colleagues, the reasoning was clear. Siding with the party's leadership against the Graefe-Goldebee/ Wulle group would help re-establish a united front and prevent any further damage to the party's public image and political influence. A campaign against the newly formed DVFP might also lend the Pan-Germans and their allies increased legitimacy in established conservative circles. Furthermore, the Pan-German League's position offered yet another crucially important advantage. With the DNVP cleared of the renegade racists, many Pan-Germans saw a real opportunity to increase their own direct influence within the party.[25] Freytagh-Loringhoven and his allies hoped that their increased role in the DNVP might one day provide them with the opportunity to unseat party moderates and firmly establish a radical anti-Weimar political party.

In August 1923, Freytagh-Loringhoven and Heinrich Claß discussed Pan-German support for the DNVP and emphasized the necessity of "proceed[ing] ruthlessly against Wulle [and the DVFP]."[26] Particularly, Freytagh-Loringhoven and the League's leadership agreed to use the *Deutsche Zeitung* to support this campaign. In an overtly partisan fashion, the League's leadership agreed that the Pan-German League must do everything it could to fight the DVFP and defend the DNVP.[27] Indeed, this was the case as the *Deutsche Zeitung* and the *Alldeutsche Blätter* subsequently published a series of articles attacking Wulle,

---

[24]   See Chapter 1.

[25]   This approach bore some early fruit in September 1923 when Claß received a request from the chairman of the DNVP's Hamburg chapter requesting Claß's advice on a candidate for the chief business manager position of the chapter. See: Dr. U. Lienau, Chairman of the Landesverband Hamburg der DNVP to Claß, 5 September 1923, BARCH R8048/209, 204.

[26]   Freytagh-Loringhoven to Claß, 6 August 1923, BARCH R8048/209, 177.

[27]   Vietinghoff-Scheel to Freytagh-Loringhoven, 11 August 1923, BARCH R8048/209, 184.

Graefe-Goldebee, Henning and the DVFP.[28] In the paranoid world of post-war right-wing politics, political control ultimately mattered more than ideological agreement.

In the wake of this crisis, the Pan-German League's influence within the DNVP increased not only because of its public support for the party, but also because of several key League members' involvement in the party's newly formed National Völkisch Committee. This committee was established at the Görlitz party congress in October 1922 to deal systematically with anti-Semitism and other racial issues. The party hoped to provide an official forum for resolving its stance on the Jewish question, while avoiding a repetition of the public embarrassment caused by the earlier conflict over similar issues with the Graefe-Goldebee/Wulle group.[29]

Pan-German League members dominated the DNVP's newly formed Völkisch Committee. The chair Walther Graef (Thüringen), and vice-chair Axel Freiherr von Freytagh-Loringhoven were both prominent Pan-German League members. Additionally, Graef, Freytagh-Loringhoven, and Baron von Vietinghoff-Scheel, the Pan-German League's head business manager and a close confidant of Heinrich Claß, directed the influential subcommittee for "national affairs." Roughly half of the 35 members of the Committee's national organization were also Pan-Germans.[30]

The Committee held its formal organizational meeting in Berlin on 22 April 1923.[31] At this meeting, the Committee established its official structure within the party and considered proposals for a specific platform. The Committee consisted of one representative from each of the DNVP's state party organizations (*Landesverbände*), along with one alternate. The executive committee reserved the right to appoint certain "particularly well-known völkisch oriented individuals" within the party.[32] The group also voted to allow other party representatives to attend any of the meetings in an advisory capacity.

---

[28]   See for example: "Und trotzdem: Völkische Einigung!" *Deutsche Zeitung*, 13 December 1923, 1–2; "In eigener Sache," *Alldeutsche Blätter*, 14 December 1923, 1–2; "Klarheit tut not," *Deutsche Zeitung*, 10 February 1924, 1–2; "Die Krise im völkischen Lager," *Deutsche Zeitung*, 12 July 1924, 1–2; and "Bild der Lage," *Deutschlands Erneurung*, May 1924, 318–320.

[29]   Although the committee itself was formed in 1922, some of its leading members had discussed the possibility of an internal DNVP organization devoted to the "volkisch" issue as early as 1920. See: Axel Freiherr von Freytagh-Loringhoven to Kuno Graf von Westarp, NL Westarp/25, 20 July 1920, np.

[30]   For a membership list and organizational roster of the DNVP's Völkisch Committee see: BARCH R8048/223, 6 and 59.

[31]   "Niederschrift über die Verhandlungen des Deutschvölkischen Reichsausschusses," BARCH R8048/223, 5–6.

[32]   Ibid., 5.

The Committee further agreed to serve as an advisory board on racial questions within the DNVP's national, regional, and local organization. Additionally, the Committee would be responsible for a "public information campaign" (*Volksaufklärung*) that distributed flyers, posters, and pamphlets concerning the DNVP's stance on völkisch politics generally, and the Jewish Question specifically.[33]

The Committee received a range of suggestions over the next several weeks regarding its official policy on racial questions. Some extreme proposals suggested a focused campaign against the Jews that in some ways resembled later Nazi racial legislation.[34] This would include an immediate stop to the influx of so-called "Eastern Jews," an official census which clearly separated Jews from members of pure German lineage, and financial incentives for large "German" families.

Ultimately, the Committee had to strike a balance between the various anti-Semitic attitudes within the DNVP. By the beginning of 1924, Baron von Vietinghoff-Scheel and several other Committee members drafted a working document entitled "Guidelines of Völkisch Philosophy and Politics."[35] They distributed the document to all committee members for immediate consideration at the upcoming February meeting. The "Guidelines" focused on three major areas: the German people, the state, and the economy. The German people's primary responsibility, the document stated, was the "preservation of their peculiarly Nordic-race heritage passed down to them from their Germanic forefathers." The German state should be grounded on the protection of this "racial heritage" and deny citizenship to any individual of "different, non-German extraction." Therefore, based on this notion, the state could not be formed "mechanically" by outside forces, but rather should grow organically from the "particularly Germanic essence" of its people.[36]

True Germans, the document continued, would participate in a government system based in part on elections, but also on "direct" citizen participation in important foreign and domestic policy decisions to help shape the future of the "organic state." This state would ideally be headed by the institution of hereditary monarchy that would represent the essence of the German people in its truest, purest form.[37] Finally, economic policy would be guided not merely by selfishness or the desire for maximum profit, but rather for the good of the

---

[33] Ibid.

[34] See the motion proposed at the organizational meeting by the DNVP member Dr. Gerstenhauer: "Antrag Gerstenhauer," 22 April 1923, BARCH R8048/223, 7.

[35] "Leitsätze der völkischen Welt- und Staatsanschauung," BARCH R8048/223, 33–35.

[36] Ibid., 33.

[37] Ibid., 34.

German people as a whole. All major aspects of the economy, including land ownership, agricultural and industrial regulation, and trades and crafts would be controlled and protected for the greatest benefit of the entire people, not simply for the special interests of one group.[38] After limited debate and minor modification, the Committee approved the document, distributed it to party members, and published it in the press.[39]

In addition to approving the draft document, the Völkisch Committee gained an important personal endorsement for its work from party chairman Oskar Hergt at their February 1924 meeting.[40] Hergt valued the group's work. He pointed out that even though economic issues had recently taken center stage in the party's deliberations, he believed that the key to the party's long-term success lay in addressing crucial ideological questions (*Weltanschauungsfragen*). The top priority on the list of these ideological issues was the "racial question."[41]

Hergt explained that because of the party's original program and recent "unfortunate personal animosities"—a reference to the feud with Graefe-Goldebee, Wulle and the DVFP—the DNVP had not dealt systematically with the racial question. Now the time had come, Hergt argued, to deepen and clarify the party's commitment to this issue. However, Hergt cautioned that he had encountered "a certain nervousness" within the party concerning the Völkisch Committee's intentions. Therefore, it was imperative not to present the racial issue as a platform to increase the Committee's influence, but rather as a truly ideological platform that the entire party must embrace. Hergt assured the Committee that what they decided on that day would be presented to the country as the party's "powerful slogan." While the DNVP could not "over-trump" the DVFP, Hergt was confident that the Committee's work would insure that the DNVP would never be questioned about its "spiritual commitment" to the racial question.[42]

In addition to drafting the DNVP's völkisch goals, the Committee's February meeting also produced an official policy regarding Jewish membership in the DNVP. Committee Chairman Walther Graef revealed that Hergt had assured him that some form of a "Jewish Paragraph" would officially be voted into the

---

[38]   Ibid.

[39]   The revised formal declaration appeared in the *Deutsche Zeitung* about two weeks later. See: "Die völkischen Ziele der Deutschnationalen Volkspartei," *Deutsche Zeitung*, 4 March 1924, 3.

[40]   BARCH R8048/223, 41–42. Hergt had previously demonstrated little interest in a DNVP völkisch program. With the DVFP's founding, however, he clearly realized the potential of such an official program.

[41]   BARCH R8048/223, 41.

[42]   Ibid.

party's statutes at the upcoming April party gathering in Hamburg.[43] After some debate, the Committee finally approved two possible options. The first and most extreme proposal denied party membership "to all Jews, mixed-Jews, and those married to Jews." In the case that the party meeting was unwilling to except this extreme position, a second proposal banned only "full Jews and those married to Jews" from the party.[44] Ultimately, the DNVP approved the second version of the Jewish clause at its April meeting.

In the short term, the National Völkisch Committee played a key role in clarifying the DNVP's stance on Jewish membership and völkisch politics generally. Oskar Hergt's speech at the Committee's February meeting gave some indication of the extent to which even important party moderates were willing to go to solidify the DNVP's official stance on the völkisch issue. Certainly, the DVFP's threat to the DNVP's control over völkisch politics played no small role in Hergt's willingness to support the Völkisch Committee's work. The DNVP's leadership realized that it could not afford to relinquish entirely the propaganda value of anti-Semitism and völkisch ideology to the DVFP or other fringe groups like the Nazi Party.

After completing the Jewish Clause and the Völkisch Platform, the Völkisch Committee devoted its energies primarily to election propaganda and speeches at local and national DNVP rallies. The Committee had regional representatives and active members in almost all major local and regional DNVP chapters and sought to focus attention on the issue of racial politics. The Committee sponsored yearly "Völkisch Weeks" like the one in Berlin in June 1924.[45] These meetings featured speeches and round-table presentations by prominent DNVP, Pan-German, and other allied right-wing leaders including Freytagh-Loringhoven and Paul Bang. The presentations covered diverse topics including race, religion, land ownership, culture, and of course, politics and economics.[46] The National Völkisch Committee played its largest public role in the coming years in this capacity as a propaganda arm for the DNVP and its völkisch program.

All of this activity was, of course, welcome news to the Pan-German League in its growing connection to the DNVP. Indeed, the National Völkisch Committee was significant for the Pan-German League's influence on the development of the DNVP in two major ways. First, the committee kept alive the issue of anti-Semitism and hashed out broader questions concerning the place of

---

[43] Ibid., 43.

[44] Ibid., 44.

[45] For an advertisement of this event, see: National Völkisch Committee to all DNVP Regional Chapters and the Members of the Völkisch Committee, 23 May 1924, BARCH R8048/223, 57.

[46] Ibid.

völkisch politics in the party more generally. The party's adoption in 1924 of the völkisch program and the Jewish clause was clear evidence of the Committee's influence—and through it the Pan-German League's—on DNVP policy. Secondly, although it was relatively small, the Committee established itself in numerous local party organizations. In this capacity it served as a platform for the promotion of the Pan-German agenda within the party, particularly from 1924 to 1928 when the League's intransigent anti-government stance was less acceptable to many party moderates. Baron von Vietinghoff-Scheel, one of the Völkisch Committee's leaders, summed up these points in a detailed letter to a Pan-German/DNVP colleague in Dresden:

> My collaboration with the [National Völkisch] committee ... has been driven by the desire to establish the deepest possible roots for the völkisch ideal among the voters and members of the party so that one day the current party leadership will be replaced by a genuinely völkisch one ... While the Pan-German League's duty and responsibility is unquestionably the dissemination of the völkisch ideal ... in all groups, we must particularly attempt this with the best available forces in the German National Peoples' Party.[47]

Ironically, the Committee's basic goals and attitudes concerning anti-Semitism did not differ substantially from the Graefe-Goldebee/Wulle group that originally split from the party in 1922. The real difference came in political tactics and the strategies used for eventual implementation of völkisch goals. While the DNVP simply could not tolerate a widely publicized split within its own ranks over the racial question, it did not want to ignore the political value of the issue or surrender completely the rhetoric of anti-Semitism to other more radical parties on the Right.

In that sense, the National Völkisch Committee satisfied the party's needs. The Committee's existence within the formal party structure also provided a number of individual Pan-German League members with yet another platform to promote their ideas not only concerning anti-Semitism and the racial question, but also the DNVP's stance on parliamentary politics and government participation more broadly. The influence of many individual Völkisch Committee members and other Pan-Germans on the course of DNVP policy would become increasingly apparent throughout the period between 1924 and 1930.

---

[47]   Vietinghoff-Scheel to Korvettenkapitän Maßmann, 27 March 1924, StADresden ADV-OD/5, 245–246.

Internal and External Challenges to the DNVP in 1924

With several important early conflicts now largely resolved, the DNVP felt increasing pressure from within and outside the party to participate more actively in the political system. This pressure was particularly strong from a growing contingent of moderate conservatives within the DNVP. By 1924 a significant number of party members had grudgingly warmed to the notion of increased participation in the Weimar government. Part of this change had to do with the simple realization that the new Republic was more durable than many had originally thought. The system had already survived major Putsch attempts from the Left and Right, and the terrible economic uncertainty that had plagued the Republic from its earliest days seemed to be stabilizing. All of this brought many influential party members to the realization that outright opposition and political obstructionism had accomplished very little and would probably continue to be ineffective. For many party moderates, government participation now seemed to offer a better opportunity to achieve their political goals than remaining permanently in the opposition.[48]

Many constituencies within the DNVP demanded increased influence over governmental decision-making by the spring of 1924. The hyper-inflation of 1923 seriously affected the personal savings and professional careers of large numbers of white-collar workers and civil servants within the party. Even more significantly, industrial interests suffered increasingly from the French occupation of the Ruhr and the inflation. Influential agricultural interests within the party also complained about the shortage of capital and demanded increased protection from foreign competition. In spite of these glaring problems, the DNVP had refused to take on the responsibility of government for fear that its participation would provide the Republic with the legitimacy in right-wing circles that the state needed to survive. At the same time, growing numbers of party moderates also began to realize that their continued absence from crucial decisions on issues like currency stabilization, passive resistance, and tax, tariff, and trade agreements, could well destroy both the party and the interests it represented.[49] The results of the May 1924 Reichstag elections, and the intense debate over the Dawes Plan, brought this basic party conflict to a boiling point.

---

[48]   On the DNVP's change in attitude toward government participation, see: Dörr, *Deutschnationale Volkspartei*, 60–80; Robert Grathwol, *Stresemann and the DNVP: Reconciliation or Revenge in German Foreign Policy* (Lawrence, 1980), 15–41; Kevin Repp, *Westarp, Hugenberg and Control of the DNVP* (MA Thesis, Washington State University, 1987), 9–10; and Scheck, *Alfred von Tirpitz*, 144–145.

[49]   Repp, *Westarp, Hugenberg*, 9–10.

The DNVP emerged from the May elections with roughly 15 percent of the total vote and 96 seats in the new Reichstag. Even though the SPD's 100 seats outnumbered the DNVP by itself, the conservatives controlled an additional 10 seats won by the allied Agrarian League (*Landbund*). Although the Agrarian League ran its candidates independently, it chose to sit with the German Nationalist Reichstag delegation. This brought the party's total count up to 106 seats, making it the largest party in the Reichstag.[50] All of this seemed to indicate that the DNVP could no longer be excluded from serious consideration for governmental participation. While the pressure for such a move increased from moderate elements within the DNVP itself, the party's leadership engaged in serious negotiations with the Center Party and the German People's Party (*Deutsche Volkspartei* or "DVP")regarding the DNVP's entry into a coalition. It soon became clear, however, that the success of these negotiations depended largely on the party's stance toward the most crucial economic issue of 1924: the Dawes Plan. Ultimately, it was this issue which precipitated a major crisis within the DNVP by the summer's end.[51]

The Dawes Plan was an economic proposal designed to facilitate Germany's reparations payments to the victorious Allies, while providing an infusion of capital into the German economy. On the positive side, the Plan provided for a massive loan to Germany and an abatement of German reparation payments in the first four years after the agreement's enactment. It also held out the possibility of an early end to the Allied occupation of German territory. The proposal did not, however, truly provide a viable long-term solution to the question of German reparations payments.[52] From the fall of 1928 on, Germany would be required to begin massive annual payments (roughly 2.5 billion Marks), with the possibility of additional amounts calculated according to the health of the German economy. With this repayment schedule, the Allies were assured to reap major benefits from any significant German economic recovery. Nonetheless, the promise of immediate and substantial credit to the German economy, combined with the temporary easing of international tensions and an end to France's Ruhr occupation, was too much for all but the staunchest radicals on the German political scene to reject.[53]

For the DNVP's moderate majority, the Dawes Plan provided even further incentive for governmental cooperation. In practical financial terms, the Dawes

---

[50]   Grathwol, *Stresemann and the DNVP*, 16–17; Liebe, *Deutschnationale Volkspartei*, 77–78 and 181, n481.

[51]   Repp, *Westarp, Hugenberg*, 11.

[52]   Ibid.

[53]   Scheck, *Alfred von Tirpitz*, 138. On the Dawes Plan and the international community see: Mommsen, *Rise and Fall of Weimar Democracy*, 173–177.

Plan credits would be a huge help to the struggling East Elbian agricultural sector. Many industrialists and workers' representatives in the party also felt strongly that the Dawes Plan represented the best possible bulwark against further loss of profits and the very real potential of mass unemployment. Industrialists in the occupied western zones also saw promise in a proposed French evacuation of the Ruhr as part of the Dawes Plan.[54] Finally, many party moderates assumed that their acceptance of the Dawes Plan might lead to the DNVP's participation in a future coalition government that would allow the party to exert even greater influence over broader policy issues.[55]

However, the mere possibility of a coalition with parties to the left of the DNVP, or any serious discussion of support for the Dawes Plan infuriated the Pan-German League and its radical party allies. Plastered triumphantly across the front page of the Pan-German League's *Deutsche Zeitung* May 1924 election evening edition was the caption: "The Great Coalition Annihilated."[56] Quoting Otto von Bismarck, the lead article warned "Don't allow those to the Left to ensnare you." The paper's editor Max Maurenbrecher argued that the election demonstrated the people's desire to oppose any government action, particularly the foreign policy decisions of Foreign Minister Gustav Stresemann, which endangered Germany's status and security as a world power.[57] Therefore, the DNVP could not allow itself to enter into negotiations with those parties to its Left, especially the Center and the DVP. The DVP had suffered the consequences of its support for Stresemann's "fulfillment policy" concerning the

---

[54]　Repp, *Westarp, Hugenberg*, 12. As Heidrun Holzbach points out, however, not all DNVP industrialists were prepared to accept the Dawes Plan. A relatively small group called the "Deutsche Industriellen-Vereinigung" led by the prominent Pan-German Paul Bang categorically rejected the proposal. The vast majority of these "anti-Dawes" industrialists were representatives of medium- and light industry that stood to gain relatively little from the Dawes Plan. Thus, their opposition to the Plan on largely ideological grounds was much easier to maintain than that of many representatives of heavy industry within the DNVP. Most, but not all, heavy industrialists represented by the "Reichsverband der Deutschen Industrie" stood to benefit from the Dawes credits and were, therefore, reluctant to oppose it. See: Heidrun Holzbach, *Das "System Hugenberg." Die Organisation bürgerlicher Sammlungpolitik vor dem Aufstieg der NSDAP* (Stuttgart, 1981), 168–172.

[55]　For a clear explanation of the pro-Dawes Plan point of view, as well as the DNVP's desire for government participation, see the unpublished history of the Württemberg DNVP and its leader Wilhelm Bazille in the holdings of the Württemberg State Library in Stuttgart: Ernst Marquardt, *Kämpfer für Deutschlands Zukunft und Ehre: Umrisszeichnungen aus der Geschichte der deutschnationalen Volkspartei Württembergs*, 47–52.

[56]　*Deutsche Zeitung*, 6 May 1924, 1.

[57]　Ibid.

Allies and reparations. And even worse, according to Maurenbrecher, was the Center Party's inability to escape its past:

> From July 1917 to April 1924 the Center has incessantly pursued a policy of fulfillment ... are we now to assume that new personalities have changed the party so much that it would now support a policy of national liberation? The Center would only hinder ... nationalist politics. To enter into a government with the Center would ultimately blur the clear message of this election.[58]

What, then, was the course to follow for the DNVP? Maurenbrecher proceeded to lay out, in an uncharacteristically public fashion, the Pan-German strategy for the party. He argued that if the party truly hoped to live up to the message it received from the voters, it must seek to create a "unified front" with only those forces that demonstrated an unwavering opposition to the "politics of fulfillment." The DNVP could neither support, nor take part in, a government of the bourgeois middle. In spite of past differences and significant personal animosities, the DNVP must turn in friendship to the groups on its Right.

This would mean uniting the DNVP's combined 106 delegates with the Völkisch-Social Bloc (32 delegates), the Bavarian People's Party (15 delegates), Bavarian Farmers' League (10 delegates), the German-Hannovarians (five delegates), and the German Socialist Party (four delegates) to create a "strong nationalist working community" of 172 delegates. Although not nearly a majority in the new 465-member Reichstag, this group would present itself as a unified force and demand that President Ebert turn over the chancellorship to a DNVP member and allow him to form the new cabinet with no other demands. After filling all the posts with "absolutely reliable men" this cabinet would then present itself to the Reichstag.

If faced with a vote of no confidence, Ebert would be forced to dissolve the Reichstag and within "a few weeks" call for a new election. If Ebert refused this demand, a national referendum would be called to demand new presidential elections. Finally, if this plan failed, then the "nationalist bloc would turn to outright obstruction of parliamentary activity, blocking all debate and effectively undermining the Reichstag's authority. This action, combined with the "ruthless engagement of extra-parliamentary economic forces that stand behind [the 'nationalist bloc]" would ensure the victory of the nationalist cause.[59] Only through this course of action could the DNVP be assured of fulfilling the "peoples' will." "The DNVP," Maurenbrecher concluded, "cannot allow itself to

---

[58]   Ibid.
[59]   Ibid.

be counseled by those who think only in parliamentary terms ... and forget that the real power of our society lies outside the walls of parliament."[60]

Maurenbrecher's far-fetched plan deserves closer attention for several reasons. First, it clearly articulated the broader Pan-German strategy for the DNVP at a time when the party's size virtually demanded inclusion in a national government. Second, the plan demonstrated the extent to which the Pan-German League despised and arrogantly dismissed the basic functioning of parliamentary democracy. Finally, it indicated that the Pan-Germans still harbored some slim hopes for reconstructing a united right-wing political bloc.

The Pan-German League clearly believed that the party's moderate majority seriously compromised the DNVP's position following the May elections. Moderate pressure for "constructive cooperation" led the party so far astray from its original mandate that it actually considered taking part in the Marx–Stresemann government. In a speech at a June Pan-German gathering in Zell am See, Heinrich Claß pointed out that this would have dealt the DNVP a "fatal blow" because the party would have had no one but itself to blame for its cooperation with those "guilt-laden party men."[61] Furthermore, Claß suggested that this sort of cooperation would surely have been purchased at the price of DNVP support for the Dawes Plan and, with it, the "destruction of the German economy."[62]

Claß argued that the Dawes Plan would do nothing but further humiliate and weaken Germany in relation to the Allied powers. Indeed, Dawes himself was nothing more than the "representative of American high-finance seeking [through the Dawes Plan] a decisive stroke for the implementation of its own form of finance-imperialism."[63] In addition to the financial havoc the Dawes Plan would allegedly inflict on the German economy, Claß pointed out the Plan's focus on the issue of German war-guilt. Although this aspect of the agreement was still allegedly being debated by German representatives in London, Claß was convinced that the Marx–Stresemann government would simply not have the fortitude to demand the removal of the war-guilt clause as part of the measure. All of these elements made it perfectly clear, Claß concluded, that the Pan-German League and its allies must do all they could, both from within and outside of the DNVP, to insure that the German people gain the leadership that they truly deserve.[64]

---

[60]   Ibid.

[61]   *Deutsche Zeitung*, 25 June 1924, 3–4.

[62]   Ibid., 3.

[63]   Ibid.

[64]   Claß reiterated these points even more emphatically one month later as it appeared that moderate DNVP members might support the Dawes Plan even though the party leadership still

With strong pressure then both for and against approval of the Dawes Plan within the DNVP, the party's leadership failed to negotiate the party's inclusion in a new coalition government. In spite of the DNVP's electoral success only weeks before, the re-formed minority Marx cabinet presented itself to the Reichstag on 4 June 1924 without the Reichstag's single largest party. In spite of the German People's Party's (DVP) best efforts to build a bridge between the middle parties and the DNVP, the attempt failed. The DNVP's confused stance regarding the Dawes Plan made concrete cabinet negotiations with them virtually impossible. The DNVP's vacillation also seemed to indicate that the party might eventually split over the Dawes Plan anyway, thus reducing the immediate need for inclusion of the party in government and seriously weakening the conservative party's bargaining position.[65]

As a result of the party's exclusion from the new government, DNVP leaders now faced a difficult choice. The party could opt to commit publicly and privately to total opposition to the Dawes Plan and Gustav Stresemann's foreign policy decisions. Conversely, it could attempt to combat the strident Pan-German minority demanding outright rejection, and attempt to reach a compromise solution. This might allow the party to approve the Dawes Plan and save face, thus opening the door to the middle parties to expand the new minority government to include the DNVP.[66] In effect, the party's leadership was unable to provide any clear public indication to the government or party members which direction the DNVP would ultimately choose.

Faced with the prospect of completely losing control over government policy and potentially losing millions in desperately needed loans, DNVP moderates began to place serious pressure on the party leadership. The National Agrarian League (*Reichslandbund* or "RLB"), one of the most influential economic interest groups within the DNVP, began to push actively for the Dawes Plan's acceptance. The National Federation of German Industry (*Reichsverband der deutschen Industrie* or "RDI"), which held strong ties to both the DVP and the DNVP, also supported the Dawes Plan. Additionally, the DNVP's leadership received numerous telegrams from regional and local

---

officially opposed it. See: "Die nächste Pflicht der nationalen Opposition," *Deutsche Zeitung*, 20 July 1924, 1.

[65]   Grathwol, *Stresemann and the DNVP*, 27–28.

[66]   Ibid., 29. The most significant factor in this "compromise" scenario was the issue of German war guilt. Many party leaders, including Oskar Hergt, felt that if Foreign Minister Stresemann could produce a disavowal of the war-guilt clause and secure the evacuation of French forces from the Ruhr, the DNVP could hold its nose and vote for the Dawes Plan, assured that German honor had been upheld in the negotiations.

party organizations, particularly in the western occupied areas, encouraging the party to support the legislation.[67]

In spite of this support, party chairman Oskar Hergt continued to hold a defiant official party line. He was convinced that some concessions might be secured from the Allies at the last minute. However, the stance of official opposition belied the real intentions of many party moderates. On 27 August, only two days before the scheduled Reichstag vote, a delegation from the party's moderate groups privately informed Hergt that about 30 DNVP representatives, including everyone from the occupied territories and others connected to the RLB and RDI, were prepared to vote for the plan.[68] Hergt, however, remained convinced that even these deputies would submit to party discipline at the last minute and vote down the measure. Because of the need to obtain a two-thirds majority to get the Dawes Plan through the Reichstag, both the Marx government and the DNVP leadership recognized the significance of party's ultimate decision. On 29 August when the official tally on the Dawes Plan vote was taken, 48 of the DNVP's 106 delegates voted in favor.[69] The Plan passed in the Reichstag by a total of 15 votes; the DNVP moderates had indeed made a difference. The DNVP would now have to address an open split within the party and deal with the lack of strong, decisive leadership.[70]

From the Dawes Plan Vote to the December 1924 Elections

The disastrous split over the Dawes Plan vote haunted the DNVP from that day forward. Most historians widely regard the vote as a crucial turning point in the party's history.[71] A long and heated debate following the split vote ensued between radicals and moderates. This division weakened the party's public image and deeply affected the confidence of party members at the regional and local level. It seemed certain in the immediate wake of the Dawes Plan vote that party unity would never again be possible.

---

[67]   Repp, *Hugenberg, Westarp*, 14.

[68]   Grathwol, *Stresemann and the DNVP*, 49–50.

[69]   Ibid., 50–52. For a complete list of DNVP candidates and their votes see: Liebe, *Deutschnationale Volkspartei*, 168–170.

[70]   The memoirs of Saxon DNVP representative Albrecht Philipp offer valuable insight into the pressures that caused delegates to vote in favor. See: "Philipp Memoirs," SHStA Dresden, NL Philipp/4, 143–147.

[71]   As historian Robert Grathwol put it, the Dawes vote split "laid bare the fundamental divergence between those Nationalists who were willing to come to terms with the political realities of the moment and those who were not." Grathwol, *Stresemann and the DNVP*, 210.

Not surprisingly, the Pan-German League and its allies were the most vocal critics of the DNVP's collapse. Only three days after the vote at the Pan-German League's Stuttgart gathering, several members, including Heinrich Claß, harshly condemned the DNVP. The Pan-Germans attacked the party's lack of leadership and the deplorable nature of "party-politics" in general that allowed 48 DNVP delegates, who claimed to place the "Fatherland above the party," to "pull off the unimaginable" and vote for the Dawes Plan.[72] Several days later, the prominent Pan-German DNVP member Karl Lohmann penned a stinging front page article in the *Deutsche Zeitung* blasting the pro-Dawes Plan representatives (the so-called *Ja-Sager*) for failing the party. According to Lohmann, they had ignored the mandate given to the DNVP in May by millions of voters who wanted the party to fight against the politics of compromise and fulfillment.[73] Many Pan-Germans also agreed with fellow member Gertzlaff von Hertzberg who interpreted the Dawes debacle as the bankruptcy of "western, Jewish parliamentarianism," the complete failure of the DNVP, and the inherent corruption of the party system.[74]

Baron von Vietinghoff-Scheel echoed the League's general sense of frustration with the DNVP's action:

> One can only be deeply saddened by the current state of domestic political affairs. What will come of this is still not clear because the horse-trading changes things everyday. We do know that a deep-seated indignation exists within the DNVP, and there is great dissatisfaction with the party's leadership.[75]

Vietinghoff-Scheel argued further that one of the most significant problems with the party, as recent events had demonstrated, was its lack of truly inspired leaders. Oskar Hergt's inability to maintain party unity against the Dawes Plan clearly indicated that he was not the leader the party desperately needed, and by the end of October Hergt had resigned.[76]

The topic of party leadership and the new direction the DNVP might take following Hergt's resignation took center stage at the Pan-German League's

---

[72]   For a detailed report on the meeting see: "Wege zum Wiederaufbau," *Deutsche Zeitung*, 2 September 1924, 1–4.

[73]   "Warum es geht," *Deutsche Zeitung*, 7 September 1924, 1–2.

[74]   "Nüchtern und sachlich," *Deutsche Zeitung*, 10 September 1924, 1–2.

[75]   Leopold von Vietinghoff-Scheel to Konstantin von Gebsattel, 20 October 1924, BARCH R8048/210, 97.

[76]   The League reiterated this point openly three days later. See: "Die Parteileitung der DNVP," and "Zum Führerwechsel in der Deutschnationalen Partei," *Deutsche Zeitung*, 23 October 1924, 1–2.

Management Committee meeting on 25–26 October 1924.[77] The members first addressed the possibility of founding a new political party. Some DNVP and Pan-German League members had already called for the creation of a new party that would have effectively split the DNVP along pro- and anti-Dawes Plan lines. The League's leadership was in constant contact with party allies—most notably the old hardline conservatives represented by the German Conservative Caucus (*Deutschkonservativen Hauptverein* or "DKHV")—about the feasibility of forming a new party and allowing the DNVP moderates either to wither away or join with the DVP.[78] After considerable deliberation, the Pan-German League's leadership decided that a better course of action would be to push for a "cleansing" of the DNVP rather than the founding of an entirely new party. Heinrich Claß expressed the common consensus by arguing that the creation of a completely new party apparatus in a short period of time would have been nearly impossible and ill-advised in light of the impending December elections.[79]

Instead, the Pan-German leadership and its associates determined that all effort must be put forth to weaken the party's moderates and strengthen the intransigent position. Heinrich Claß encouraged members to focus intently on "cleaning up" the party. With its DNVP allies, particularly in the party's regional and local organizations, Claß proposed that the League work to defeat the leading figures of the party's moderate faction by undermining their support in the provinces.[80] This effort would emphasize agitation in local chapters and active support for alternative candidates, although Claß and others in attendance expressed concern that it was probably too late to implement this strategy to affect the upcoming December Reichstag elections significantly.[81] The Pan-German/DNVP members Gottfried Gok and Karl Lohman confirmed that everything possible must be done to insure that

[77] SGA, 25/26 October 1924, BARCH R8048/140, 49–71.

[78] On the DKHV and its often antagonistic relationship to the DNVP see: Jens Flemming, "Konservatismus als 'nationalrevolutionäre Bewegung'. Konservative Kritik an der Deutschnationalen Volkspartei 1918–1933," in *Deutscher Konservatismus im 19. Und 20. Jahrhundert: Festschrift für Fritz Fischer zum 75. Geburtstag und zum 50. Doktorjubiläum* (Bonn, 1983), 295–331.

[79] SGA, 25/26 October 1924, BARCH R8048/140, 52.

[80] The League consistently pushed this approach in its correspondence with local Pan-German organizations. For example: Leopold von Vietinghoff-Scheel to Herrn von Klitzing (Köln), 29 October 1924, BARCH R8048/210, 107.

[81] On the same day that Claß presented this strategy to the assembled League members in Berlin, Claß's colleague Gertzlaff von Hertzberg published an article covering precisely the same issue in the *Deutsche Zeitung*. Hertzberg argued that the DNVP's regional organizations must be prepared to replace the *Ja-Sager* candidates with truly "reliable" nationalists. See: "Die Landesverbände haben das Wort!" *Deutsche Zeitung*, 26 October 1924, 1–2.

the largest possible number of reliable (i.e. Pan-German oriented) delegates appeared on election tickets in the future.

After a lengthy discussion that included numerous reports on the status of local and regional DNVP chapters, Heinrich Claß closed the meeting and reaffirmed the importance of the Pan-German League's task. "We must fight with all severity against those who have the DNVP's collapse on their conscience." In addition to active attention to the election lists and the regional DNVP chapters, the League and its press planned to "name names in public through published letters, newspaper articles, etc. That is the only thing that these people fear."[82]

This October 1924 Pan-German League meeting was of great significance in light of the DNVP's later history. It was at this meeting that the League outlined in clear terms its strategy for undermining moderate conservatism and driving the DNVP permanently toward the anti-democratic Right. However, while the League's long-term strategy of influencing the party at the regional and local level would take effect in the coming years, very little could be done in the coming weeks to change the DNVP's entire candidate list for the December elections.[83] In a frustrated letter to a Pan-German League member in Nürnberg, Heinrich Claß lamented that "the outcome of the Reichstag vote cannot now be seriously affected ... I fear that even the Lord himself can't help the German Nationals right now."[84]

The election results confirmed many of the Pan-German League's fears. In spite of the Dawes Plan fiasco and the failed government negotiations earlier that year, the DNVP actually strengthened its total vote count and increased its number of seats to 111.[85] Overall, the numerical balance of the Reichstag had changed, however. The SPD made significant gains over the May elections and finished with 131 seats.[86] Nonetheless, the DNVP still wielded considerable influence as the largest non-socialist party in the Reichstag. Although tough negotiations lay ahead, it now seemed fairly likely that the next coalition government could well include the DNVP. In two elections in one year, the party had proven itself to be a major force in national politics.

---

[82]   SGA, 25/26 October 1924, BARCH R8048/140, 70–71.

[83]   Some limited action was taken at the local level in the weeks leading up to the election. In Dresden, for example, the local Pan-German League chapter held a large election rally in conjunction with the United Patriotic Leagues of Dresden on 27 November. Axel Freiherr von Freytagh-Loringhoven was the key speaker. See: StADresden ADV-OD/6, 26.

[84]   Claß to Wolfgang Kürzel, 1 November 1924, BARCH R8048/210, 109.

[85]   This total again included the Agrarian League's mandates. On its own, the DNVP still gained ground and finished with 103 seats. See: Liebe, *Deutschnationale Volkspartei*, 181, n481.

[86]   Ibid.

With these developments, the Pan-German League faced the end of 1924 with deep concern about the DNVP's future. Heinrich Claß reiterated his conviction that the DNVP's participation in a coalition government would never produce any sort of truly nationalist oriented solution to Germany's troubles.[87] Nonetheless, most Pan-Germans expressed cautious optimism that the disaster of 1924 would eventually force the party to confront its very nature. In the short term, practical financial and political pressures had triumphed over hard-line ideological principles in the DNVP. The Pan-Germans felt that it would take time to enact their strategy to weaken the moderate forces within the party at the local, regional, and ultimately, national levels. The League hoped that the coming year would present an opportunity to alter the DNVP's course and force the party to realize that it could not afford to pursue the politics of fulfillment. As the year-end edition of the *Deutsche Zeitung* put it "1925 must produce the decisiveness that lies not in compromise, but rather in this distinct choice: Black-Red-Gold or Black-White-Red!"[88]

1925: The DNVP in Government

Clearly, the DNVP's stance toward the Weimar Republic at the end of 1924 remained unclear. The Dawes Plan vote publicly exposed the deep divisions between several major factions within the party and by the beginning of 1925, the DNVP's fundamental dilemma remained the same. Either the party could enter into government, thereby tacitly lending support to the Weimar state but nevertheless hoping to influence foreign and domestic policy in favor of conservative interests, or it could take the ideological high road and remain in the opposition in spite of its recent substantial electoral gains. The latter of these two options would mean opposition at all costs, denying the Weimar Republic any measure of support or legitimacy at a crucial moment not only in its domestic affairs, but even more importantly in its relation to the other major European powers.[89]

---

[87] Claß to Alfred Roth, 12 December 1924, BARCH R8048/210, 151.

[88] "Deutschland an der Jahreswende: Opposition und Regierung," *Deutsche Zeitung*, 31 December 1924, 1. This statement referred respectively to the colors of the new national flag of the Weimar Republic and the old Imperial Flag embraced by many conservatives.

[89] Party leaders received numerous letters from the provinces before and after the December elections speaking out for and against the party's potential participation in a coalition government. For example, see: DNVP Kreisverein Zehlendorf (Berlin) to Hergt, 26 September 1924, NL Westarp, np; DNVP Landesverband Hamburg to Westarp, 12 December 1924, NL Westarp, np; and DNVP Landesverband Potsdam II to Westarp, 31 December 1924, NL Westarp, np.

Before January was through, the DNVP's leaders made their decision and staked the party's fortunes on participation in a new national government. The party's moderate nationalist majority backed this crucial decision and hoped as a result to gain substantial influence over a wide range of governmental policies. However, the party's radical minority, supported by the Pan-German League, immediately decried the move as destructive not only for the legacy of German conservatism and the development of the DNVP, but also for the fate of the German nation itself. Ultimately, the League's conflict with the DNVP severely weakened the party's long-term stability by further exposing its deep-seated internal divisions. Furthermore, this conflict paved the way for a decisive transformation of the party's platform, membership, and place in party politics between 1925 and 1930.

Even before the formal resignation of Wilhelm Marx's minority cabinet on 15 December 1924, many political observers believed that the newly enlarged and powerful DNVP would play a decisive role in the upcoming negotiations leading to the formation of a new national government. While there was a pause at the end of December, negotiations intensified during the first two weeks of 1925. Initially, while the Center Party's Wilhelm Marx sought to form a cabinet of experts based primarily on leaders from the German Democratic Party (*Deutsche Demokratische Partei* or "DDP"), the Center, and elements of the ministerial bureaucracy, the DVP made it clear that it could not accept "a disguised cabinet of the middle."[90] DVP leaders further demanded that only a firm bourgeois majority, most assuredly including the increasingly powerful DNVP, was the only real solution to the government crisis. Faced with increasing parliamentary opposition and fundamentally opposed to his party's inclusion in a government with the DNVP, Marx resigned his commission on 9 January 1925.[91]

Upon Marx's resignation, the responsibility to form a new government fell to Finance Minister Hans Luther. After negotiations with Martin Schiele, the new chairman of the DNVP's Reichstag delegation, and after further discussions with several other parties, Luther presented the Reichstag on 15 January with a cabinet that included leaders from the DNVP, DVP, the Center Party, and the Bavarian People's Party. One week later on 22 January, Luther's proposal was approved and the search for a new cabinet had finally come to an end.[92] However, this new cabinet was one of "personalities" and not a cabinet based on an actual working majority in the Reichstag. Martin Schiele, a DNVP

---

[90]   Larry Eugene Jones, *German Liberalism and the Dissolution of the Weimar Party System, 1918–1933* (Chapel Hill, 1988), 240.

[91]   Ibid.

[92]   Grathwol, *Stresemann and the DNVP*, 61.

moderate who had not participated in the disastrous Dawes Plan vote, took over as minister of the interior. Otto Gessler stayed on as minister of defense, but not as a formal representative of the DDP in the cabinet. The Center Party sent Heinrich Brauns under the same conditions, and most significantly, Gustav Stresemann retained his post as foreign minister.[93]

Stresemann and his allies in the DVP had hoped for some time to bring the DNVP into the national government so that they could share formal responsibility for all aspects of his foreign policy decisions and not merely attack from the luxury of opposition. Stresemann also hoped that the inclusion of the DNVP moderate Martin Schiele in the cabinet might be evidence of the DNVP's turn away from the radical right's extreme policy concerning Germany's relationship with the other European powers, particularly France and Britain. In short, Stresemann clearly sought the emergence of a moderate DNVP that would carry the mantle of a functional state-supporting conservative party so desperately needed in Weimar Germany.[94]

The DNVP's leaders understood the risk of participation in a coalition government. In a 20 January Reichstag speech, Kuno Graf von Westarp, the DNVP's newly appointed Reichstag delegation leader, walked a fine line between the traditional conservative responsibility to support the state and the DNVP's freedom of action to address the most pressing political issues in the best interest of the fatherland:

> We recognized our participation [in the Luther cabinet] as a duty to our Fatherland which currently finds itself in the midst of a difficult and decisive crisis in both foreign and domestic policy and in need of a functional government. Our participation in this government represents a last attempt to achieve stable conditions for the current system to accomplish practical parliamentary work. If this attempt fails, it is the system that is to blame.[95]

Interestingly, Westarp provided the DNVP with an exit strategy of sorts. The party's leaders would try their best to make the government address Germany's pressing needs. However, if their efforts were not successful, Westarp made it clear that it was the republican system itself and not the party that would be at fault. Clearly, the DNVP's participation in government marked an important outward change in policy. Nonetheless, as Westarp's speech indicated, concerns

---

[93]   Ibid.

[94]   Ibid., 61–62, Henry Ashby Turner, *Stresemann and the Politics of the Weimar Republic* (Princeton, paperback edn 1965), 175–176, 187–188, and Jonathan Wright, *Gustav Stresemann: Weimar's Greatest Statesman* (Oxford, 2002), 292–296.

[95]   Westarp quoted in: Dörr, *Deutschnationale Volkspartei*, 96–97.

still lingered among conservatives about the party's decision to participate in government and this decision's potentially negative implications for the party's nationalist image. His concerns were well founded as the furious response from the Pan-German League and its radical party allies would soon demonstrate.

Two major factors dominated the Pan-German League's opposition to the DNVP's decision to join the Luther cabinet. The first centered on the party's very existence as a nationalist force. The League's leaders simply could not comprehend how a party that claimed to stand for the "German national" interests of the country could ever be successful in the long run by pursuing any course other than outright opposition to the "illegal" Weimar state. The second issue centered on the specific complications of the DNVP's participation in a cabinet that included the League's outright enemy, Gustav Stresemann.[96] The Pan-Germans consistently denounced Stresemann's foreign policy as a national disaster and a betrayal of German interests to the Western powers. In the following months, these two issues, often closely intertwined, dominated Pan-German debates and propaganda, eventually forming the basis for concrete action against the DNVP's moderate majority which, according to the League, had led the party terribly astray.

Immediately following the announcement of the new government, the League's press swung into action. Fritz Baer's article "Shaky Ground" headlined the *Deutsche Zeitung*'s 16 January 1925 edition's front page coverage of the new cabinet.[97] Baer dismissed the DNVP's participation in the new cabinet as shortsighted and highly detrimental to the party. The same traitorous leaders, especially Stresemann, would continue to exercise the real power even with the DNVP's participation. Nothing good could come from the Nationalist's participation, Baer concluded, and the shame and embarrassment of responsibility for Stresemann's disastrous policies would only tarnish the party's image in the eyes of true Germans.[98] The League's own newsletter, the *Alldeutsche Blätter*, also ran a lead article decrying the DNVP leaders' entrance into a government so fundamentally opposed to their true interests. The article held out slim hope that the German National leaders would "make the timely decision to separate

---

[96]   Stresemann had been a Pan-German League member before World War I. He broke with the League during the war primarily over the contentious war-aims issue. The League's pamphlet series entitled "Wehr und Gegenwehr," devoted an entire issue to the group's history with Stresemann starting before World War I and leading up to 1925. The pamphlet stated that Stresemann had fallen so far from his original Pan-German allegiance that he was now "the unquestioned leader of the politics of fulfillment, the heir to Eisner, Erzberger, and Rathenau." See: "Stresemann," *Wehr und Gegenwehr*, Nr. 6, 1926, R8048/532, 2–8.

[97]   "Schwankender Grund," *Deutsche Zeitung*, 16 January 1925, 1.

[98]   Ibid.

themselves from such a fundamentally unnatural and dishonorable 'community,' so that at least part of the terrible consequences, which we fear from their entry into the Luther cabinet, can be prevented."[99]

At the League's executive committee meeting on 31 January–1 February 1925, Heinrich Claß and many other members echoed these public statements with further concerns regarding the DNVP's recent actions.[100] Claß condemned the entire affair and pointed directly to the Luther cabinet's intention to pursue a Stresemann-dominated foreign policy. Claß argued that this approach was "unbearably pacifistic for any truly nationally-oriented German," and he asserted that it set the stage for another national humiliation. Worst of all, the DNVP cabinet members had tied themselves to this program, and thereby insured that they would also be held accountable for its shortcomings.[101]

In spite of this blunt Pan-German attack, the DNVP's leadership had to move forward with their work in the new coalition government. The most difficult challenge for the Nationalists in the new Luther cabinet was Gustav Stresemann's foreign policy. From the cabinet's inception, Stresemann intended to pursue further the strategy of normalizing relations with the Allies that had already begun with the Dawes Plan.[102] While the DNVP cabinet members officially confirmed their support for the basic outlines of the Dawes Plan, privately many DNVP leaders expressed considerable reservations about the future of a Stresemann-dominated foreign policy.[103]

In addition, the Nationalists quickly found themselves in a difficult position because of the way that Stresemann's recent negotiations with the Western powers had become public. Stresemann's overarching goal, as it had been for some time, was a gradual revision of the most extreme stipulations of the Versailles Treaty by first calming French and British concerns regarding future German aggression.[104] This would, he believed, lead sooner rather than later to the withdrawal of French and British forces from the Ruhr, Rhine, and Cologne occupation zones, and it would eventually ensure Germany's re-emergence as an equal power in Europe.

In January and early February 1925, Stresemann circulated a security pact offer to London and then to Paris that guaranteed Germany's western borders with France and Belgium. This meant, in effect, abandoning German claims

---

[99]   "Die neue Regierung," *Alldeutsche Blätter*, 17 January 1925, 9–10.

[100]   SGA, 31 January–1 February 1925, BARCH R8048/141, 36–39, 41–44.

[101]   Ibid., 38–39.

[102]   For Stresemann's role in the Dawes Plan negotiations and their impact on domestic politics see: Turner, *Stresemann*, esp. 163–181; and Wright, *Stresemann*, 267–270 and 286–307.

[103]   NL Philipp/4, SHStA Dresden, 178.

[104]   Turner, *Stresemann*, 175.

to Alsace-Lorraine and a general acceptance of the western border as it stood, without agreeing to anything concrete regarding Germany's eastern borders. Although Stresemann made this offer with Luther's approval, he did not pre-circulate it among the other cabinet members for fear of Nationalist alterations or outright opposition.[105] However, the Paris press corps quickly picked up news of the plan, and members of the British House of Commons made reference to the proposals during open debate on 5 March.[106] These revelations forced Stresemann's hand and on 7 March he called a press conference to trace the background of his proposals, as well as the larger political significance of his initiatives. The foreign minister argued that he had operated secretly only because of previous commitments and the exceedingly delicate nature of the negotiations. The proposal did include a renunciation of Alsace-Lorraine, he admitted, but in return Germany stood an excellent chance of securing an end to the military occupation of the Rhineland while lessening the direct threat of French military force on Germany's borders.[107]

The DNVP's leadership now stood at a crossroads. Stresemann's policies challenged the Nationalists to resolve their bitter conflict with the "enemy" over the hated Versailles Treaty not through open, belligerent defiance, but rather through negotiation and compromise.[108] For the first time since the party's founding, its moderate leaders seemed willing to tolerate temporarily Stresemann's foreign policy proposal to see if important concessions could be gained later from the Western Allies. However, Stresemann's foreign policy would not be so readily accepted by the more radical elements within the DNVP's rank and file.[109]

In the face of Stresemann's announcement, the Pan-German League redoubled its efforts to discredit both the foreign minister's entire policy and the DNVP's moderate strategy. In conjunction with its allies in the DNVP's Reichstag delegation, regional party organizations, and the United Patriotic Leagues of Germany (*Vereingte Vaterländiche Verbände Deutschlands* or VVVD), the Pan-German League launched an extensive public campaign denouncing Stresemann's entire policy and placing renewed pressure on the DNVP's moderate leadership. In early March, the League drafted a strongly worded circular and immediately distributed it to all local and regional League

---

105   Mommsen, *Rise and Fall of Weimar Democracy*, 198.

106   Grathwol, *Stresemann and the DNVP*, 66.

107   Ibid., 66–67.

108   Ibid., 75.

109   The *Vossische Zeitung* correctly predicted the extreme difficulty that the DNVP faced in dealing with Stresemann's foreign policy and the politics of compromise. See: "Der vertagte Kampf: Die Krise der Deutschnationalen," *Vossische Zeitung*, 26 March 1925, 2.

offices in advance of the League's upcoming national meeting in Dresden later that month.[110] The statement boldly announced that any individual who even tolerated Stresemann's policies would bear direct responsibility for "the final sacrifice of [his] fellow Germans ... the eternal enslavement of German blood ... and a curse on future generations." The statement concluded that "[s]uch a storm of outrage must arise that no politician and no president would dare to contradict ... the honor and the dignity of the German people."[111]

The League published this statement initially in the *Alldeutsche Blätter*.[112] The declaration also appeared on the front page of the *Deutsche Zeitung*'s 14 March edition, along with a further front page commentary entitled "Stresemann's Subjugation Offer."[113] Only days later one of the League's most prominent DNVP members, Axel Freiherr von Freytagh-Loringhoven, published yet another stinging indictment of Stresemann's entire policy.[114] It was clear that the League and its allies were prepared to hold Stresemann publicly accountable for what they perceived as an unconscionable betrayal of German interests. On 21–22 March 1925, the League gathered in Dresden to accelerate its campaign against Stresemann and the DNVP moderates.

The Dresden meeting began with a closed-door leadership session to discuss Stresemann's motives and goals, as well as the DNVP's unacceptable response.[115] The assembled members heard reports from Karl Lohmann and Carl Gok, both DNVP Reichstag representatives, on their assessment of the party's conduct during this entire affair. Lohmann decried what he perceived to be a clear "misperception" on the part of the DNVP's leadership to assume "that there was no cause for alarm."[116] Gok concluded even more forcefully that "it is time to sound the alarm ... and insure the German Nationalists won't be pushed around anymore."[117] As Heinrich Claß put it, "the German National People's Party ... must be forced to show their true colors."[118] After tabling a proposal to place Stresemann on trial for treason, the leadership committee finally agreed that the League's main task was to make it clear to the public

---

[110]   See the cover page and the resolution entitled "Der Alldeutsche Verband zum Stresemannschen Sicherheits-Angebot," StADresden ADV-OD/7, 172–174.

[111]   Ibid., 173.

[112]   *Alldeutsche Blätter*, 21 March 1925, 58–59.

[113]   *Deutsche Zeitung*, 14 March 1925, 1–2.

[114]   "Völkerbund und Sicherungspakt," *Deutsche Zeitung*, 21 March 1925, 1–2.

[115]   SGA, 21–22 March 1925, BARCH R8048/142, 78–91.

[116]   Ibid., 88–89.

[117]   Ibid., 90.

[118]   Ibid., 84.

that "a minister [Stresemann] who proceeds as he has, cannot remain minister for one day longer."[119]

That same evening the League held a large public gathering in Dresden's Wettiner Hall.[120] The event, arranged as a "German Evening" by the League's Dresden chapter, drew over one thousand participants, including a wide range of other local right-wing groups, such as the United Patriotic Leagues of Dresden, as well as hundreds of League members from various parts of the country. Speeches by Heinrich Claß and Carl Gok highlighted the evening and excoriated Stresemann and the entire course of Germany's foreign policy.[121]

In the weeks following the gathering, the League's Dresden chapter distributed in mass numbers the pre-prepared League statement against Stresemann issued earlier on 14 March. Members posted the statement in a variety of public places and published it as an insert in two large circulation local papers, the *Dresdner Nachrichten* and the *Dresdner Anzeiger*.[122] Furthermore, in conjunction with the United Patriotic Leagues of Dresden, the Dresden Pan-Germans arranged for yet another large public gathering on 28 May 1925 to protest Stresemann's actions. The organizers made it clear that they wanted the meeting to send a message to the DNVP's leaders, letting them know that "the largest nationalist party in the Reichstag and in our struggle cannot leave us in the lurch again as with the Dawes Plan ... without arousing substantial dissatisfaction in our ranks."[123] The League organized similar protest meetings in many other parts of Germany as well. One report that arrived at League headquarters in Berlin described "a rally of several thousand" in Königsberg's main exhibition hall on 28 March 1925. The Pan-German League and the United Patriotic Leagues of East Prussia organized the gathering. The official statement issued from the meeting condemned Stresemann's policies as a "disgrace," and his behavior as "spineless."[124]

---

[119]   Ibid., 85.

[120]   On the meeting see: *Jahresbericht* 1924/25, StADresden ADV-OD/50, 152.

[121]   Claß was generally pleased with the impact of the Dresden gathering and the "alarm call" which it generated against Stresemann's foreign policy. See: Claß to Justizrat Petzoldt, 26 March 1925, R8048/613, 10.

[122]   *Jahresbericht* 1924/25, StADresden ADV-OD/50, 153. The Dresden chapter also issued its members a special set of guidelines for the campaign against Stresemann and the DNVP moderates. See: StADresden ADV-OD/7, 107.

[123]   *Jahresbericht* 1924/25, StADresden ADV-OD/50, 153. For meeting preparations see: StADresden ADV-OD/7, 105.

[124]   For the report submitted by Siegfried Graf zu Eulenburg-Wicken on the gathering see: BARCH R8048/211, 112–113.

Throughout the spring of 1925, the League and its party allies continued their campaign to discredit Stresemann and increase pressure on the DNVP's leadership to separate itself from the government. In late March, Claß explained to one Pan-German member that the League would "move heaven and earth to push through [its] agenda in the DNVP."[125] In this spirit on 3 April 1925, the League's local group in Hamburg issued a clear and extreme challenge to the DNVP's leadership. The declaration read:

> [We] expect the leadership of the German National People's Party to disassociate itself publicly from Mr. Stresemann and his security pact offer, that the party acknowledge this offer as degrading and therefore unacceptable for the German people, and that [the party] declare that if Minister Stresemann follows through with his offer, the German National ministers will immediately be withdrawn from the cabinet by the party leadership.[126]

This trend of direct and open confrontation not only with Stresemann and his policies, but also increasingly with the DNVP's leadership continued throughout the spring and into the summer. Each week, several new lead articles covering various aspects of the crisis appeared in the pages of the Pan-German *Deutsche Zeitung*.[127] The League's goal was consistent, constant pressure on DNVP leaders and a high public profile for the intransigent, anti-government position. Certainly, even the casual reader of the newspaper could not help but be bombarded with a constant stream of anti-Stresemann propaganda, as well as numerous challenges to the DNVP's moderate leadership to forgo their accommodation with Stresemann's policies.[128]

The impact of this approach soon became evident. Throughout the summer months, the pages of the *Deutsche Zeitung* were awash with anti-Stresemann/DNVP articles and editorials.[129] Several Pan-German members also reported

---

[125]   League Headquarters to Hugo Göring, 30 March 1925, BARCH R8048/211, 126.

[126]   Quoted in: StADresden ADV-OD/7, 122.

[127]   For example, see the following *Deutsche Zeitung* articles: "Glück im Unglück," 24 May 1925, 1–2; and "Der Irrtum," 7 June 1925, 1–2.

[128]   The Pan-German League's anti-Stresemann attacks became so intense that they resulted in at least one law suit. Leading Pan-German member Gertzlaff von Hertzberg sued Walter Hermann, the general secretary of the German People's Party (DVP), for libel. The suit claimed that Hermann publicly accused Hertzberg of defaming Gustav Stresemann and lying about his policies at a Pan-German League rally in late May 1925. The suit was later dismissed, but it indicates the heated nature of the attacks surrounding Stresemann's foreign policy. See: Nachlass Gertzlaff von Hertzberg, BARCH N2353/1, 75–81, 87, 103.

[129]   For example: "Gegen den Stresemann-Geist," 5 July 1925, 1; "Neue Zwangsläufigkeit?" 26 July 1925, 1–2; and "Gradlinig zum Abgrund," 2 August 1925, 1–2.

success in influencing local DNVP chapters to take up the Pan-German cause. For example, two executive committee members reported that leaders of the DNVP's state organization in Braunschweig and the Dresden chapter firmly supported the Pan-German position. The Braunschweig leadership made it perfectly clear that for its members, Stresemann's security pact "was not even an issue."[130] If the party's leadership went forward with their support for Stresemann, their members would have nothing more to do with the party. Most importantly, the Braunschweig chapter would make sure that, in the future, no moderate candidates would be presented on the electoral list.[131]

Frequently in conjunction with local Pan-German League members, many of the DNVP's regional party associations also began to express their extreme displeasure with the moderate leadership's stance. Protest letters and resolutions from individual members and local groups appeared in increasing numbers at DNVP offices in Berlin. For example, party headquarters received a resolution in June 1925 passed by the combined regional party organizations of Hamburg, Hannover Ost, Osnabrück, Oldenburg, Ostfriesland, and Bremen.[132] According to the statement, Stresemann's policies represented a "shameful betrayal" of "German brothers" fighting desperately for their very existence. Stresemann's security pact proposal represented "nothing more and nothing less than a renewed, voluntary signature on the Versailles Diktat."[133] The statement demanded that the DNVP's leadership immediately reject any agreement that sacrificed "German honor and German land."[134]

As Stresemann's negotiations intensified throughout the summer, the Pan-German League and its allies remained firmly committed to this uncompromising stance. This strategy made it increasingly difficult for the DNVP's moderate leadership to hold the line in the event that Stresemann accomplished some sort of substantial breakthrough with his French and British counterparts. And while the Pan-German League's campaign to discredit Gustav Stresemann and the DNVP's moderate leadership gained even greater momentum in the summer of 1925, its effects had already become apparent within the government by March 1925.

On 17 March, Gustav Stresemann and Martin Schiele had a pointed exchange over the potential complications of the radical nationalist campaign against the DNVP's position. Schiele made it clear that Pan-German allies within the party, especially Walther Graef, would handle Stresemann's foreign policy "in such a

130   SGA, 4 September 1925, BARCH R8048/143, 39.
131   Ibid., 39–40.
132   NsäStA-Osnabrück C1/1, 13–14.
133   Ibid., 14.
134   Ibid.

way as to make the entire affair very difficult for the [DNVP]."[135] Only weeks later in April, several party members openly accused the Pan-German Reichstag representative Karl Lohmann of leaking confidential information from the party's Reichstag delegation meetings to Heinrich Claß and the Pan-German League.[136]

By July, the Pan-German League's intense pressure forced Kuno von Westarp and several other DNVP leaders to meet with Heinrich Claß for a frank discussion concerning the League's public stance. As Claß recounted to the League's leadership, this meeting with "several of the DNVP's most influential leaders" was clearly meant to silence the Pan-German League.[137] The DNVP's leaders made it clear to Claß that a "frontal assault" on Stresemann was simply not the answer. Such an approach only threatened to "tear apart" the coalition before other important issues like the pending changes to tax and tariff legislation, from which many of the DNVP's members stood to benefit, could be passed.[138] The League needed to see the broader picture and not treat Stresemann's foreign policy in isolation. Furthermore, the DNVP leaders made it clear to Claß that the League's actions would surely alienate Luther and create further tension within the cabinet. The League, they maintained, needed to place its trust in Schiele and believe that he would prevent Stresemann from "doing any real harm."[139] Despite this advice, Claß asserted that the League would continue its public attacks and that it would certainly not back away from applying pressure on the foreign minister or the DNVP moderates.

Only days later an article appeared in the *Deutsche Zeitung* that openly called the DNVP to account for its failure to oppose Stresemann and his policies. The article listed the names of DNVP leaders that could be considered "trustworthy" representatives of the "national opposition."[140] The implication, of course, was that those not mentioned could no longer be considered reliable nationalists. This article infuriated many moderate members within the DNVP's Reichstag delegation and led to demands to break once and for all with the *Deutsche*

---

[135]   Document #50 "Besprechung im Reichstagsgebäude. 17 März 1925, 18.45 Uhr, Anwesend: Luther, Stresemann, Schiele; Protokoll StS Kempner," in Karl Dietrich Erdmann (ed.), *Akten der Reichskanzlei-Weimar Republik: Die Kabinette Luther I und II, Bd. I Januar 1925 bis Oktober 1925* (Bopard am Rhein, 1977), 183.

[136]   For a detailed account of this event, along with Lohmann's defense, see: Karl Lohmann to Kuno von Westarp, 29 April 1925, NL Westarp.

[137]   SGA 4 September 1925, BARCH R8048/144, 10.

[138]   For more on the tax and tariff issue and the DNVP's position see: SHStA Dresden, NL Phillip/4, 172a. See also: Stürmer, *Koalition und Opposition in der Weimarer Republik*, 101–103.

[139]   SGA, 4 September 1925, BARCH R8048/144, 11.

[140]   Grathwol, *Stresemann and the DNVP*, 103.

Zeitung and the Pan-German League.[141] Outraged, the party's Reichstag delegation voted to block DNVP members from publishing further articles in the *Deutsche Zeitung*. This measure was clearly aimed at regular Pan-German DNVP contributors to the paper like Axel Freiherr von Freytagh-Loringhoven, Carl Gok, Walther Graef, and Karl Lohmann. Furthermore, the DNVP's leadership decided to exclude permanently the *Deutsche Zeitung*'s reporter from further party meetings if the paper did not stop its assault.[142] One week later on 24 July, Kuno von Westarp invited Major von Sodenstern from the *Deutsche Zeitung*'s editorial board to a private discussion and informed him of the party's decision should the paper continue to publish such open attacks.[143]

In light of these events, the Pan-German leadership informed Kuno von Westarp and the rest of the DNVP that the *Deutsche Zeitung* could not be pressured or blackmailed because of its political stance. The Pan-Germans felt that they had no other choice but to air the entire conflict with the DNVP so that the "nationalist public" would be made aware of what the German Nationalists were doing.[144] In a detailed letter to an angry party moderate who accused the League of "seriously endangering" the DNVP's position within the government, the League's business manager Leopold von Vietinghoff-Scheel vigorously defended the Pan-German position and the *Deutsche Zeitung*. "Are we [the Pan-German League] simply expected to give up our public and deeply felt opposition only because it happens to run against the desire of the party majority?" As independent political actors, Vietinghoff-Scheel concluded, the Pan-German League and the *Deutsche Zeitung* had the right and the duty to raise objections against the party's leadership regardless of risk.[145]

This response infuriated several of the DNVP's top leaders and seemed to push the crisis to a breaking point. At this juncture, Alfred Hugenberg stepped in to placate the outraged party moderates. While Hugenberg's newspaper empire had actively denounced Stresemann's negotiations with the Western powers from the beginning, Hugenberg, already a close confidant of Heinrich Claß and a co-founder of the Pan-German League, had not yet played a direct personal role in the growing party crisis during the summer of 1925.[146] Nonetheless, at the

---

[141]   SGA, 4 September 1925, BARCH R8048/144, 11.

[142]   Ibid.

[143]   Ibid., 12. See also: Freytagh-Loringhoven to Westarp, 27 June 1925, NL Westarp/56, np; Freytagh-Loringhoven to Westarp, 26 July 1925, NL Westarp/57, np; and Westarp to Freytagh-Loringhoven, 27 July 1925, NL Westarp/57, np.

[144]   Ibid. See also: Editor of the *Deutsche Zeitung* to Kuno von Westarp, 5 August 1925, NL Westarp, np.

[145]   Leopold von Vietinghoff-Scheel to Herr Leopold, 3 August 1925, NL Westarp, np.

[146]   Holzbach, *System Hugenberg*, 180–181.

high point of the Pan-German League's conflict with the DNVP, Hugenberg finally arranged a second meeting between Claß and Kuno von Westarp that produced an uneasy truce between the League and the DNVP.[147]

Several things should be noted about the conflict between these two groups. First, it is clear that the League's efforts to undermine the DNVP's leadership had a significant impact on the relationship between the DNVP cabinet members and their colleagues concerning Stresemann's foreign policy specifically, and the functioning of the Luther government generally. While not immediately forcing a showdown between the foreign minister and the DNVP, the League's constant propaganda made it increasingly difficult for party moderates to remain in the cabinet to influence substantially Stresemann's negotiations with the Western powers. Kuno von Westarp's willingness to meet with Claß was a clear indication of the DNVP's growing concern about the impact of the Pan-German campaign against the moderate leadership.[148]

Another important result of the League's feud with the DNVP was Alfred Hugenberg's emergence as a clear Pan-German ally. Heinrich Claß commented that "our friends in the Reichstag delegation have gained an important ally in Privy Councilor Hugenberg."[149] Claß believed that the intra-party feud was a crucial step in Hugenberg's emergence as a leading figure of the party's "Pan-German" wing. This occurrence would be of utmost importance for the League's campaign within the DNVP in the next several years.

All of these developments indicate that the Pan-German campaign was having a significant impact on the DNVP. The League's leadership was proud of its significant and influential representation at a meeting of the DNVP's opposition state party organizations in Berlin on 1–2 September.[150] Karl Lohmann, who was present at the meeting, recounted the "extraordinarily decisive and determined" spirit of opposition against any further cooperation of the DNVP with the Luther government.[151]

---

[147]   SGA, 4 September 1925, R8048/144, 13.

[148]   Stresemann recalls in his memoirs Westarp's frustration with this situation. Westarp compared his struggle against critics of the Reichstag delegation's relationship to Stresemann and the government as "a battle with a Hydra." "As soon as you lop off one head," Westarp lamented, "two new ones emerge." Gustav Stresemann, *Vermächtnis, volume II* (Berlin, 1932), 145.

[149]   SGA, 4 September 1925, R8048/144, 15.

[150]   Ibid., 37.

[151]   Ibid. The Center Party newspaper *Germania* published a front page article commenting on the national impact of the opposition from the DNVP's regional groups: "The real question now is how long Mr. Schiele will be able to cooperate with the foreign policy of the Luther Cabinet, while a boundless German National demagogy creates disorder throughout the country. Needless to say, such a divided German Nationalist policy—[i.e.] a desire for official cooperation in Berlin accompanied simultaneously by wild opposition ... in other parts of the country—

It was clear that the DNVP's leadership had a potential revolt on its hands. Westarp, Schiele, and other party leaders received a disturbingly large number of angry complaints from individuals and local and regional party chapters demanding the DNVP's withdrawal from the government.[152] In mid-September, Westarp received a detailed letter from his colleague Oskar Hergt describing the outrage over government policy at a recent meeting of the DNVP's Landesverband Ostsachsen.[153] Within two months, it was precisely these regional and local party organizations, with significant Pan-German support, that brought the crisis between Stresemann and the DNVP to a head.

Withdrawal from the Luther Cabinet

Gustav Stresemann and Hans Luther returned on 18 October from the Locarno meeting of foreign ministers. The Locarno meeting was the result of Stresemann's months-long negotiations with Britain and France to reach agreement on several important issues critically affecting Germany's relationship to the Western powers. At Locarno, Belgium, France, and Germany renounced forceful revision of their common borders without any binding agreement concerning possible future revisions to Germany's eastern border with Poland. Britain and Italy would act as guarantors. This arrangement also meant that Germany had to recognize officially its new western border as stipulated in the Versailles Treaty, including forgoing any future claims to Alsace-Lorraine. Stresemann had pushed hard for an end to the occupation of the Ruhr and the early withdrawal of Allied troops from the Rhineland, but he did not get the firm guarantees on specific timetables he had expected. Nonetheless, the Locarno Accords eventually helped normalize relations between Germany and the former Allies, and paved the way for Germany's admission to the League of Nations by 1926.[154]

While the Locarno meeting represented an important turning point in Germany's post-war diplomacy with the Western powers, Germany's radical nationalists viewed the conference as nothing short of a second humiliating Versailles. The DNVP's leadership, therefore, was prepared for the worst as

---

represents a great burden for Germany." See: "Deutschnationale Zwiespältigkeit," *Germania*, 17 September 1925, 1.

[152]   For example see: DNVP Landesverband Potsdam II to Westarp, 11 September 1925, NL Westarp/56, np, and DNVP Landesverband Sachsen to Westarp, 17 September 1925, NL Westarp/94, np.

[153]   Oskar Hergt to Westarp, 16 September 1925, NL Westarp/53, np.

[154]   Mommsen, *Rise and Fall of Weimar Democracy*, 197–208, Turner, *Stresemann*, 182–219, and Kolb, *Weimar Republic*, 61–63.

Luther and Stresemann returned. The pressure from the party's Pan-German wing, in conjunction with many of the party's regional organizations, had grown so intense that Westarp, Schiele, and others now feared that acceptance of the Locarno Accords would be virtually impossible. Although Luther and Stresemann had accomplished a great deal at Locarno, and had secured a number of important proposals which would help Germany's return as an equal power in Europe, the DNVP's leadership faced a serious crisis. While Martin Schiele initially approved of the overall tenor of the Locarno agreements and thanked Stresemann for his efforts, he made it clear at the Luther cabinet's first post-Locarno meeting that he could not guarantee how the party itself would respond.[155] In particular, Schiele was concerned about the treaty's details concerning the permanent acceptance of Germany's new western border, Germany's entry into the League of Nations, and the timetable for French withdrawal from the Rhineland occupation zones.[156]

In effect, Schiele, Westarp, and the rest of the DNVP's moderate leadership were trapped. Privately, they saw some potential in the results of the Locarno meeting, even if they could not accept the agreement as it currently stood. Nonetheless, while they still hoped to stay in the cabinet and buy time to attain further French and British concessions and 'monitor' Stresemann's behavior, Schiele and his colleagues could not stem the growing frustration with the foreign minister from the Pan-German League and regional party organizations. Less than one week after Stresemann and Luther had returned from Locarno, the DNVP's leaders ran out of time.

On 23 October, the DNVP's executive committee, along with the chairmen of the state party committees, gathered in Berlin for a showdown with the party's moderate leaders.[157] One day before the meeting, the Pan-German dominated National Völkisch Committee issued a statement to be read directly to the party leadership and the heads of the state party chapters meeting the next day. The statement demanded that the party leave the government and openly reject the Locarno Accords, thus preventing any further embarrassment to the party.[158]

In this tense climate, the DNVP's top leadership began its October meeting in Berlin. During the morning session, Westarp and Schiele tried desperately to convince the assembled representatives that the DNVP needed to stay in the government until a final decision on the Locarno agreements had been made. This strategy offered the party the best hope of forcing either revision or outright

---

[155]   Stresemann, *Vermächtnis, volume II*, 247.

[156]   For a detailed treatment of the DNVP's position during, and its response to, the Locarno negotiations see: Grathwol, *Stresemann and the DNVP*, 121–144.

[157]   Ibid., 140.

[158]   For a copy of the resolution, see: BARCH R8048/223, 96.

rejection of the accords. Westarp and Schiele assured the delegates that the party would absolutely oppose the government if their demands for revision to the Locarno Treaty were ignored.[159]

In spite of these promises from Schiele and other members of the Luther cabinet, nothing further could be done. The provincial leaders believed that Schiele and his colleagues had compromised too much already. The time had come to end the DNVP's role in the Luther government. The Executive Committee and the provincial party leaders demanded the immediate withdrawal of DNVP support for the government, including the removal of the DNVP ministers. Echoing the Pan-German line, the assembled party delegates argued that the Locarno Accords were completely unacceptable to the party organization as a whole. The delegates sent a clear message that the party could not tolerate further accommodation with the so-called "politics of fulfillment."[160] Faced with the probability of yet another public split in the party only a year after the disastrous Dawes Plan vote, Kuno von Westarp recommended on 25 October that the Reichstag delegation formally vote to break with the government and recall its ministers. The Reichstag delegation approved the measure and the DNVP's first governmental experience came to an ignominious end.[161]

The DNVP's reaction to this decision revealed a range of opinions.[162] The party's moderate leaders were deeply disturbed by the radical Pan-German course endorsed by the rank and file membership. Choking back tears in his parting message to his cabinet colleagues, Martin Schiele insisted that he and his colleagues had been "overwhelmed by a tidal wave" from the party's regional organizations.[163] Looking back later on the decision, Kuno von Westarp observed:

---

[159]   Grathwol, *Stresemann and the DNVP*, 140.

[160]   Ibid., 141–142.

[161]   Ibid., 142. For an official statement from one of the DNVP's regional groups explaining its demand for the DNVP's cabinet members withdrawal, see: "Die sächsischen Deutschnationalen zum Rücktritt der Reichsminister," *Deutsche Tageszeitung*, 27 October 1925, 2.

[162]   The DNVP's opponents began to attack the party even before it had withdrawn its ministers from the cabinet. An article in the Socialist *Vorwärts* newspaper juxtaposed a positive statement regarding Locarno made by party moderate Oskar Hergt with a quote from the radical Freytagh-Loringhoven decrying Stresemann's entire foreign policy. The article concluded: "Hergt declares his willingness to accept what Freytagh-Loringhoven dismisses as delusional. Unity of the German Nationalists in the name of delusion!" See: "Hergts Irrwahn von Freytagh-Loringhoven bewiesen," *Vorwärts*, 7 October 1925, 2.

[163]   For Stresemann's account of Schiele's emotional parting cabinet speech see: Stresemann, *Vermächtnis, volume II*, 206–207. For Schiele's complete parting statement see: Document #208 "Ministerrat vom 26. Oktober 1925, 12 Uhr," in Karl Dietrich Erdmann (ed.), *Akten der Reichskanzlei-Weimar Republik: Die Kabinett Luther I und II, Bd. II 2 Oktober 1925 bis Mai 1926*,

After the withdrawal of our ministers, a new constellation emerged in which the government came to rely on the Social Democrats and the Democrats [DDP]. The nationalist opposition against the calamity of the Locarno accords, which led to Germany's unconditional acceptance of [the treaty's] demands ... had a decisive impact. The Executive Committee and the leaders of the party's regional organizations gave up the fight in the cabinet and the coalition five minutes before midnight. One can only imagine how differently the reparations negotiations of 1930 might have gone if the Saar and Rhineland had already been cleared in 1925 and 1926.[164]

Westarp's observations echoed other contemporary concerns about the DNVP's decision to withdraw from the Luther cabinet. Some moderate DNVP members expressed their outrage to party leaders that the radicals had effectively hijacked the DNVP. One party member chided Kuno von Westarp for the party's decision to leave the government over Locarno:

The German people already lost the war once. We must now, even with gnashing of teeth, yield to this reality and use all our abilities to reestablish confidence [in Germany] abroad. We Germans who have lived abroad for many years judge the psyche of foreigners much differently than the German beer-bench politicians from the provinces.[165]

President Hindenburg, elected only months earlier, was also upset by what he perceived to be the Nationalists' irresponsible behavior, claiming that they were the ones who had convinced him to serve the government, and now they had left him high and dry.[166] For their parts, Luther and Stresemann were furious with the Nationalist betrayal, but were able to keep the cabinet functioning until the end of the year.[167] In spite of initial opposition they also secured approval of the Locarno Accords with help from the Social Democrats on 27 November.

On 1 December 1925, the Locarno Accords were officially signed in London. It soon became clear that the DNVP gained nothing from its withdrawal from the government. The party lost its ability to affect the course of further foreign and domestic policy negotiations from within the government. Furthermore,

---

803–804. Schiele closed by observing that he was "not convinced that a calm wait-and-see attitude [on the part of the DNVP's leadership] might not have led to a general agreement concerning Locarno." He "sincerely regretted" that this opinion was not shared by others in the party.

[164] Kuno von Westarp quoted in: SHStA Dresden, NL Phillip/4, 182–183.

[165] Paul Kratzmann (Berlin) to Westarp, 12 November 1925, NL Westarp, np.

[166] SHStA Dresden, NL Phillip/4, 183.

[167] Stresemann, *Vermächtnis, volume II*, 248. Stresemann referred to a "general sense of indignation" regarding the DNVP's departure from the Luther government.

in the wake of the embarrassing Dawes' vote split, the DNVP was again faced with an internal feud that threatened to divide it even further. By bowing to the radicals, the party went back over to the opposition with very little to show for its roughly nine months in power.

However, all of this was welcome news to the Pan-German League. The League welcomed the DNVP's decision openly on the front page of the *Deutsche Zeitung*. In an article entitled "German and Nationalist" ("*Deutsch und National*"), Fritz Baer extolled the DNVP for its decision to leave the government. Although some of the party's leaders hoped to stay in the government to "prevent the worst" from occurring, Baer pointed out that the worst had already occurred in the form of Stresemann's entire foreign policy.[168] It was now up to the party to insure that, in the future, there could be no compromise on questions of "life-or-death" importance for the German people.

According to Baer, the DNVP was "free again" to return to the opposition and to demonstrate its resolve to remain in the opposition unless a new government was formed, composed only of individuals committed to "conducting truly German nationalist policies."[169] Baer believed that the DNVP's return to opposition did not in any way mean a loss of power. On the contrary, the party had regained a position of power upon which its true supporters could rely. The DNVP's leaders had finally listened to their constituents and made the correct decision; now the party would carry on the fight in parliament and represent the true will of the people rather than the spirit of party politics. Baer concluded that the DNVP could now pursue "a policy which would never sacrifice that which was German, but rather preserve it as a non-negotiable right ... for the German nation!"[170]

Not even the Reichstag's approval of the Locarno Accords in November dampened the Pan-German League's enthusiasm for the DNVP's decision. The Pan-German League argued that the Reichstag's vote simply proved the corrupt nature of the political system. Despite the Reichstag's tragic mistake, the League took great pleasure in the fact that the DNVP "found the courage to draw a clear line in the sand" in opposing Stresemann's policies.[171] The Pan-German leadership further clarified its position in a detailed letter to the head of the Pan-German League's Marburg chapter.[172] The letter described the League's relationship to the DNVP, observing that: "The best friend is the friend who speaks the truth." In that sense, the Pan-German League was indeed the DNVP's

---

[168]   "Deutsch und National," *Deutsche Zeitung*, 15 November 1925, 1–2.

[169]   Ibid., 1.

[170]   Ibid., 2.

[171]   Admiral von Roeder to G. Nißen, 24 November 1925, BARCH R8048/211, 375–376.

[172]   Admiral von Roeder to M. Mauß, 25 November 1925, BARCH R8048/211, 386–387.

"best friend" because it "point[ed] out openly and honestly that which [was] not truly völkisch and must, therefore, be changed."[173] The DNVP's size alone was never the key issue. The letter explained that pure strength in numbers would be useless if the party strayed from its true "nationalist" calling. "Unity alone accomplishes nothing if it is not rooted in a völkisch foundation."[174]

Heinrich Claß echoed these sentiments at the League's year-end executive committee meeting in mid-December 1925. Despite the fact that President Hindenburg had failed in his national duty to reject the Locarno Accords—a failure which Claß likened to Kaiser Wilhelm II's "breakdown" in 1918—the Pan-Germans were still truly pleased that at least the DNVP had seen the light at the last minute.[175] The League could be proud of its work, Claß continued, particularly at the local level in its increased connection to many of the DNVP's regional groups that brought the party around to this crucial decision. The DNVP was "safe" for the time being, but Claß admonished the League's members to remain vigilant in the future. As the party developed in the next three years, this Pan-German vigilance would be repeatedly tested.[176]

Reflecting on the tumultuous events of 1925, Axel Freiherr von Freytagh-Loringhoven pointed to the DNVP's struggle with Stresemann's foreign policy as a key turning point in the party's history.[177] As Freytagh-Loringhoven put it, the party simply could not have gone along with a treaty that so deeply offended Germany's honor. The Locarno Accords represented nothing less than the final abandonment of Germany's "stolen" western border areas. If the party as a whole had approved this, Freytagh-Loringhoven concluded, the DNVP would have ceased to exist as "the bearer of nationalist resistance ... and would have merely gone the same way as the DVP years earlier."[178]

Freytagh-Loringhoven saw this tragic conflict between the party's membership and the moderate leadership as an unfortunate, but ultimately necessary development. Martin Schiele and his colleagues had to be recalled from the cabinet because they simply could not be relied upon any longer to stop Stresemann. Their apparent willingness to go along with the foreign minister's policy decisions did not represent the true desire of most rank and file party members. Had the party continued on the course that Schiele and his fellow party moderates supported, both the DNVP and the entire nationalist

---

[173]   Ibid., 386.

[174]   Ibid., 387.

[175]   SGA, 12 December 1925, BARCH R8048/145, 33.

[176]   Ibid., 32.

[177]   Freytagh-Loringhoven, *Deutschnationale Volkspartei*, 38–39.

[178]   Ibid., 38.

movement would have suffered "a defeat from which it might never have recovered."[179]

The conflict that Freytagh-Loringhoven described might never have occurred without the constant pressure of the Pan-German League. To be sure, the League did not attain all the goals it set throughout 1924 and 1925. It ultimately failed to prevent national approval of the Dawes Plan, the Locarno Accords, and Germany's eventual entrance into the League of Nations in 1926. However, the League did succeed in its campaign to drive the DNVP away from any significant responsibility for these developments. While the League and its party allies viewed this outcome as a real victory, historians should consider it in a much different light.

Without the Pan-German League's relentless pressure, DNVP moderates may well have been able to preserve the party's position and gradually increase its image as a reliable coalition partner. There was certainly support for government participation within the party at a time when certain domestic issues, like taxes and tariffs, directly affected the livelihood of agrarians and industrialists alike. However, in the realm of foreign policy the party's moderate leadership simply could not make a strong enough public case to account for a "surrender" of German lands in order to remain in a government which some party members already despised. On the other hand, members of the party's radical wing and the Pan-German League presented regularly and openly a wide range of reasons why the DNVP should reject out of hand any accommodation with the "politics of fulfillment."

The Pan-German League and its allies in the Reichstag delegation, regional party groups, and allied patriotic organizations, undermined the DNVP's moderate leadership at a crucial time in the Republic's history. The Pan-German League's extremist propaganda campaign leveled against party moderates left the DNVP's cabinet ministers with few options. As a result, they stepped down precisely as the specific structure and ultimate outcome of the Locarno Accords hung in the balance. As Martin Schiele correctly observed in his parting cabinet statement, it was truly unfortunate that more party members could not agree to support the DNVP and its important role within the cabinet.[180]

The Pan-German League's relentless public attack against the DNVP's leadership ultimately had a debilitating effect on Weimar Germany's largest conservative party. The public feud over the Dawes Plan vote in 1924 publicly exposed the lack of DNVP solidarity. The crisis precipitated largely by the Pan-German League and its allies over Stresemann's foreign policy and the DNVP's

---

[179]   Ibid., 39.
[180]   See above, footnote 163.

participation in the Luther cabinet in 1925 seemed to confirm the party's inherent instability. While this alone did not prevent the DNVP's inclusion in one further national government in 1927, it severely tarnished the party's image as an effective, unified political force.

Despite the DNVP's numerical strength between 1924 and 1928, there was a huge discrepancy between the will of the moderate national leadership and the uncompromising demands of the party's vociferous and influential Pan-German wing. The DNVP's clear inability to reconcile these two dominant currents robbed the Weimar Republic of something that it desperately needed: a state-supporting, conservative party willing to work within the framework of the constitution and enter fully into the life of party politics. As the events of 1924–1925 suggest, the Pan-German League played an important role in ensuring that precisely such a party would not emerge.

Chapter 5

The Campaign for Alfred Hugenberg, 1926–1928

At the beginning of 1926, the German Right faced an uncertain political future. Extremist elements stretching from völkisch paramilitary militias to the upstart Nazi Party had largely discredited themselves in various poorly-planned attempts to overthrow or violently destabilize the Weimar Republic. On the other hand, the dominant conservative party, the DNVP, was deeply divided about its fundamental responsibility to the republican system. Within the previous 18 months, the DNVP careened between the extremes of substantial electoral success and open division over the Dawes Plan vote to participation in a national coalition government and an embarrassing cabinet departure by the end of 1925. The Pan-German League played an important role in these developments within the DNVP, particularly during the turbulent years of 1924 and 1925.

However, the League's strategy during 1924–1925 produced only mixed results. In the broadest sense, the League and its allies failed to prevent the adoption of the Dawes Plan, the Locarno Accords, or Germany's eventual participation in the League of Nations by 1926. However, the League had helped force an open confrontation within the DNVP over the Dawes Plan vote, and played an undeniably important role in driving the DNVP out of Luther's 1925 coalition government in response to Gustav Stresemann's foreign policy and the Locarno Accords. Yet with each of these partial "successes," the League also realized that it had failed to accomplish its ultimate goal of helping to create a truly radical DNVP that would never again entertain the notion of participating in the Weimar system. To accomplish this task, the Pan-German League began revising its strategy regarding Germany's largest conservative party in early 1926.

Alfred Hugenberg was the centerpiece of the Pan-German League's new approach to transform the DNVP.[1] Heinrich Claß and many other leading Pan-

---

[1] Born in Hannover in 1865, Hugenberg had served as director of the Krupp steel works before investing sizeable amounts of money to build up a right-wing press and media empire that he used relentlessly to attack the Weimar Republic. He was Heinrich Claß's long-time friend and a co-founder of the Pan-German League. Although Hugenberg did not actively participate in

Germans now believed that the only way to transform the party permanently was to promote Hugenberg as the chairman. With the Pan-German ally Hugenberg at the helm, the League could devote its remaining influence to removing other moderate conservatives from the party and help to create a unified, intransigent force of the nationalist opposition that would never again compromise with the Weimar system. As events unfolded, the Pan-German League did, in fact, play an important role in promoting Alfred Hugenberg's election as party chairman while also helping to drive out moderate conservatives. The departing DNVP moderates ultimately split off between 1929 and 1930 either to form new political organizations like the Conservative People's Party (*Konservative Volkspartei*—hereafter "KVP"), or to return permanently to private life, disgusted with the DNVP's new radical stance.[2]

Seen more broadly, however, the Pan-German campaign for Alfred Hugenberg and a "purified" radical DNVP ultimately proved disastrous for the overall course of right-wing politics in the Weimar Republic. The Pan-German League's machinations helped undermine any real hope for the emergence of a responsible, popular, governmental conservatism that might have offered a more effective alternative to the Nazi Party after 1930. In this regard, Heinrich Claß and the Pan-German League bear significant responsibility for the radicalization of conservative politics and the fracturing of the German Right generally in the later years of the Weimar Republic. This chapter examines the Pan-German League's role in these events during the key period between 1926 and 1928.

Laying the Foundation: Heinrich Claß and Personal Political Influence

There is little question that the Pan-German League's chairman Heinrich Claß played an important personal role in Alfred Hugenberg's ascent to the chairmanship of the German National People's Party. While several major

---

League meetings and events during the Weimar period, he maintained close personal ties to his Pan-German allies including Claß, Paul Bang, Karl Lohmann, Carl Gottfried Gok, and Axel Freiherr von Freytagh-Loringhoven. For more on Hugenberg's political career generally and his place within the DNVP, see: John Leopold, *Alfred Hugenberg: The Radical Nationalist Campaign Against the Weimar Republic* (New Haven and London, 1977). Reinhold Quaatz, a Hugenberg supporter within the DNVP and a former DVP member, also provides ample evidence of Claß's close working relationship with Hugenberg in the final years of the Weimar Republic. See: Hermann Weiß and Paul Hoser (eds), *Die Deutschnationalen und die Zerstörung der Weimarer Republik: Aus dem Tagebuch von Reinhold Quaatz 1928–1933* (Munich, 1989).

[2]   For more on the DNVP's departures and the KVP's formation see: Erasmus Jonas, *Die Volkskonservativen 1928–1933: Entwicklung, Struktur, Standort und staatspolitische Zielsetzung* (Düsseldorf, 1965).

factors ultimately contributed to Hugenberg's victory, including his own influential press empire, Claß and his Pan-German associates were directly involved in much of the behind-the-scenes political maneuvering that made Hugenberg's success possible.[3] Claß set to work already at the end of 1925. In late December, Claß traveled to Hugenberg's home to discuss the possibility of his taking control of the DNVP. Hugenberg initially displayed little willingness to run for the party's top spot. He explained to Claß that he stood in a minority within the party and that many of his colleagues perceived him as too extreme on a number of key political issues. Claß countered that he would help Hugenberg recast his image to make him appear more "personable" and politically appealing to a wider segment of the population. As a result of Claß's personal insistence during the course of their discussion, Hugenberg finally agreed to consider the possibility over the Christmas and New Year holidays.[4]

Claß's next step came at the end of January 1926. Hugenberg, who had been taking a cure for several weeks in Kreuth, invited Claß back for further discussions at his country estate at Rohbraken. Claß succeeded first in assuring Hugenberg's wife that her husband was physically prepared to undertake such an arduous political commitment and that, with the proper backing, he would also enjoy sufficient support within and outside of the DNVP to make his candidacy a success.[5] Hugenberg explained to Claß that, in principle, he was indeed prepared to challenge Kuno von Westarp for the DNVP chairmanship. This could only happen, however, with stronger support for Hugenberg within and outside of the party and with a reliable network of trustworthy confidants. Claß explained that Hugenberg would enjoy the League's full support and its members would be placed "unconditionally at his disposal."[6] Claß singled out Paul Bang as an ideal liaison between Hugenberg and the Pan-Germans. Bang was Claß's close friend, a member of the League's leadership and executive committees, and a respected nationalist expert on economics.[7] Hugenberg and Claß agreed that Bang would provide the type of expertise Hugenberg would need on economic issues within the party and would also serve as an important

---

[3]   Claß, *WdS v. II*, 843. Much of the following account of Claß's personal campaign for Hugenberg is taken from Claß's unpublished memoirs. These memoirs provide a unique perspective on the personal politics that resulted in Hugenberg's election as party chairman.

[4]   Ibid., 851.

[5]   Ibid., 853.

[6]   Ibid.

[7]   Bang was one of the youngest and most radical members of the Hugenberg/Claß circle. Born in Saxony in 1879, Bang served as an economics advisor in the Saxon Ministry of Finance until 1919. He joined the League in 1915 and became an influential member of the League's Leadership committee by 1920. See: Holzbach, *System Hugenberg*, 170 n22.

connection between Hugenberg and his supporters within the party and the Pan-German League.[8]

Buoyed by Hugenberg's commitment to challenge for the DNVP's leadership, Claß immediately began to drum up support for Hugenberg within the party. However, the Pan-German leader realized that this effort might take a considerable amount of time. With the instability of the Luther cabinet in the first weeks of 1926, Claß came up with an even more direct approach to propel Hugenberg into a position of national leadership. In early January 1926, Claß began to work with his closest advisors to influence President Paul von Hindenburg to appoint Hugenberg directly as leader of a new right-wing government. This government would replace Hans Luther's "cabinet of personalities" as soon as it collapsed.[9]

Claß believed that since Luther's cabinet already drew its authority from President Hindenburg and not an outright parliamentary majority, Claß could attempt to convince the president to appoint another such cabinet composed of right-wing nationalist notables headed by Hugenberg.[10] As implausible as this plan might seem, Claß and his associates pushed forward during the first few months of 1926 to convince Hindenburg of the plan's feasibility. Although Claß and the Pan-German League had not given up on their long-term goal to place Hugenberg at the head of the DNVP, they felt they had a unique opportunity in early 1926. If their short-term strategy proved successful, Hugenberg would move into a national leadership position without the immediate need for parliamentary support.

Claß worked quickly to strengthen his contacts with President Hindenburg through trusted Pan-German associates Prince Otto zu Salm-Horstmar and General Wilhelm von Dommes. Furthermore, Claß found strong support for his plan in another ally outside the League, Elard von Oldenburg-Januschau. As Claß recounted, all three of these men agreed with Claß's assessment of Hugenberg's abilities and supported his attempt to promote Hugenberg as chancellor. Of all the men, Oldenburg-Januschau provided the best hope for influencing the president. Claß believed Januschau's frequent formal and informal discussions with Hindenburg would provide the ideal opportunity to promote Hugenberg as a suitable political leader.[11]

---

[8]   Claß, *WdS v. II*, 854.

[9]   Ibid., 856.

[10]   Ibid.

[11]   Ibid., 856. Oldenburg-Januschau was an arch-conservative East Prussian noble, a member of the pre-war German Conservative Party and the post-war DNVP, and a confidant of President Paul von Hindenburg.

Claß's plan had three major components. First, Hindenburg would appoint Hugenberg to form a nationalist cabinet that could attempt to secure the support of enough parties including the DNVP, the DVP, the BVP, and perhaps the Center Party. If this nearly impossible scenario failed, Hindenburg would re-form a cabinet of rightist "personalities" following the example of the current Luther cabinet. This would, of course, require at least the toleration of a majority in the Reichstag. If this option failed, Claß expected Hindenburg to turn to the provisions of Article 48 of the Weimar Constitution and appoint Hugenberg as leader without formal parliamentary approval or even toleration. Claß believed this latter option might be possible because of what he characterized as the growing threat of the extremist Left in Germany.

Once the president was convinced of Hugenberg's abilities, Claß hoped that he would appoint him according to Article 48 with the full justification that such a move would prevent a Leftist takeover of power in Germany. Claß referred to what he saw as a heroic, historical precedent for his attempts to influence the political situation. He argued that his own efforts, along with those of Oldeburg-Januschau, to convince the President of Hugenberg's abilities were similar to "Minister of War von Roon's campaign to convince his King to clear the way for Otto von Bismarck to become Minister President of Prussia."[12]

Despite Claß's grandiose historical assessment of Hugenberg's potential impact on the German political scene, President Hindenburg did not see things in the same light. At the end of March 1926, Claß received a "full report" from Oldenburg-Januschau concerning his recent private discussions with Hindenburg. Although Hindenburg believed Hugenberg would be thoroughly suited to serve as finance minister in a new cabinet, the president felt that Hugenberg could not be entrusted with the chancellorship, and certainly not under the extreme conditions implied by the use of Article 48.[13] In spite of this disappointing news, Claß still believed that Hugenberg could serve, even if he began in the cabinet merely as finance minister. Claß believed that for the time being, he needed to find someone who might be more acceptable to President Hindenburg and who would be willing to work with Hugenberg as finance minister.

Claß then turned his attention to one of his oldest friends, the Lübeck Mayor Johann Neumann. Although hardly a prominent figure on the right-wing scene, Claß oddly believed that Neumann possessed sufficient leadership experience and respect in right-wing circles to serve as chancellor with President Hindenburg's approval. After discussing this option with Hugenberg and

---

[12]   Ibid., 857.

[13]   Ibid.

receiving his assent to proceed, Claß contacted Neumann and proposed to him the idea of a chancellorship. Claß assured Neumann that when the time came for a formation of a rightist cabinet, Hugenberg would make sure that only the "best men" would stand at his disposal. Neumann's main responsibility, Claß explained, would be "to represent the cabinet calmly and securely."[14] Neumann's final answer came several weeks later. At the end of April 1926, Neumann informed Claß that he had spoken with Hugenberg and had considered the offer, but ultimately he decided to reject it. Neumann explained that he already had too many responsibilities as mayor of Lübeck. Additionally, he was having an exceedingly difficult time with opposition parties in his own government and he simply did not want to turn away from such a responsibility to present himself as a candidate for chancellor of a new nationalist cabinet.[15] Although Claß does not mention it in his memoirs, it is reasonable to assume that Neumann was simply not prepared to take such a plunge without greater assurance that a concrete schedule existed, or that the formation of a nationalist cabinet would actually work under Claß's far-fetched scenario.

Faced with President Hindenburg's reluctance to appoint Hugenberg directly, and Neumann's unwillingness to serve in a cabinet largely as a figurehead chancellor, Claß and the Pan-German League reverted to their original, more modest goal of securing Hugenberg as leader of the DNVP. However, as Claß was soon to discover, his secretive negotiations with Hindenburg, Hugenberg, Neumann, and other prominent right-wing leaders had not gone unnoticed. Indeed, other political leaders, including Foreign Minister Gustav Stresemann, had heard rumors for some time concerning Claß's attempts to influence the president to form a new right-wing government. Whatever Claß's true intentions were in the opening months of 1926, by the end of May he faced charges of high treason for attempts to lead a coup d'état against the government. Revelations of a so-called "Claß Putsch" exploded onto the already tense Weimar political scene and drew sensational press coverage across the country. The affair also had a profound impact on the Pan-German League's broader campaign to influence the course of right-wing politics, especially with the DNVP.

The "Claß Putsch" and Right-Wing Politics, 1926–1927

Although the so-called Claß Putsch received a great deal of public attention from late spring 1926 until the end of 1927, scholars have largely overlooked

---

[14]   Ibid., 859.
[15]   Ibid., 860.

or misinterpreted this event.[16] As the historian Heidrun Holzbach points out, part of this has to do with what has appeared to be the lack of a clear-cut picture of Claß's intentions, and the intensely polemical nature of the political responses to the allegations against Claß and other right-wing leaders.[17] Therefore, it is important to explore all sides of this event to determine its real significance, particularly within the broader context of contemporary German right-wing politics.

As the complete evidence now demonstrates, there really was no "Claß Putsch" in the sense of an organized, imminent threat to overthrow the government. In reality, by 1926 Heinrich Claß and many of his alleged associates like Johann Neumann of Lübeck simply did not possess the political authority or, most importantly, the military backing that they would have required to pull off a coup d'état. While Claß certainly discussed various scenarios in which the parliamentary system might be neutralized or suspended through Article 48—as he had done in the first months of 1926 concerning Hugenberg—he and the Pan-German League simply did not have the resources or backing to implement such a direct assault against the national government. Nonetheless, the question remains why the so-called Claß Putsch received so much public attention throughout 1926 and 1927. We will explore that dimension of this misunderstood episode in the following pages.[18]

The government's response to rumors of a rightist Putsch came very quickly in the second week of May 1926. Acting on a seemingly reliable tip from an obscure right-wing agitator named Dietz, the SPD-led Prussian coalition government launched a series of house searches on 11 May to uncover evidence of plans for a rightist attack against the state. Dietz alleged that Heinrich Claß, Alfred Hugenberg, Johann Neumann, and several other prominent right-wing leaders and businessmen had been plotting to create a directory headed by Hugenberg, approved by Hindenburg, and enforced by an array of illegal paramilitary organizations.[19]

---

[16]   See: Hering, *Konstruierte Nation*, 148–149; and Chamberlin, *Enemy on the Right*, 342–403. Chamberlin's dissertation examines the Putsch in some detail, but does so without use of important government sources, especially the key files of the *Reichsjustizamt/-ministerium* (hereafter "BARCH R30.01") and the *Reichskommisar für Überwachung der öffentlichen Ordnung* (hereafter "BARCH R1507"). Lack of access to these invaluable sources caused Chamberlin to overestimate significantly the Putsch's organization and its overall impact.

[17]   Holzbach, *System Hugenberg*, 195.

[18]   The Claß Putsch attracted comprehensive national media attention. The files of the "Reichskommisar für Überwachung der öffentlichen Ordnung" provide some sense of the extensive coverage this affair received. See: BARCH 1507/228, 19–50, 56–65, and 72–156.

[19]   For the government's actions in this case see: Dietrich Orlow, *Weimar Prussia 1925–1933: The Illusion of Strength* (Pittsburgh, 1991), 78–80. For the role of the Prussian police and

Interestingly, Gustav Stresemann became immediately involved in the police action. Although he had no formal standing within the internal Prussian police and security structure as sitting foreign minister, he took a particularly strong interest in the right-wing Putsch rumors. On 11 May, concerned about rumors that had persisted regarding right-wing negotiations with President Hindenburg and the possibility of a Putsch, Stresemann contacted Dr. Ferdinand Friedensburg, the vice-president of the Berlin police. Friedensburg informed Stresemann that according to a police witness, a wide scale Putsch had been planned.[20] Allegedly, the plot involved the president's removal and the appointment of a national commissioner, who would in turn have appointed commissioners for all of the constituent states, and ruled as dictator without parliamentary support. Upon hearing this information, Stresemann encouraged the police to proceed quickly against this scheme. Stresemann later commented in his memoirs that he took action that "any supporter of the constitution" would have taken.[21] Later that evening, Stresemann contacted Friedensburg again after the police raids to congratulate him and the rest of the police force for their quick strike to prevent an "internal political catastrophe."[22] Stresemann added further that, in the event that those connected with the alleged Putsch were political figures or Reichstag delegates, parliamentary immunity should not affect the prosecutor's case. "In my opinion, immunity comes to an end when there is a question of treason," Stresemann suggested.[23]

The government's quick strike took Claß and his allies by surprise. Claß contacted Hugenberg and several other colleagues to assure them that he had planned nothing of the sort. Claß dismissed the entire affair as "laughable" and decried the "characteristically Jewish and exaggerated" press coverage the police action had received.[24] Prussian authorities uncovered one of the few allegedly solid pieces of evidence when they searched Claß's home. It was a list of 12 members, primarily from Rhenish-Westfalian industrial circles, belonging to the

---

the Ministry of Interior especially, see: Thomas Albrecht, *Für eine wehrhafte Demokratie: Albert Grzesinski und die preußische Politik in der Weimarer Republik* (Bonn, 1999), 136–139. Other paramilitary organizations also came under suspicion in this episode, including the Vereinigte vaterländische Verbände Deutschlands, the Sportverein Olympia, and the Wiking-Bund. See: Internal Report of the Reichskommisar für Überwachung der öffentlichen Ordnung from 12 May 1926 in: BARCH R1507/228, 7–8.

20   Stresemann offers a detailed account of these events in a memo dated 5 June 1926. See: Nachlass Stresemann, Auswärtiges Amt-Politisches Archiv (hereafter "AA-PA")/38, 000273–000276.

21   Stresemann, *Vermächtnis, v. II*, 403.

22   Ibid., 404.

23   Ibid., 405.

24   Claß, *WdS v. II*, 864.

so-called "Economic Association."[25] Prussian authorities initially claimed that this list represented a collection of co-conspirators for Claß's planned action against the state. In reality, the list was prepared during World War I to provide names and addresses of potential Pan-German League contributors.[26] Beyond that, police searches uncovered no concrete evidence linking Claß or anyone else to a planned Putsch.

Claß reserved special scorn for Gustav Stresemann's role in the entire affair. In sharp contrast to Stresemann's account, Claß believed that the foreign minister had far more than a patriotic motive for his surprisingly direct involvement in this domestic political matter. In fact, Claß and several of his close political allies believed that Stresemann engineered the government's action against Claß to prevent any future discussions with President Hindenburg regarding a right-wing cabinet and to discredit Pan-German efforts on behalf of Hugenberg's leadership of the DNVP. Claß further believed that it was Stresemann who encouraged the police to move so aggressively on the basis on one witness and a set of unfounded rumors.[27] The immediate press attention that the entire affair received was, Claß claimed, also the result of Stresemann's connections in his own party and with the Prussian Ministry of the Interior.[28] Claß also believed that Stresemann used his influence in the Ministry of the Interior to leak the story to the press in order to discredit the Right generally, and Hugenberg specifically as a potential national leader.[29] Several other prominent right-wing leaders shared Claß's own suspicions concerning Stresemann's role in the affair.[30]

After the initial investigations had ended, Claß was the only member of the alleged rightist conspirators to be formally charged.[31] In his deposition, Claß did not shy away from discussing his plans for the establishment of a right-wing cabinet, or from asserting the possibility that Article 48 might be

---

[25] Ibid., 866.

[26] Ibid.

[27] Ibid., 867.

[28] Ibid.

[29] In fact, Stresemann recounts in his memoirs that he contacted the press with information regarding the police action the day after the raid. See: Stresemann, *Vermächtnis, v. II*, 403.

[30] Leo Wegener, a close associate of Hugenberg and Claß, believed strongly that Stresemann had engineered the Prussian state's response to prevent a cabinet or government of the Right from being formed. Referring directly to Stresemann, Wegener wrote in November 1927: "Who was the strong man who alerted the police within 24 hours of this 'criminal activity?' It must have been someone who stood to gain a great deal. What advantages were there for the taking? A new cabinet position or an attempt to maintain the old one?" See: Leo Wegener to Claß, 19 November 1927, BA-Koblenz, N1003 Nachlass Leo Wegener/23, 454.

[31] The official summary of the state's case against Claß can be found in: BARCH 30.01 Reichsjustizamt/-Ministerium (hereafter "30.01")/21430 (5063/9), 3–81.

a necessary measure to ensure the survival of such a cabinet in the face of Leftist parliamentary or extra-parliamentary opposition.[32] Claß argued, however, that such a measure was legal, constitutionally sound, and did not imply the creation of a permanent dictatorship or a forceful overthrow of the established state order.[33]

Ultimately, the state failed to prove any conspiracy even existed. No one even came to trial in connection with the case. Even Claß, the only suspect to be formally charged, was finally cleared for lack of sufficient evidence to suggest that he or his alleged co-conspirators had prepared a Putsch against the government.[34] Nonetheless, this event had a far-reaching impact on Heinrich Claß, the Pan-German League, and the development of the German Right in the coming months.

Looking back on the entire episode almost a decade later while writing his memoirs, Claß came to a very clear set of conclusions. Most importantly, he believed that the affair had been artificially created to stimulate such a public outcry against him, Hugenberg, and other nationalists so that no rightist government could be formed for a substantial period of time. As Claß put it, it was no mere coincidence that the "smear campaign" launched against him in May 1926 came only days after the so-called "Flag crisis" which precipitated the collapse of the second Luther government.[35] As he and his allies had stated publicly and privately from the beginning, Claß still maintained that:

> It was a political affair ... The entire process was prolonged precisely because of political considerations. The purpose of this exercise was to separate the Reich President from the Right or, more precisely, to keep him separated. The governing parties recognized the danger that, under the correct conditions, Mr. von Hindenburg could appoint a right-wing government ... [The governing parties] further realized that prominent members of the Right were in frequent contact with him [Hindenburg] and were attempting to influence him in such a direction. So they concluded that as long as the

[32] Claß, *WdS v. II*, 870. For the official transcript of Claß's complete deposition see: BARCH 30.01/21430 (5063/9), 49–52.

[33] Ibid., 49.

[34] The government found no evidence that Claß, Hugenberg, or anyone else originally accused had agreed to any plan to overthrow the Republic. For the state's official statement releasing Claß and closing the investigation on 15 October 1927, see: BARCH 30.01/21430 (5063/9), 83.

[35] Claß, *WdS v. II*, 875. The "flag decree" authorized the use of the old black-white-red commercial banner of the Second Empire at Germany's trade establishments abroad. The DDP and the Center Party vigorously protested what they believed to be a direct concession to Germany's extremist nationalists. The ensuing political crisis drove Luther from office and ultimately led to the formation of a Marx minority cabinet. Mommsen, *Rise and Fall of Weimar Democracy*, 209.

process was still pending, the Reich President could not receive, or even consult for advice, anyone who was in any way connected to the alleged high treason.[36]

Although Claß and his political allies were notorious for their often far-fetched political schemes and paranoid conspiracy theories, in this particular case their assessment of the political motivation behind the Putsch affair had some merit. Even the Reich Commissioner for Monitoring Public Order (Reichskommissar für Überwachung der öffentlichen Ordnung) internally acknowledged that Claß and the Pan-Germans were in no position to mount any sort of large scale assault against the Weimar Republic:

> I do not accord this issue [the Putsch allegations] any great significance … Certainly such 'mobilization preparations' are disconcerting, but they are often merely childish games. Because these right-wing groups are disorganized and would never attempt something without the certain support of the Reichswehr, and because the Reichswehr will move decisively against any putschist attempt against the government, no realistic threat exists from these right-wing groups. The excitement that has developed in the Reichstag is likely the result of the press attention [this event has received].[37]

Based on internal government documents, then, it is much more likely that the exaggerated response to the Putsch rumors was at least in part intended to discredit Claß and his associates. Although Stresemann never formally admitted his actual intentions concerning Claß and Hugenberg, his extraordinarily strong interest in this specific case while serving as foreign minister only seems to make sense in this regard. Further evidence from Stresemann's own private papers sheds additional light on his involvement in this affair. In early June, Wilhelm Abegg, the state secretary in the Prussian Ministry of the Interior, wrote Stresemann to discuss criticism of the Prussian government occurring in the Landtag over the alleged Claß Putsch. Abegg felt compelled to defend his government's swift action against Claß and his alleged co-conspirators in part

---

[36]   Claß, *WdS v. II*, 878. The *Deutsche Zeitung* also ran numerous articles pointing out the "obvious" political motivation behind the police action. For an excellent example of this approach, see: "Politische Hintergründe," *Deutsche Zeitung*, 15 May 1926, 1–2. Another *Deutsche Zeitung* article modified the title of Heinrich Claß's popular *Wenn ich der Kaiser wär* (Leipzig, 1912), to apply to Stresemann. The article, which the foreign minister retained in his personal papers, attacked Stresemann's entire foreign and domestic policy. See: "Wenn ich Stresemann wäre …," *Deutsche Zeitung*, 17 November 1926 in: NL Stresemann, AA-PA/46, 000141.

[37]   Reichskommissar für Überwachung der öffentlichen Ordnung to Reichsministerium des Innern, Reichswehrministerium, Staatssekretär in der Reichskanzlei, Herrn Min. Stresemann, 12 May 1926, BARCH R1507/228, 6.

by explaining that the police intervention had been "briskly supported ... and encouraged" by a "prominent member of a right-wing party." Abegg apologized that Stresemann's name had subsequently been revealed in this connection though "other sources."[38]

Another memo dated 5 June 1926 from Ferdinand Friedensburg, the vice-president of the Berlin police, detailed a private conversation between Friedensberg and Stresemann on the evening of 11 May 1926 in which the foreign minister revealed a specific interest in Hugenberg's role in the alleged plot. Friedensburg explained that the government was concerned about far-reaching action against Hugenberg because of his immunity as a Reichstag member. According to Friedensburg, Stresemann replied "if you have any problems with [Hugenberg's] immunity status, I will go to my party's caucus to encourage that immunity be lifted." Friedensburg concluded that the entire conversation seemed very "personal and secretive" and that Stresemann must have assumed that "the details of the conversation would not be made public."[39]

As Stresemann and other reasonable political leaders surely recognized, Claß, Hugenberg, and their allies still maintained their connections to President Hindenburg. Moreover, the Pan-German League and its radical party allies posed an ongoing threat to the emergence of a moderate DNVP, as the recent Locarno fiasco demonstrated. While swift police intervention to prevent a right-wing Putsch seemed reasonable on its own terms, it is likely that political considerations also played a role. A key internal Berlin police report from June 1926 clearly reinforces this notion:

> Police efforts have sharply reduced the political influence of the accused ... within the nationalist movement. The delegates of the German National People's Party who value the parliamentary system are certainly not upset about this action against [Heinrich] Claß, the man who is often referred to as the 'uncomfortable agitator.' The party itself seems to view Claß's setback as not entirely inconvenient, because it will allow [the DNVP] to proceed with its politics of the possible with considerably less criticism.[40]

While Heinrich Claß and his allies primarily blamed Gustav Stresemann for the overreaction to the Putsch rumors, the foreign minister was not the only one to come under fire from the Pan-German press. Claß believed that Arthur Mahraun, one of the leaders of the Young German Order (Jungdeutsche Orden—hereafter

---

38   Wilhelm Abegg to Gustav Stresemann, NL Stresemann, AA-PA/38, 000277–000278.

39   "Niederschrift des Polizeivizepräsidenten Dr. Friedensburg," NL Stresemann, AA-PA/ 38, 000280–000282.

40   "Lagebericht des Pol. Präs. Berlin vom Juni 1926: II. Die rechtsradikale Bewegung," BARCH R1507/228, 106.

"Jungdo"), had purposely tipped off Prussian authorities and Stresemann about a potential rightist plot to overthrow the government.[41] Although there is no concrete evidence that Mahraun or other Jungdo leaders had contacted the authorities prior to the police action, Claß and his allies still believed that this was indeed the case. Claß and the Pan-German press lambasted Mahraun and the Jungdo for their alleged betrayal of the nationalist cause.[42] This feud spilled over and produced a complete split between the Pan-German League and the Young German Order from 1926 forward.[43] Again, the paranoid, conspiratorial world of right-wing politics played an important role in this split between these two prominent nationalist organizations.

The Claß Putsch affair also provoked highly charged responses from Claß's supporters and detractors in the Reichstag. On several occasions, the Claß case became a major topic for Reichstag debate. On 18 May 1926, delegates hurled accusations at one another concerning the recent house searches of Claß and his associates.[44] The Claß affair also inspired surprisingly intense debate months after the entire case was dismissed. These exchanges, which took place in the Reichstag in late January 1928, featured charges and recriminations from Left and Right concerning the broader significance of the Claß Putsch case for the German legal system.[45]

---

[41]   The Jungdeutsche Orden was a nationalist paramilitary organization with a substantial following in the Weimar Republic. By the mid-1920s however, its leader Arthur Mahraun had begun to push the organization more to the political center, rejecting what he perceived to be the extremism of the Right. For more on the Jungdo and its activities at the time of the Claß Putsch, see: Klaus Hornung, *Der Jungdeutsche Orden* (Düsseldorf, 1958), esp. 62–65. For Mahraun's stance on state authority and putschist politics in the Weimar Republic, see also Clifton Ganyard, *Artur Mahraun and the Young German Order: An Alternative to National Socialism in Weimar Political Culture* (Lewiston, 2008).

[42]   In this regard see the following *Deutsche Zeitung* articles: "Die Denkschrift des Jungdeutschen Ordens," 18 May 1926, 1–2; "Der Lügenfeldzug gegen Heinrich Claß," 20 May 1926, 1; and "Nochmals: Die Denkschrift des Herrn Mahraun!" 4 June 1926, 1–2.

[43]   See the extensive correspondence between the Pan-German League and the Jungdo during and after 1926 in: BARCH R8048/427, especially 23, 27–30, 34–41, and 43–45. For the regional impact of the Pan-German/Jungdo conflict on the radical nationalist movement in Saxony from 1926 until 1928, see: StADresden ADV-OD/10, 221 and 227–230; StADresden ADV-OD/11, 5–8, 64–65, 77, 151, and 161–163.

[44]   *Stenographische Berichte des Reichstags*, 204 Sitzung, 18 May 1926, esp. 7271–7310. In this exchange, Arthur Rosenberg, a Communist Party delegate, attacked Claß for his purported plans and excoriated the legal system and the Prussian government for their timid response to the looming threat from the Right. Predictably, Axel Freiherr von Freytagh-Loringhoven rose to Claß's defense and dismissed Rosenberg's charges out of hand.

[45]   *Stenographische Berichte des Reichstags*, Sitzungen 367–369, 25 January–27 January 1928.

Ultimately, after all of the accusations surrounding the so-called Claß Putsch had subsided, two things were clear. First, the Pan-German League and its prominent leader had suffered a significant public-relations setback. Although his acquittal bolstered his reputation in certain circles on the extremist Right, the sensationalist press coverage for much of the rest of the country helped perpetuate an even more sinister image of Claß and the Pan-German League. Even though the charges against Claß were dismissed, this newest accusation further tarnished the League's national image.

Second, and perhaps most significant, the Putsch affair effectively quashed any further negotiations with President Hindenburg regarding the possible formation of a rightist cabinet. As a result, Claß's plan to promote Alfred Hugenberg in the short term as head of a rightist government had utterly failed. Claß described the period from May 1926 until roughly October 1927 as largely a "dead time" for the nationalist opposition.[46] Claß counted those 17 months as "lost in the sense of any great political activity" as part of the broader campaign to promote Hugenberg as DNVP chairman. "When I received the court's decision [to drop the charges] I knew I would have to start all over again."[47]

By the fall of 1927, Claß and his allies within and outside of the Pan-German League were, therefore, firmly convinced that the only way to position Hugenberg in the national political spotlight was to expand his role within the DNVP itself. The ultimate goal of this campaign would be Hugenberg's election as party chairman. Faced with this challenge, Claß again turned his complete attention, as well as the concerted efforts of the Pan-German League, to the task of uniting the party behind Hugenberg.

Toward a Change in DNVP Leadership, 1927–1928

Seeing clearly that his direct attempts to influence President Hindenburg to appoint a right-wing cabinet had failed, Claß now turned to what he saw as the last hope of the nationalist opposition. Hugenberg had to be elected party chairman as soon as possible to make the DNVP a truly effective platform for unrelenting nationalist opposition against the Weimar Republic. However, the party's course throughout much of 1926–1927 certainly did not bode well for Claß and his Pan-German colleagues. Despite the DNVP's initial opposition to Stresemann and his alleged betrayal of German national interests at Locarno, moderate conservatives still largely retained control of the party. By the time of

---

[46]   Claß, *WdS v. II*, 878–879.

[47]   Ibid., 879.

the DNVP's Cologne party congress in October 1926, Kuno von Westarp, the party's chairman and Reichstag delegation leader, again committed the DNVP to seek another opportunity to enter the national government.[48]

The greatest roadblock to the DNVP's renewed participation in a coalition government was its continued intransigence on the issue of foreign policy. The party voted against the Locarno Accords in December 1925 and Germany's entry into the League of Nations in 1926. This public stance, however, belied an increasing willingness to sacrifice certain ideological principles in order to return to government. Privately some party moderates were growing frustrated with the impact of the DNVP's near fixation on Stresemann's foreign policy at the expense of addressing pressing economic issues or the much greater threat posed by the political Left.[49] Finally, on 26 January 1927, to the chagrin of party radicals and the Pan-German League, and to the delight of party moderates and many economic interests, the DNVP announced that it had again entered into a national government. The coalition government, headed by Wilhelm Marx, was comprised of the Center Party, the DVP, and the BVP.[50]

In spite of the moderate conservatives' desire to focus on other pressing issues, the DNVP's leaders still had to clarify the party's official stance on Germany's recent foreign policy decisions. After much intra-party hand-wringing and discussion with their future coalition partners, the DNVP's leaders not only recognized the validity of the Weimar constitution and the republican system, but they also acknowledged the Locarno Accords as internationally binding and the basis for future German policy.[51] In effect, the DNVP's leaders surrendered two of the party's most cherished principles in their desire to gain influence over national policy in a coalition government.[52]

However, the party's moderate leaders did not stop there. A further challenge to the DNVP's continued participation in the cabinet was the looming vote to

---

[48]   On Westarp's position and the Cologne party congress, see: Dörr, *Deutschnationale Volkspartei*, 251–253.

[49]   For a detailed discussion of moderate frustration over the DNVP's focus on Stresemann and the continuing impact of the party's radical Pan-German wing, see: Walter Rademacher to Kurt Philipp, 7 October 1926, NL Westarp/81, np.

[50]   On the formation of the Marx cabinet, see: Jones, *German Liberalism*, 291–293.

[51]   For the background to these negotiations see: Dörr, *Deutschnationale Volkspartei*, 265–270; and SHStA Dresden, NL Philipp/4, 191–196.

[52]   This abrupt departure from earlier policy led to sharp criticism of the party leadership from many local chapters and from the Pan-German controlled National Völkisch Committee. See: Landesverband Danzig to Kuno von Westarp, 5 February 1927, NL Westarp, np; and Axel Freiherr von Freytagh-Loringhoven (on behalf of the National Völkisch Committee) to Kuno von Westarp, 9 February 1927, and Westarp to Freytagh-Loringhoven, 17 February 1927, both letters in: NL Westarp/59, np.

extend the "Law for the Protection of the Republic" (*Republikschutzgesetz*). Originally passed in July 1922 after Walter Rathenau's brutal murder, the law allowed for special courts to deal with politically motivated violence, severe penalties for political murders, and government authority to suspend or ban altogether extremist organizations on the Left or the Right. In an effort to reinforce the Republic's political authority and undermine monarchist radicals, the law also severely limited the ability of Germany's former ruling families, especially the exiled Kaiser, from returning to Germany.[53] This last clause infuriated many DNVP monarchists and caused them to vote against the law originally in 1922.

In 1927, with the law up for renewal after its initial five-year period, the DNVP faced a difficult decision within the context of their new government coalition. They could either vote for the law's extension, thereby continuing the Emperor's effective exile from Germany and going against the party's monarchist sentiments, or face a break-up of the coalition and a return to opposition. On 17 May 1927, the party chose the former option and voted for the law's extension. Even this piece of openly pro-Republic legislation was not enough to deter the party's moderates from their goal of keeping the DNVP in power.[54] In spite of the DNVP's fairly remarkable public reversals on both Stresemann's foreign policy and the *Republikschutzgesetz*, the Marx coalition government would eventually break apart over yet another difficult domestic policy matter.

The primary issue that ultimately split the cabinet was the formation of a national school bill. The negotiations that led to the Marx cabinet in January 1927 in part focused on the common desire of both the Catholic Center Party and the heavily Protestant DNVP for significant reform in the realm of cultural and educational policy. Specifically, both parties hoped to expand denominational schools (*Konfessionsschulen*) throughout Germany, thus undermining existing Weimar-era educational policy that had favored common schools (*Simultanschulen*) where students of different faiths would receive religious instruction.[55] In July 1927, the government's interior minister, Walter von Keudell of the DNVP, submitted a draft of a new school law to the Reichstag

---

[53]   Kolb, *Weimar Republic*, 45, and Repp, *Westarp, Hugenberg*, 34. On the background of the Republikschutzgesetz, see: Jasper, *Der Schutz der Republik*, esp. 56–91. For a detailed analysis of the intra-party conflict over this issue, see: Dörr, *Deutschnationale Volkspartei*, 303–313.

[54]   Repp, *Westarp, Hugenberg*, 35. The party's radical wing was furious with this decision. See: Kuno von Westarp to Oskar Hergt, 20 May 1927, NL Westarp/60, np. The Pan-Germans tried to convince the DNVP's leadership not to go along with the extension. See: Alldeutscher Verband-Ortsgruppe Osnabrück to Kuno von Westarp, 12 May 1927, NL Westarp/59, np.

[55]   Jones, *German Liberalism*, 295–296. For the Center Party's educational policies and its relationship to the DNVP on this issue, see: Günther Grünthal, *Reichsschulgesetz und*

that sought to fulfill earlier Center Party/DNVP demands to greatly expand denominational education.[56] This directly contradicted liberal educational policy formulated throughout the Weimar era and offended many of Keudell's coalition partners in the DVP.

As a national debate raged over Keudell's proposed bill, the consequences within the Marx coalition government were severe. In late November 1927, the DVP came out firmly against the major provisions of the Keudell bill and in support of existing liberal educational policy that favored common schools and state control over educational matters.[57] Between December 1927 and February 1928, the Marx government faltered as the DVP, Center, and DNVP pulled further apart over the negotiations surrounding the school bill. With little apparent room for compromise, the Keudell bill was finally withdrawn.[58] Then, on 15 February 1928, the Marx government itself came to an end.[59] For the DNVP, this second failed experiment with the parliamentary system had far-reaching consequences.

During the roughly 14 months of the DNVP's participation in the Marx government, moderate conservatives largely held the upper hand. This did not mean, however, that party radicals and their allies in the Pan-German League were not actively plotting ways to undermine the DNVP's moderate course. Throughout much of 1926 and 1927, the Pan-German League and its party allies were forced to deal with the fallout from the Claß Putsch affair while trying to organize an effective critique of the DNVP's participation in the Marx government. They eventually adopted a two-pronged approach that featured a public print campaign against party moderates and the Marx government, along with a renewed private focus on specific strategies to radicalize the DNVP especially at the local and regional level.[60] It was this two-pronged

---

Zentrumspartei in der Weimarer Republik (Düsseldorf, 1968). On the DNVP's role in this crisis see: Dörr, *Deutschnationale Volkspartei*, 355–361.

[56] Marjorie Lamberti, *The Politics of Education: Teachers and School Reform in Weimar Germany* (New York and Oxford, 2002). Lamberti offers a thorough analysis of the controversy surrounding the Keudell school bill and the crisis in the Marx cabinet on pages 170–184.

[57] Jones, *German Liberalism*, 296.

[58] The recriminations over the failed school bill continued to haunt the DNVP in the following years. See: Hauptvorstand des Deutschnationalen Lehrerbundes to Parteileitung der DNVP, 4 October 1928, NL Westarp, np; Reinhard Mumm to Kuno von Westarp, 18 October 1928, NL Westarp, np; and Westarp to Hauptvorstand des Deutschnationalen Lehrerbundes, 19 October 1928, NL Westarp, np.

[59] Dörr, *Deutschnationale Volkspartei*, 360.

[60] The League hoped generally to revitalize its local organizational structure and increase its financial reserves in the wake of the Claß Putsch affair. One of the leadership's main proposals called for the creation of a "Group of One Thousand" (*Tausendschaft*), consisting of particularly

approach that finally contributed to Alfred Hugenberg's election as party chairman in October 1928.

Publicly, the Pan-German League took a predictably defiant, intransigent stance against the DNVP's decision to enter the government in January 1927. As it had done in the past, the *Deutsche Zeitung* published a series of articles condemning the party and the entire state of parliamentary democracy in Germany.[61] Three articles in particular boldly declared the Pan-German League's disgust with the recent developments. On 3 February, the newspaper published an article that likened the relationship between Stresemann, who remained foreign minister in the new cabinet, and the DNVP ministers to that of a streetcar conductor and his passengers.[62] The second article, written by Paul Bang, openly encouraged all of those "still reliable" nationalist elements within the party to unite and revolt against the tyranny of the party's moderate leadership.[63] Finally, on 14 February, the Pan-German League issued a front-page declaration to all those true nationalists within the party to organize a nation-wide opposition under Pan-German leadership to prevent the "advanced state of decay in our national life."[64]

While important to the overall campaign against the party moderates, this public propaganda was accompanied by the development of a systematic strategy to alter permanently the composition and leadership of the party as a whole. This approach was more comprehensive than previous attempts that focused more narrowly on accomplishing specific goals (e.g. rejection of the Locarno

---

loyal and active Pan-German League members who would raise funds and motivate other members at the local and regional level. For further details about this plan, see: BARCH R8048/6.

[61]   See the following *Deutsche Zeitung* articles: "Die neue Reichsregierung: Ernste Befürchtungen," 29 January 1927, 1; and "Die deutschnationale Beteiligung an der Reichsregierung," 30 January 1927, 1–2.

[62]   "Der neue Regierungkurs: Straßenbahnschaffner und Fahrgast," *Deutsche Zeitung*, 3 February 1927, 1.

[63]   "Nun erst recht!" *Deutsche Zeitung*, 7 February 1927, 1–2.

[64]   "Alldeutsche Kundgebung zur Lage," *Deutsche Zeitung*, 14 February 1927, 1. The League produced this formal declaration at their 12–13 February 1927 Executive Committee meeting in Berlin. This meeting featured a particularly extensive debate on the future of the DNVP as a nationalist force. For more detail, see: SGA, 12/13 February 1927, BARCH R8048/149, esp. 42–77. The League also drafted several declarations to the national government concerning its alleged betrayal of German interests. On one occasion, the Pan-Germans actually asked Kuno von Westarp to sign on to such a declaration as a show of good faith from the party's leadership. Westarp rejected the League's request, citing the impossibility of formally supporting a document that criticized the very government in which the DNVP was participating. See: Leopold von Vietinghoff-Scheel to Kuno von Westarp, 14 November 1927, NL Westarp, np; and Westarp to Vietinghoff-Scheel, 17 Novemember 1927, NL Westarp/59, np.

Accords). By the end of 1927, Heinrich Claß and his colleagues within and outside of the League had developed a strategy to help transform the DNVP completely as a political force.

In addition to promoting Hugenberg as the top party leader, the Pan-Germans also sought to reinforce Hugenberg supporters within the party, particularly at the local level. To implement this campaign, the Pan-German League's executive committee laid down a set of guidelines at its November 1927 meeting in Berlin.[65] Claß recalled in his memoirs that this set of guidelines provided the necessary blueprint for League members throughout the country to "set to work with the greatest zeal" to push through Hugenberg's agenda at the local level so that "his takeover of the party and the Reichstag delegation would be assured."[66]

The guidelines stressed five basic approaches to transforming the DNVP.[67] First, League members would seek a greater role within the party's regional associations in the nomination of individual candidates for electoral lists. With national elections slated for May 1928, this approach would have to begin immediately. Second and third, the League would not approve or support any candidate who had already "failed" according to Pan-German expectations, or who blindly accepted the status quo moderate party line. Fourth, the League demanded that any candidate it supported must be prepared to remain in constant contact with his local constituency and not allow himself to be guided merely by the party's moderate national leadership. Finally, each candidate approved by the League must be ready to fight the parliamentary system as it currently existed.[68]

On a personal level, Heinrich Claß was also hard at work. Claß spoke with Hugenberg on several occasions throughout the summer of 1927, and both leaders agreed that personal connections with close Pan-German/DNVP allies needed to be solidified if Hugenberg were to gain the party chairmanship. In addition to working with several long-time Pan-German stalwarts like Karl Lohmann, Carl Gok, and Axel Freiherr von Freytagh-Loringhoven, Hugenberg was particularly keen on maintaining Paul Bang's support. Realizing the advantage of having as many allies as possible within the party, Hugenberg insisted Bang run as a DNVP candidate in the upcoming May 1928 elections.[69] By mid-April 1928, Bang had been added to the DNVP's electoral list in East Saxony and Claß and Hugenberg had secured Bang's promise to stand as a

---

[65]   SGA, 26/27 November 1927, BARCH R8048/152, 19–25.
[66]   Claß, *WdS v. II*, 880.
[67]   SGA, 26/27 November 1927, BARCH R8048/152, 23.
[68]   Ibid., 23–24.
[69]   Claß, *WdS v. II*, 880.

candidate and serve if elected. Hugenberg explained that he absolutely needed experts like Bang as allies within the party. Without them, Hugenberg felt he would be unable to succeed on his own.[70]

However, Bang's candidacy in the district of East Saxony did not sit well with party moderates in the region. As a leader of the contentious German Industrialists Association (*Deutsche Industriellen-Vereinigung*), representing mostly light industry, Bang spoke out strongly against the Dawes Plan and often opposed the interests of larger industrialists in the National League of German Industry (*Reichsverband der Deutschen Industrie*) and many party moderates.[71] Bang's membership in the Pan-German League and his close ties to Claß and Hugenberg also caused concern.

Leading Saxon DNVP moderates like Kurt Philipp, Siegfried von Lüttichau and Walter Rademacher were convinced that Bang's candidacy was nothing more than a thinly veiled attempt to increase Pan-German influence within the party. Rademacher claimed that Bang was relatively unknown in Saxon politics outside of radical völkisch circles, and his candidacy was a "brutal snub" to the vast majority of Saxon industrialists.[72] Rademacher bluntly summarized his position in a letter to party leader Kuno von Westarp: "Bang's candidacy is political ... and represents the Pan-German position of a large part of the party, particularly in the city of Dresden."[73] Despite continued strong reservations on behalf of many local party moderates, and even the resignation of Kurt Philipp as chair of the East Saxony state party organization, Bang remained on the electoral list.[74] He was elected to the Reichstag in May 1928 and subsequently

---

[70] Ibid., 881.

[71] See above, Chapter 4, and Holzbach, *System Hugenberg*, 168–172.

[72] Rademacher to Westarp, 20 March 1928, NL Westarp, np. For further criticism of Bang's candidacy see also: Lüttichau to Westarp, 27 March 1928, NL Westarp, np.

[73] Rademacher to Westarp, 3 April 1928, NL Westarp, np. Westarp acknowledged Rademacher's concerns about Bang, but pointed out the party's need for votes and especially for financial support, which Bang provided, for the troubled East Saxony state party association. See: Westarp to Rademacher, 7 April 1928, NL Westarp, np. According to historian John Leopold, industrial candidates like Bang paid between 50,000 and 100,000 Marks for a secure position on an electoral list. Hugenberg helped fund his close allies Bang in East Saxony and Reinhold Quaatz on the national DNVP list. The significance of Hugenberg's financial support for Bang's candidacy is echoed in a letter from Lüttichau to Westarp, 17 April 1928, NL Westarp, np.

[74] Philipp resigned in outrage over the Pan-German League and Hugenberg's attempts to shape the Saxon electoral lists. See: SHStA Dresden, NL Philipp/4, 278; Kurt Philipp to Kuno von Westarp, 3 July 1928, NL Westarp, np.

proved to be a major asset to Hugenberg and the Pan-Germans in their quest to radicalize the DNVP.[75]

In spite of Paul Bang's personal success, the 20 May 1928 vote did not go well overall for the DNVP. The party lost over one-quarter of its Reichstag seats, dropping from its previous total of 111 to 78.[76] Much of this loss came as a direct result of deep-seated agrarian disaffection in the countryside and the creation of several new splinter protest parties. Although the DNVP had attempted to secure agricultural prices and government support, many German farmers felt the party had failed to take their interests seriously. This frustration exploded by early 1928 in the form of the Agrarian People's Movement (*Landvolkbewegung*). The DNVP, which had previously gained substantial support from farmers, was hit hard. This agricultural disaffection also led to the formation of several new parties like the Christian National Farmers and Peasants Party (*Christlich-Nationale Bauren- und Landvolkpartei* or "CNBL"). In short, these protest parties robbed the DNVP of considerable votes in the countryside.[77]

The Pan-German League and its allies saw several advantages to the election results even with the party's extensive losses. First, most of the League's candidates survived the election intact and Paul Bang was elected in East Saxony. As Claß put it, Hugenberg could now count on a more reliable following within the party.[78] Secondly, the party's agricultural support, which had traditionally

---

[75]   When Bang formally announced his DNVP candidacy for the East Saxony district, the local Pan-German chapter in Dresden campaigned vigorously for him. The Dresden chapter published a special flyer and newspaper insert on 30 April 1928 highlighting Bang's agenda and encouraging all Pan-Germans and other nationalist-minded voters to support Bang. See: StADresden ADV-OD/10, 67. Bang also spoke at a number of gatherings, including a Pan-German-sponsored rally in Dresden at the Sarasani Circus hall on 14 May 1928. A crowd of nearly 3,000 gathered to hear Bang's promise to reform the DNVP and the nation. For a full account of the rally, see: "Appell Dr. Bangs an die Wähler," *Deutsche Zeitung*, 14 May 1928, 1–2.

[76]   For election results, see: Dörr, *Deutschnationale Volkspartei*, 387.

[77]   The party's leadership had been aware for some time of the looming threat posed by agrarian interest politics to the DNVP. The difficulty came in resolving increasingly critical economic concerns in the countryside within the broader framework of the DNVP's coalition policies in the Marx government. See: Siegfried von Lüttichau to Kuno von Westarp, 9 March 1928, NL Westarp, np; Albrecht Philipp to Westarp, 24 March 1928, NL Westarp, np; and Philipp to Westarp, 17 April 1928, NL Westarp, np. For a more detailed analysis of the DNVP's agricultural policy in the period leading up to the May elections, see: Dörr, *Deutschnationale Volkspartei*, 339–346. On the *Landvolkbewegung* and its political impact, see: Gerhard Stoltenberg, *Politische Strömungen im schleswig-holsteinischen Landvolk 1918–1933. Ein Beitrag zur politischen Meinungsbildung in der Weimarer Republik* (Düsseldorf, 1962). For the CNBL see: Markus Müller, *Die Christlich-Nationale Bauren- un Landvolkpartei 1928–1933* (Düsseldorf, 2001).

[78]   Claß, *WdS v. II*, 863.

pushed the moderate leadership for government participation, had been seriously weakened. Thirdly, whether it was actually the case or not, Hugenberg and his Pan-German allies saw in the election results a propaganda opportunity to link the party's losses to Kuno von Westarp's weak leadership.[79]

In addition to the DNVP's poor electoral showing in May, the party endured another public controversy during the last half of 1928 that greatly assisted the Hugenberg/Pan-German faction within the party. The "Lambach Affair," as it was known, yet again exposed the deep-seated divisions within the DNVP and created a perfect opportunity for party radicals to attack Westarp and other moderates. Walther Lambach was a leading DNVP member and a spokesman for the German Nationalist Commercial Employees Union (*Deutschnationaler Handlungsgehilfenverband*). On 14 June 1928, he published an article entitled "Monarchism" that blamed the DNVP's recent electoral losses on the party's blindness to the growing acceptance of the republican system among the German people, especially the youth. In order to expand the DNVP's appeal and establish it as a true "people's party," its leadership needed to focus more attention on the nationalist youth, small business owners, and workers. In sum, Lambach suggested that the party could not merely continue to hold on to its old loyalties and needed to accept the realities of the new republican system.[80]

Despite Kuno von Westarp's attempts to defuse this explosive situation, the intra-party feud over the Lambach affair quickly spun out of control.[81] Alfred Hugenberg jumped at the chance to exploit Lambach's alleged betrayal of monarchist loyalties within the DNVP and used the affair to highlight the dangers of the party's moderate policies. In reality, this conflict had less to do with the actual issue of monarchist loyalties, and far more to do with the future of the

---

[79]   The Pan-German press, including some of Hugenberg's staunchest DNVP supporters like Paul Bang and Axel Freiherr von Freytagh-Loringhoven, took advantage of this opportunity. For a sample of the anti-Westarp articles that appeared throughout the summer, see: "Die deutsche Frage: Enttäuschung?" *Deutsche Zeitung*, 27 May 1928, 1; "Erkenntnis und Folgerung aus der Wahl," *Deutsche Zeitung*, 7 June 1928, 1–2; and "Völkische Aufgaben," *Deutsche Zeitung*, 14 June 1928, 1–2.

[80]   Repp, *Westarp, Hugenberg*, 63. For a copy of the "Monarchismus" article from the 14 June 1928 *Politische Wochenschrift* IV/24, see: Dörr, *Deutschnationale Volkspartei*, 554–556. Dörr also provides a thorough discussion of the Lambach Affair and its aftermath on 391–430.

[81]   See Westarp's lengthy letter to the leaders of the party's state organizations explaining his response to the Lambach issue. Westarp to the Landesverbandsvorsitzenden, 12 July 1928, NL Westarp, np. Westarp also tried to intercede, with little effect, in the growing personal conflict between Paul Bang and Lambach regarding the DNVP's direction. See: Bang to Westarp, 26 June 1928, NL Westarp/70, np; Bang to Westarp, 12 September 1928, NL Westarp/70, np; Westarp to Bang, 15 September 1928, NL Westarp/70, np; and Westarp to Bang, 10 October 1928, NL Westarp/70, np.

party's leadership. Indeed, Hugenberg and his allies cynically used Lambach's article to advance their own position within the party to great success.[82]

Directly supporting Hugenberg, the Pan-German League exploited the Lambach affair and converted it into a litmus test for political leadership in the DNVP. The *Deutsche Zeitung* quickly published a series of anti-Lambach/Westarp articles that supported Hugenberg's position within the party.[83] Another important article by Axel Freiherr von Freytagh-Loringhoven appeared on 25 July 1928 on the front page of the newspaper *Der Tag*.[84] In this article, entitled "Not a Large, but a Strong Right," Freytagh-Loringhoven claimed that if the DNVP continued on its present course dictated by party moderates, the party would simply dissolve into the other bourgeois "centrist" parties and thereby lose its distinctiveness and calling. The DNVP could continue to strive for compromise and even larger numbers as much as it wanted, but if it betrayed its true calling as a party of the nationalist opposition, its large size would mean nothing. Instead, Freytagh-Loringhoven proposed "a goal-oriented, fundamentally sound, strong Right, ready in the decisive hour to take on the leadership itself." Only by staying true to its core principles and not traveling the road of compromise and accommodation, could "the Right," embodied in the DNVP, truly succeed.[85]

Party moderates decried the clearly political nature of the Pan-Germans' distorted attacks and the impact of their campaign in favor of Hugenberg. For example, the state employees sub-committee of the DNVP's Düsseldorf-East chapter published a resolution backing Lambach's position and blasting demands that Lambach be removed from the party. The resolution exposed the real motivation behind the vicious attacks on Lambach by focusing on the intra-party conflict that threatened to tear the DNVP apart. "We must emphatically point out that a victory of the social reactionary group of Hugenberg-Bang would result in the loss of the last remaining workers within the party. As a result, the party would lose its identity as a true 'people's party.'"[86]

Lambach himself also condemned the Pan-German League's politicized attacks against him and his party allies. In a letter to select DNVP colleagues,

---

[82]   Dörr, *Deutschnationale Volkspartei*, 396.

[83]   See the following *Deutsche Zeitung* articles: "Monarchismus und Deutschnationale," 29 June 1928, 1–2; "Kampfansage der Gewerkschaften an die Deutschnationalen," 25 July 1928, 1; "Eine Richtigstellung zum Fall Lambach," 28 July 1928, 1–2; "Die Deutschnationalen am Scheideweg," 28 August 1928, 1; and "Wo liegt der Irrtum?" 31 August 1928, 1–2.

[84]   "Nicht Große, sondern starke Rechte," *Der Tag*, 25 July 1928, 1–2.

[85]   Ibid., 2.

[86]   Entschliessung des Landesangestellten-Ausschusses des Landesverbandes Düsseldorf-Ost, 11 August 1928, NL Westarp, np.

Lambach defended his position in favor of expanding the party and moving away from a reliance on the politics of the past. At the same time, he pointed out the severity of Pan-German attacks against him and pleaded for the re-election of Kuno von Westarp as party leader later that month:

> I have recently received a large number of written and oral reports concerning developments within the party throughout the country. [These reports] make clear that the Pan-Germans have unleashed a real propaganda campaign with a formidable structure to achieve control of the party in Hugenberg's favor. Accompanying this is the increasingly grotesque agitation against me [within the party] ... In light of these developments it is absolutely essential that everything be done to secure Westarp's re-election as party chairman.[87]

Others also decried the seemingly endless Pan-German agitation at local DNVP meetings. Still fuming over Paul Bang's election, moderate members of the DNVP's East Saxony organization complained to Kuno von Westarp about the constant agitation by Bang, Heinrich Claß, and other Pan-Germans covering a range of political issues. By September, the situation had become so unbearable that the leaders of the East Saxony party organization formally requested that the DNVP party leadership draw a clear line between the party and the Pan-German League:

> The national party leadership needs to publish a communiqué as soon as possible clearly stating that the Pan-German League has no formal relationship to the party and that the party does not allow the League to exert any influence over it. Because the [DNVP] simply recognizes the Pan-German League leaders as passionate patriots consumed with a burning love of the Fatherland, the party has developed no specific policy to identify the attacks of [Heinrich] Claß as an unfortunate derailment [of our party's goals].[88]

In the face of these angry protests against the League's increasingly influential role in DNVP politics, the Pan-Germans continued their efforts to shift support within the party toward Hugenberg through direct contact with party members, especially at the local level. The League's headquarters sent out a form letter requesting that each local DNVP leader provide a complete list of

---

[87] Walther Lambach to Otto Rippel (Hagen) and Wilhelm Koch, 11 October 1928, NL Westarp, np.

[88] Deutschnationale Volkspartei-Landesverband Ostsachsen to Kuno von Westarp, 12 September 1928, NL Westarp, np. See also: Kurt Philipp to Westarp, 5 October 1928, NL Westarp, np.

newly elected local DNVP representatives.[89] These lists allowed the League to contact representatives directly to push for Hugenberg's support. In addition, the League's local chapters increased publication of pro-Hugenberg flyers, newspaper articles, and rallies/speeches.[90] In conjunction with the League's national propaganda campaign, and its newly instituted electoral strategy, these measures helped promote Hugenberg's name and position within the party at a crucial moment in the leadership struggle.

For Claß and the Pan-German League, all of these efforts were finally rewarded on 20 October 1928 when the party narrowly elected Alfred Hugenberg as its new chairman. Although the vote was quite close and many within the party were still intensely loyal to Westarp and his vision for the party, the Pan-German League and its party allies had helped to give Hugenberg the upper hand.[91] The *Deutsche Zeitung* praised Hugenberg's triumph in the party as "a testimonial ... to the desires of the entire truly nationalist population."[92] The *Alldeutsche Blätter* also highlighted another important aspect of Hugenberg's election as party chairman. After praising Hugenberg's accomplishments, the article pointed out that, as a result, the Pan-German League had "solidified its relationship to the strongest nationalist group of our Reichstag."[93]

Beyond the League's effusive public acclamation of Hugenberg's success, Heinrich Claß and his colleagues also took great private satisfaction in the new party leader's success. In a letter to his close associate Leo Wegener, Claß reveled in the fact that even though it had been several years since the League decided to put all its effort into Hugenberg's election, "he [Hugenberg] had finally come into the position that he deserved."[94] Wegener replied shortly thereafter to Claß

---

89   SHStA Dresden, NL Philipp/22, np.

90   Claß, *WdS v. II*, 883. In fact, much of this type of campaigning for the Pan-German/ Hugenberg agenda within the party had been going on for some time in many local DNVP chapters. For example, the local Pan-German League found a great deal of success with this approach in the DNVP's Osnabrück chapter. See: Herr Stachow to Herr Hagen, 20 August 1927, NsäSTA-Osnabrück C1/1, 58; and Herr Hagen to Herr Stachow, 29 August 1927, NsäSTA-Osnabrück C1/1, 59.

91   At the last minute, Westarp decided not to run for the position and left Hugenberg alone to attempt to secure an outright majority. Hugenberg succeeded, but only narrowly. Hugenberg's success lay in his strong support from the members of roughly 17 state party associations. For a thorough discussion of the final vote and the intense intra-party strife that preceded it, see: Dörr, *Deutschnationale Volkspartei*, 442–451; and Holzbach, *System Hugenberg*, 192–253. For a contemporary account of the Hugenberg victory, see: SHStA Dresden, NL Philipp/4, 284–286.

92   "Hugenberg deutschnationaler Parteivorsitzender," *Deutsche Zeitung*, 21 October 1928, 1.

93   "Zur Zeitgeschichte," *Alldeutsche Blätter*, 27 October 1928, 1.

94   Claß to Wegener, 22 October 1928, BA-Koblenz, NL Wegener/23, 98.

that, without question, the Pan-German League "accomplished a great deal that led directly to 'The Success' [Hugenberg's election]."[95]

However, all of this celebration in the Pan-German camp was tempered by the sobering notion that a great deal of work remained to be done.[96] Within the party itself, Westarp retained his position as Reichstag faction leader, and there was still considerable support within the party for the moderate, pro-government position. Hugenberg's narrow margin of victory provided ample evidence that the party was not yet completely in his control. As Chapter 6 explains, Heinrich Claß and the Pan-German League still had an important role to play not only in the final radicalization of Hugenberg's DNVP, but also in the broader developments of the German Right that led to Adolf Hitler's appointment as chancellor in January 1933.

---

[95]   Wegener to Claß, 1 November 1928, BA-Koblenz, NL Wegener/23, 99.

[96]   Ibid. See also: Freytagh-Loringhoven to Baron Vietinghoff-Scheel, 24 November 1928, BARCH R8048/219, 3–4.

Chapter 6
The Collapse of the Non-Nazi Right, 1929–1939

Alfred Hugenberg's election as DNVP party chairman in October 1928 marked an important milestone for the Pan-German League in the Weimar era. Since 1925 the League had devoted most of its remaining political influence to achieve a radicalized DNVP under Hugenberg's unquestioned leadership. While that goal was not yet completely accomplished in late 1928, it would be realized in the wake of moderate conservative defections that shook the DNVP in the following 18 months. Hugenberg's political success, and his continued close ties to several key Pan-German leaders like Heinrich Claß and Paul Bang, also assured the League some measure of national political influence in the final tumultuous years of the Weimar Republic. So even as the League's membership continued to decline, its leaders retained an important place in the national councils of the German Right.

Overall, the Pan-German League's history from 1929 until 1939 can be best divided into three major periods. The first, stretching from 1929 through 1930, witnessed the League's cooperation in Alfred Hugenberg's right-wing campaign against the Young Plan and Pan-German involvement in the moderate conservative defections from the DNVP in December 1929 and July 1930. The second period from 1931 through January 1933 witnessed the increasing fragmentation of the German Right and included Pan-German participation in the right-wing "Harzburg Front," the complex negotiations surrounding the 1932 presidential elections, and the growing conflict between the NSDAP and the non-Nazi Right in the final months before Hitler's seizure of power. In the third and final period the League struggled for survival after January 1933 until it was disbanded by Nazi security forces in March 1939.

Throughout this entire period, the Pan-German League's actions generally exacerbated the growing conflict between the established political Right and the rapidly growing Nazi Party. The League's leaders, especially Heinrich Claß, maintained a deep and unshakable faith in Alfred Hugenberg as the only leader capable of solving Germany's growing political and economic crisis. For a brief period of time between the campaign against the Young Plan and the collapse of the Harzburg Front, the League reestablished direct contact with the Nazi Party hoping that Hitler and his movement might be convinced to work more closely with the DNVP and a broader right-wing front under Hugenberg's leadership.

This goal, however, proved to be impossible as the Nazi movement maintained its political independence and refused to subordinate itself to an elitist representative of the old right-wing order like Alfred Hugenberg. Hitler's behavior in the Harzburg Front gathering in 1931, the 1932 presidential campaign, and during the final months before the seizure of power seemed to validate the Pan-German League's earlier assessment of the Nazi leader's flawed political judgment and lack of preparation to lead the country. Pan-German leaders greeted Hitler's appointment as chancellor in January 1933 with mixed emotions, emphasizing Hugenberg's vital importance to the new coalition government. This chapter will now turn to the Pan-German League's role in the process that led to the creation of the Hitler cabinet and the end of Weimar democracy.

The Anti-Young Plan Campaign and the Radicalization of the DNVP

At a series of international meetings during the first eight months of 1929, Allied and German negotiators hammered out terms of an agreement to fix a concrete, supposedly final, schedule for Germany's reparations payments. This agreement, generally referred to as the Young Plan, came into clear focus by August 1929. Although Germany had formally accepted the terms of the Dawes Plan in 1924, many international experts argued for a new schedule to regulate reparations. Concerns lingered about Germany's ability and willingness to satisfy its debts in full on a regular schedule, the country's use of foreign loans, and the continued international oversight of Germany's internal economic affairs.[1] The pending Young Plan promised to resolve these problems by reducing the total amount of German reparations and setting payments on a fixed schedule. According to the plan, Germany would pay between 2 and 2.05 billion Marks annually to satisfy its reparations debts to the former Allied powers for the next 59 years. According to this schedule, Germany would complete its payments by 1988.[2]

In exchange, Germany secured several important concessions. First, the agreement abolished foreign oversight over Germany's internal finances, including the much resented role of the reparations agent. Second, the Young Plan actually lowered Germany's total repayment amount in comparison to the terms of the 1924 Dawes agreement and allowed for a two year suspension

---

[1]   For these and other issues leading to the decision to draft the Young Plan, see: Mommsen, *Rise and Fall of Weimar Democracy*, 269–275.

[2]   Ibid., 273.

of payments in the event of a severe economic crisis. Third, and perhaps most importantly, Germany tied its acceptance of the reparations provisions in the Young Plan to an early withdrawal of remaining occupation forces from western Germany. This accomplishment, due in large measure to Gustav Stresemann's direct negotiations with French Foreign Minister Aristide Briand, produced a final deadline of 30 June 1930 for a complete evacuation of foreign troops from all Rhineland occupation zones. By most measures, the Young Plan provided important political benefits to Germany in the short term, while easing its reparations schedule in the long term.[3]

From the Pan-German League's perspective, however, the Young Plan represented yet another cruel betrayal of the nation's interests by cowardly domestic politicians and foreign powers bent on Germany's destruction. The reparations issue dominated the League's business management meetings from December 1928 through August 1929.[4] These discussions focused on the former Allied powers' continued exploitation of Germany and the cowardice of the country's current leadership in the face of this new reparations plan. League economic experts, especially Paul Bang, predicted economic catastrophe and Germany's demise if the Young Plan were accepted. The fixed repayment schedule would allegedly tie Germany to an unacceptable debt that would cripple the German economy for decades to come. Bang exhorted all Pan-Germans to fight the newest reparations proposal and to remember that they were doing so not merely for political gain, but rather for their very livelihoods and the survival of their families.[5]

The League's dire assessment of the Young Plan and its alleged consequences squared with Alfred Hugenberg's broader call for a nationalist front to prevent the German government from accepting the terms of this newest reparations agreement. Already in June 1929, the DNVP executive committee supported Hugenberg's call to create such an organization. Roughly one month later on 9 July 1929, representatives from major right-wing groups including the Pan-German League, the DNVP, the Stahlhelm, the National Rural League (*Reichslandbund*), the NSDAP, and several other smaller parties, met in the former Prussian House of Lords in Berlin to announce officially the formation of the "National Committee for the German Referendum against the Young Plan"

---

[3]   Ibid., 273–274. For Stresemann's role in the Rhineland negotiations at the August 1929 Hague Conference see: Wright, *Gustav Stresemann*, 479–482. Only weeks after these difficult negotiations, Stresemann died of a stroke on 3 October 1929.

[4]   See: SGA, 1/2 December 1928, BARCH R8048/156, 54–55; SGA, 19 January 1929, BARCH R8048/157, 10–12; and SGA, 20 April 1929, BARCH R8048/158, 109–112; SGA, 30 August 1929, BARCH R8048/159, 4–12.

[5]   SGA, 30 August 1929, BARCH R8048/159, 9.

(*Reichsausschuss für das deutsche Volksbegehren*—hereafter "Reichsausschuss").[6] While this group intended to present a united nationalist front to the German government as it weighed the terms of the Young Plan, the reality behind the scenes of the Reichsausschuss was much different. Indeed, political divisions developed in the nationalist bloc as the campaign moved from vague public pronouncements to drafting more specific policy.

Several leading Pan-Germans, including Heinrich Claß, Paul Bang, and Leopold von Vietinghoff-Scheel, played an important role in the Reichsausschuss. In particular, Heinrich Claß was a member of the group's leadership council and he was charged with the crucial task of drafting the legal document on which the coming public plebiscite would be based.[7] Claß and his close Pan-German legal consultants favored an extreme document that would threaten any member of the government with prison time for accepting the Young Plan's terms. A draft of what would become known as the "Freedom Law" circulated first among the Reichsausschuss's leading members, and then later among the rank and file members of the committee. The sharply divergent responses to this document indicated a growing lack of cohesion within the anti-Young Plan front.

The Pan-German inspired Freedom Law had four primary points of emphasis. Article One demanded that the German government force the former Allies to reject the underlying claim of German war guilt. Article Two called for the formal removal of the "war guilt clause" itself (Article 231) from the Versailles Treaty and the immediate, unconditional withdrawal of all remaining foreign troops on German soil. Article Three rejected all new payments or debts based on the war guilt clause premise, including any new reparations agreements in the Young Plan. Article Four, soon to be known as the infamous "penal paragraph," threatened to imprison any member of the German government—including the chancellor—who disobeyed these stipulations.[8] The Reichsausschuss's leadership council met in Nuremberg on 28 August 1929 and approved the Freedom Law, including the controversial Article Four. However, the absence of two major groups from this meeting, the National Rural League and the Christian National

---

[6]   Leopold, *Alfred Hugenberg*, 59. The best overall treatment of the Young Plan and its impact on right-wing politics remains: Elizabeth Friedenthal, *Volksbegehren und Volksentscheid über den Young Plan und die deutschnationale Sezession* (PhD Dissertation, University of Tübingen, 1957).

[7]   Claß, *WdS v. II*, 901. Claß remained in close contact with Hugenberg regarding various aspects of the draft law as it took shape during July and early August 1929. Claß to Hugenberg, 26 July 1929, BARCH R8048/262, 90–92; and Claß to Hugenberg, 30 July 1929, BARCH R8048/262, 110–112.

[8]   Claß, *WdS v. II*, 903–904.

Farmer's Party (*Christlich-Nationale Bauern- und Landvolkpartei*), signaled the start of a major conflict within the movement.[9]

Martin Schiele, the moderate DNVP Reichstag deputy and leader of the National Rural League, was the key figure in the emerging split within the anti-Young Plan campaign. Schiele and his supporters refused to accept the extreme Pan-German terms of the Freedom Law contained in the "penal paragraph." He also saw an opportunity in the growing dissension over Article Four to weaken Hugenberg's leadership of the DNVP and strengthen the position of remaining party moderates.[10] By rejecting the penal statement, Schiele and other moderates forced Hugenberg not only to take a clear stand on this controversial issue, but also to seek support for Article Four outside the ranks of his own still-divided DNVP.[11] This meant that Hugenberg and his Pan-German allies had to rely on the most radical elements of the Reichsausschuss including the non-party Stahlhelm and the Nazis, who strongly supported the most extreme demands of the Freedom Law contained in the penal paragraph.[12]

For its part, the Pan-German League continued to offer its unwavering support for Hugenberg's position in the run-up to the plebiscite. The *Deutsche Zeitung* published numerous articles about the looming threat of the Young Plan and the League's efforts to prevent its adoption.[13] League headquarters also cultivated Pan-German influence in local Reichsausschuss chapters, and helped to coordinate regional and local demonstrations against the Young Plan.[14] These efforts enjoyed some success, particularly in areas where active Pan-German

---

[9]   Leopold, *Alfred Hugenberg*, 62–63.

[10]   For Schiele's behavior and the position of his agrarian allies see: Müller, *Christlich-Nationale Bauern- und Landvolkpartei*, 118–129.

[11]   In September 1929, several prominent moderate DNVP deputies including Walter von Keudell, Otto Hoetzsch, and Hans-Erdmann von Lindeiner-Wildau formally rejected the Freedom Law based on the penal paragraph. This public defiance seemed to reinforce Schiele's position and now raised the real prospect of permanent moderate defections from the party. See: Beck, *The Fateful Alliance*, 56.

[12]   On the Stahlhelm and the Young Plan, see: Volker Berhahn, "Das Volksbegehren gegen den Young-Plan und die Ursprünge des Präsidialregimes, 1928–1930," in Dirk Stegmann, Bernd Jürgen Wendt, and Peter-Christian Witt (eds), *Industrielle Gesellschaft und politisches System. Beiträge zur politischen Sozialgeschichte. Festschrift für Fritz Fischer zum siebzigsten Geburtstag* (Bonn, 1978), 431–446.

[13]   For examples of these *Deutsche Zeitung* articles see: "Volksentscheid in Gang gesetzt," 4 November 1929, 1–2; and "Falsche Signale," 7 November 1929, 1–2.

[14]   League records contain numerous examples of this coordinated effort to support the Reichsausschuss in various parts of the country. See: Leopold von Vietinghoff-Scheel to Axel von Freytagh-Loringhoven, 8 August 1929, BARCH R8048/262, 151; Freytagh-Loringhoven to Vietinghoff-Scheel, 13 August 1929, BARCH R8048/262, 164; Ortsgruppe Osnabrück to

branches still existed. For example, in Dresden where the League was well-represented in the Saxon state and local city Reichsausschuss committees local Pan-Germans helped raise money and organize a series of public presentations and newspaper articles devoted specifically to the anti-Young Plan campaign.[15]

However, in spite of the League's efforts and the saturation coverage of the issue in the Hugenberg-controlled press, the anti-Young Plan campaign results were far from impressive. By the beginning of November 1929, the initiative barely secured the 10 percent of eligible voter signatures required to move the proposal to the Reichstag for a formal vote. On 30 November, the Reichstag defeated the measure by a sizable margin. According to the constitution, the proposal now went to a direct public referendum scheduled for 22 December 1929. Formal approval of the Freedom Law required a simple majority from the roughly 42 million eligible voters. The final results of the 22 December referendum deeply disappointed Hugenberg and the Pan-German League. In the final tally, the initiative received only 5.8 million votes, or roughly 14 percent of the voter base.[16]

Not only did this vote represent the failure of right-wing efforts to block the Young Plan, which was eventually approved by a sizable Reichstag majority and signed into law by President Hindenburg in March 1930, it also ushered in an important period of political fragmentation within the DNVP.[17] Between 27 November and 4 December 1929, a total of 12 moderate conservative Reichstag members resigned from the party.[18] Furthermore, after failed efforts to forestall this split, Kuno von Westarp stepped down as Reichstag faction leader. The initial impetus for this departure came from the fierce internal debates regarding the Freedom Law and the penal paragraph, which the 12 deputies refused to support in the November Reichstag vote. Hugenberg responded to this open challenge to party discipline by initiating expulsion procedures against these

---

League Headquarters, 18 August 1929, BARCH R8048/262, 195; and Ortsgruppe Chemnitz to League Headquarters, 20 August 1929, BARCH R8048/262, 209.

[15]   *Jahresbericht* 1929/1930, StADresden ADV-OD/50, 177–180. For further details concerning the Pan-German League's Dresden chapter and the anti-Young Plan preparations see: AgS 1929–30, StADresden ADV-OD/12, esp. 5, 9–12, 32–36, 41–42.

[16]   Leopold, *Alfred Hugenberg*, 67, 70.

[17]   Ibid., 72.

[18]   This was a prestigious group of DNVP members including Gottfried Treviranus, Hans von Schlange-Schönigen, Hans-Erdmann von Lindeiner-Wildau, Walter von Keudell, Otto Hoetzsch, Reinhard Mumm, and the controversial Walter Lambach.

party moderates. By resigning, these 12 party members simply acted on their own before they were removed from the party.[19]

The Pan-German League's leadership welcomed this turn of events. At a December 1929 business management committee meeting, Heinrich Claß and Paul Bang offered their perspectives on the Reichsausschuss and the split in the DNVP. Claß praised his fellow Pan-Germans for their steadfast support throughout the anti-Young Plan campaign. He emphasized the "limitless patience and self-mastery" demanded of the Pan-German members of the Reichsausschuss in order to hold the movement together behind Hugenberg.[20] Bang identified the long-term origins of the moderate resignations in the conflict with Hugenberg over the party's future. After criticizing the delegates for their "dishonest" resignations, Bang succinctly summarized the Pan-German position regarding the departed deputies: "Thank God they are now on the outside [of the party]."[21] Publicly, the League also praised the defections. The *Deutsche Zeitung* ran a series of articles welcoming the resignations as a further "purification" of the party.[22] This unequivocal Pan-German support for an increasingly politically homogenous, radicalized DNVP at all costs soon helped to precipitate yet another disastrous party divide.

After the Young Plan's adoption in March 1930, Hugenberg and his Pan-German allies now had to reassess their attempts to sustain a workable nationalist front against the Weimar system. This planning took place as Germany experienced the economic shock waves that reverberated from the US stock market crash of October 1929. On 27 March 1930, Hermann Müller's coalition government resigned under the combined weight of the growing international economic crisis and the domestic political conflict centered on employer contributions to national unemployment insurance.[23] President Hindenburg quickly nominated Heinrich Brüning to form a new government that would deal with the serious challenges facing the country. Gottfried Treviranus, one of the recently departed DNVP deputies, and Martin Schiele were included in

---

[19]   For more detail on these first DNVP defections see: Leopold, *Alfred Hugenberg*, 68–71; and Beck, *The Fateful Alliance*, 56–58. Reinhold Quaatz, a close Hugenberg confidant, offers important insight into this affair in his personal diary: Weiß and Hoser, *Die Deutschnationalen und die Zerstörung der Weimarer Republik*, esp. 74–97.

[20]   SGA, 7–8 December 1929, BARCH R8048/160, 36.

[21]   Ibid., 37.

[22]   "Reinigung!" *Deutsche Zeitung*, 5 December 1929, 1–2. See also: "Scheidung der Geister," *Deutsche Zeitung*, 4 December 1929, 1.

[23]   William L. Patch, Jr., *Heinrich Brüning and the Dissolution of the Weimar Republic* (Cambridge, 1998), 67–71.

the new cabinet.[24] This fact, along with the government's tax and agricultural policies, set the Brüning cabinet on a collision course with Alfred Hugenberg and his Pan-German loyalists. Moreover, it set the stage for the last and the largest defection of moderate conservatives from the DNVP.

The Pan-German leadership regarded the Brüning cabinet with disdain.[25] The League argued that Brüning's decision to include several of Hugenberg's conservative opponents in the new government indicated that the chancellor intended to undermine Hugenberg's control of the DNVP. This would be accomplished in part, League leaders argued, by encouraging remaining moderate conservatives within the party to support the new government's proposals for agrarian tariffs and subsidies aimed at large-landholders in the eastern states.[26] The Pan-German League remained united behind Hugenberg and continued to support his policies and control of the DNVP actively through public press coverage and private political action. These efforts at the national and local levels kept the League at the center of the growing intra-party conflict.[27]

In the last week of April 1930, the Pan-Germans published a front-page article in the *Alldeutsche Blätter* entitled "Gründonnerstag" or "Maundy Thursday."[28] Incorporating the imagery of the Easter season, the article compared Kuno von Westarp and his moderate conservative colleagues to Judas Iscariot for their alleged betrayal of the nationalist cause. The article's hyperbolic implication was clear: there was no room for dissent within the DNVP and refusal to support Hugenberg's leadership was tantamount to treason against the party's leadership. The article clearly articulated the narrow Pan-German goal for the party's future and thus infuriated moderate conservatives with its tone and the very public nature of its accusations. For example, Curt Fritzsche, a pro-Westarp Saxon DNVP leader, blasted the "Gründonnerstag" article and attacked the local Dresden Pan-German League chapter for its intrigues within the local party structure. The irate Fritzsche wrote:

---

[24]   Leopold, *Alfred Hugenberg*, 73 and Patch, *Heinrich Brüning*, 78–79.

[25]   Heinrich Claß respected Brüning's war-time service, but believed his ties to Catholic politics and trade unions made him unfit to lead the government: Claß, *WdS v. II*, 914–915.

[26]   SGA, 17 May 1930, BARCH R8048/162, 5.

[27]   For a lengthy Pan-German response to the political implications of Brüning's attempts to engender moderate conservative support against Hugenberg in the realm of economic policy, see: Paul Bang to the Working Committee of German Nationalist Industrialists, 18 April 1930, NL Westarp/14, np.

[28]   "Gründonnerstag," *Alldeutsche Blätter*, 26 April 1930, 1. This article appeared one day after a crucial DNVP executive board meeting that reaffirmed Hugenberg's control over the party and demanded party discipline in future Reichstag votes. See: Beck, *The Fateful Alliance*, 67.

The article's tone is a slap in the face to the basic rules of polite society ... The Pan-German League has no right and no mandate to become involved in the German National party's internal affairs. [The League] degrades itself ... by descending to the lowest form of expression ... to impugn the character [of Westarp and his followers] and create suspicion.[29]

Despite Fritzsche's assertions, the Pan-Germans remained deeply involved in the party's internal affairs, even proposing detailed questionnaires to gauge DNVP delegates' loyalty to Hugenberg.[30] The League's unwavering support for Hugenberg ultimately proved to be an important factor in the chairman's showdown with remaining party moderates and precipitated the second secession of DNVP delegates in July 1930.

The immediate impetus for this final round of defections came from difficult decisions concerning the new government's economic policy. On 12 April 1930 an appropriations bill for the 1930 budget came before the Reichstag. The DNVP split its vote, as Hugenberg demanded that the party reject Brüning's economic plan completely, while moderate conservatives, especially large landowners, saw in the government's agricultural proposals an offer that was simply too good to refuse. Thirty-one party moderates voted in favor of the bill.[31] This lack of party discipline infuriated Hugenberg and his supporters, yet when a new round of appropriations came before the Reichstag on 16 July, the DNVP split yet again. This time the bill was defeated and the following day the SPD renewed a motion of no-confidence against the Brüning government. On 18 July 1930, 25 DNVP Reichstag deputies led by Kuno von Westarp voted to preserve the Brüning government, thus defying Hugenberg's demand for unanimous party support for the no-confidence measure. On that same day, those 25 members announced their departure from the DNVP.[32]

This second and final round of defections gave Hugenberg nearly complete control over the party and also satisfied the long-standing Pan-German goal of

---

[29]   Curt Fritzsche to Alldeutsche Verband, Ortsgruppe Dresden, StADresden, ADV-OD/12, 26 April 1930, 208. The League's headquarters fielded several additional complaints concerning the "Gründonnerstag" article and the fallout it produced in Fritzsche's electoral district of East Saxony. See: Leopold von Vietinghoff-Scheel to Georg Beutel (Dresden), 1 May 1930, StADresden, ADV-OD/12, 210; and Vietinghoff-Scheel to Freiherr Helmuth von Maltzahn (Radebeul), 2 May 1930, StADresden, ADV-OD/12, 213.

[30]   See the proposal of Christoph Pickel, leader of the Pan-German League's Northern Bavarian district, to all local chapters: Pickel to Ortsgruppen des Gaues Nordbayern des Alldeutschen Verbandes, 24 July 1930, BARCH R8048/441, 22.

[31]   Leopold, *Alfred Hugenberg*, 75, and Beck, *The Fateful Alliance*, 66–67.

[32]   Leopold, *Alfred Hugenberg*, 77–79, Beck, *The Fateful Alliance*, 68–69, and Patch, *Heinrich Brüning*, 93–94.

a radicalized DNVP that could serve as the core of the nationalist opposition against the Weimar system. Not surprisingly, the Pan-German League publicly welcomed the July 1930 resignations and praised the new DNVP under Hugenberg's unquestioned leadership.[33] The League also worked to ensure that local DNVP chapters would be brought in to line with the party's broader reorientation at the national level. Clear evidence of the Pan-German League's role in the purge of remaining moderate conservatives at the local level can be found in the city of Dresden.

Even with Hugenberg's election as party chairman in October 1928, moderates loyal to Kuno von Westarp still maintained influence over certain local party organizations. This was the case with the party's Dresden organization. The struggle for Pan-German control over the Dresden DNVP began with the controversy over Paul Bang's nomination as a party candidate from East Saxony for the May 1928 Reichstag elections.[34] The head of the Dresden DNVP and a member of the local Pan-German League Dr. Otto Kretschmar came under sharp criticism for promoting the candidacy because of Bang's national ties to Hugenberg and the Pan-Germans. After Kretschmar resigned for health reasons, Hugenberg's allies struggled with Westarp supporters for control over the local DNVP chapter throughout 1929.[35]

In the wake of the party's substantial losses in the Saxon state (*Landtag*) elections in June 1930 and the last moderate DNVP defections at the national level in July 1930, the Dresden Pan-Germans finally brought the local DNVP party structure firmly under their direction.[36] On 28 July, all remaining local party moderates resigned under mounting pressure from the Pan-German League and

---

[33]   See the following articles from the *Deutsche Zeitung*: "Der Abfall der Westarp-Gruppe," 18 July 1930, 2; "Die Landesverbände hinter Hugenberg," 25 July 1930, 1; and "Graf Westarps Wandlung," 26 July 1930, 1–2.

[34]   Georg Beutel to Heinrich Claß, 9 September 1930, StADresden, ADV-OD/12, 194–195. For the background to Bang's nomination in East Saxony, see Chapter 5, this volume.

[35]   Georg Reyher to Paul Bang, 30 March 1929, BARCH R8048/219, 12–13, Kretschmar to Claß, 5 June 1929, R8048/219, 33–36, and Beutel to Claß, 9 September 1930, StADresden, ADV-OD/12, 194. For the moderate conservative perspective on events in Dresden and in the East Saxon DNVP district see: Albrecht Phillip to Siegfried von Lüttichau, 9 April 1929, SHStA Dresden, NL Philipp/23, np; Kurt Phillip to Albrecht Philipp, 11 April 1929, SHStA Dresden, NL Philipp, np; and Albrecht Philipp to Wilhelm Beutler, 16 May 1929, SHStA Dresden, NL Philipp/23, np.

[36]   On the DNVP's substantial losses in the May 1929 and June 1930 Saxon state elections, as well as the broader fragmentation of the established party structure in Saxony after 1928, see: Larry Eugene Jones, "Saxony, 1924–1930: A Study in the Dissolution of the Bourgeois Party System in Weimar Germany," in James Retallack (ed.), *Saxony in German History: Culture, Society, and Politics, 1830–1933* (Ann Arbor, 2000), 336–355.

the loss of party allies at the national level.[37] On 10 August, members elected new leaders and new party councils. As a result, the local DNVP again had an active Pan-German as chairman and nine of 11 members of the executive council and 25 of 46 members of the party council were now also Pan-Germans.[38]

These results pleased Heinrich Claß and the Pan-German League's leadership. Similar reports of Pan-German success in other local party chapters reached League headquarters as well.[39] By the summer of 1930, the Pan-Germans had largely accomplished the main goal that they had set for themselves already in 1924. By working to drive out remaining party moderates and replacing them with loyal Hugenberg supporters, the League had clearly helped shift the balance of power in Berlin and in the provinces toward Hugenberg. These actions helped produce a significantly smaller, tightly organized, and increasingly intransigent DNVP. While this satisfied the Pan-German League's leaders, the DNVP's political defections seriously weakened the party and left it with few solid options for future political coalitions. The primary option left to the Hugenberg-led DNVP and its Pan-German allies was the unpredictable National Socialist movement.

From the Harzburg Front to the Nazi Seizure of Power

On 14 September 1930, the German electorate went to the polls and changed the balance of power on the German Right and across the political spectrum. The DNVP suffered further losses beyond those they had already sustained in 1928, reducing the party to 41 seats in the Reichstag with only 7 percent of the total vote. Conversely, Adolf Hitler's National Socialists scored a remarkable political victory moving from their previous total of 12 seats and 2.6 percent of the vote in 1928 to 107 seats and 18.3 percent of votes cast in 1930. In two years' time the NSDAP had gone from a fringe right-wing force to the second

---

[37]   Pan-German members maintained steady pressure on local party moderates throughout 1929 and the first half of 1930. For example, see: Fritz Goebel, 3 July 1930, StADresden, ADV-OD/12, 247–248; and DNVP Ortsgruppe Dresden to Goebel, 11 July 1930, StADresden, ADV-OD/12249–250.

[38]   Beutel to Claß, 9 September 1930, StADresden, ADV-OD/12, 194–195.

[39]   For example, see the article on leadership change in the Hamburg DNVP state party (*Landesverband*) association: "Führerwechsel bei den Hamburg Deutschnationalen," *Deutsche Zeitung*, 13 November 1930, 2. For the background on the conflict with the Pan-German faction in the Hamburg state party association see the lengthy report from the League of German Nationalist Associations Hamburg: "Verband Deutschnationaler Vereine für das Staatsgebiet Hamburg," 28 May 1929, NL Reinhard Mumm, BARCH N2203/108, 173–180.

largest party in the Reichstag, behind only the SPD with 143 seats and 24.5 percent of the vote.[40]

Remarkably, the Pan-German League's leadership interpreted the election results largely as a victory for Hugenberg and the broader nationalist front. Heinrich Claß argued that although the DNVP's total vote count had declined substantially from 1928, in reality one had to take into account the two rounds of moderate conservative defections in December 1929 and July 1930. With these moderate resignations in mind, the de facto total of DNVP deputies still loyal to Hugenberg before the September 1930 elections was only 38. The fact that the recently "purified" DNVP had just earned 41 seats indicated a net gain of three delegates rather than a loss.[41]

In addition, Claß framed the NSDAP's tremendous success within the context of a broader victory for the nationalist opposition begun by Hugenberg and the Pan-Germans in the Reichsausschuss. Rather than realistically considering the implications of such an electoral victory for Hitler's freedom of action from other right-wing forces, the Pan-Germans continued to see the primary value of Hitler's dynamic movement as an ally for Hugenberg's campaign against the current system.[42] Claß concluded that in spite of widespread attempts by political enemies to "annihilate" Hugenberg and "his" party, the DNVP leader emerged with an important mandate for action and had demonstrated his great abilities as a "statesman in the highest sense."[43] The League's goal now was to help forge a strong working relationship between the DNVP and the NSDAP, so that both parties would enter the political "battle" united in purpose. In this regard, the League's leadership placed considerable emphasis on the personal relationship between the two parties' leaders. It was crucial, the Pan-Germans claimed, that Hugenberg continue to exert a positive influence over Hitler to ensure that the Nazi leader did not fall prey to the more radical socialist elements within his own party.[44]

The Pan-German League's renewed interest in the Nazi movement resulted largely from the NSDAP's undeniable electoral success in September 1930 and

---

[40]   Kolb, *Weimar Republic*, 194–195.

[41]   SGA, 19 September 1930, BARCH R8048/163, 18.

[42]   The Nazi Party took note of Claß's interpretation of the election results and strategy for cooperation between the NSDAP and the DNVP. See: "Nicht Hugenberg oder Hitler, sondern Hugenberg und Hitler! Tagung der Alldeutschen," *Der Nationalsozialist*, 22 September 1930, 1.

[43]   SGA, 19 September 1930, BARCH R8048/163, 18–19.

[44]   Ibid., 19. See also: SGA, 17 May 1930, BARCH R8048/162, 6; SGA, 7 December 1930, BARCH R8048/164, 42; Paul Bang to Siegfried von Lüttichau, 8 April 1930, BARCH R8048/232, 30–34; and "Justizrat Claß zur politischen Lage," *Deutsche Zeitung*, 20 September 1930, 1.

also from the hope, based in part on the party's cooperation with the anti-Young Plan campaign, that Hitler and his followers had learned their political lesson in the wake of the 1923 "Beer Hall" Putsch. Strangely, Heinrich Claß was convinced that Hitler would now be willing to support a true statesman like Hugenberg as leader of the nationalist opposition against the Weimar Republic.[45] To achieve this goal, the League devoted considerable effort throughout the remainder of 1930 and much of 1931 to keep the alliance between these two groups intact.

In a broader sense, however, the Pan-German League's leaders believed that Hitler and his movement had much to learn about nuances of radical nationalist politics.[46] The Pan-Germans felt that their political acumen, social pedigree, and long experience with radical nationalist politics prepared them to educate Hitler and shape the Nazi movement. This approach, while consistent with the League's long-standing preference for working behind the scenes to influence other political groups, proved to be woefully inadequate when dealing with Adolf Hitler. The Nazis soon made it clear that they had little use for political lessons from their nationalist elders. Instead, Hitler and his party colleagues felt that the Pan-Germans' passion for the nationalist cause was wasted by the League's elitist, exclusionary attitude which did little to attract broad popular support.[47] The first significant signs of serious division between the Hugenberg/Pan-German camp and the Hitler movement came in the nationalist demonstration in October 1931 against the Brüning government at Bad Harzburg.

By the summer of 1931, the economic consequences of the Great Depression left Germany reeling. A severe banking crisis, initially sparked by the fallout from the collapse of Austria's largest bank in May 1931, besieged the country. By early July, several of Germany's biggest banks faced a flood of nervous creditors

---

[45]   Claß, *WdS v. II-addendum*, 37–40. In a letter to a Pan-German League member living in China, Claß expressed his belief that Hitler was "absolutely loyal" to Hugenberg and that it was the Pan-German League's task to maintain the connection between Hitler's "mass movement" and Hugenberg's "statesmanlike leadership." Claß to Hermann Walbaum, 3 January 1931, BARCH R8048/486, 32–33.

[46]   Indeed, in spite of League leaders' earnest attempts to encourage closer cooperation between the Nazi Party and Hugenberg's DNVP from 1930 to 1931, they still harbored private concerns about Hitler's control of his party and the NSDAP's true nationalist credentials. See: SGA, 7–8 February 1931, BARCH R8048/165, 33–34; and SGA, 25 April 1931, BARCH R8048/166, 16.

[47]   Already in 1926, Joseph Goebbels offered a stinging indictment of the League's approach to politics. About a Pan-German dedication service at Richard Wagner's grave in Bayreuth in 1926, Goebbels remarked: "[Heinrich] Claß gives a speech at Richard Wagner's grave. Around him stand 20 German men with long beards. It is shocking ... so much insight into the issues and so little action." Elke Fröhlich (ed.), *Die Tagebücher von Joseph Goebbels: sämtliche Fragmente*, part I: 1924–1941, vol. I (Munich, 1987), 206.

and customers who sought to withdraw their funds. Unable to satisfy this overwhelming demand, Germany's banks began to stop payment, leading to an emergency bank closure on 14–15 July to prevent a full-blown collapse. In addition to its mounting debts and the increasing withdrawal of foreign capital, the German government now had to make available massive funds to prop up the banking system. As a result, Germany suspended its reparations payments and the Brüning cabinet relied on emergency legislation to maintain basic government functions.[48]

The Pan-German League's leaders viewed the Brüning government's policies as an unmitigated disaster for the German people.[49] The League welcomed plans for a united nationalist demonstration against the Brüning government as an opportunity not only to reawaken the spirit of the anti-Young Plan nationalist front, but also to send a clear message to President Hindenberg that the time had come to end his support for the Brüning government.[50] The League hoped that such a public demonstration of united nationalist strength would convince the President to create a nationalist government under Hugenberg with emergency powers that might yet spare Germany from total collapse. At least initially, the League felt that plans for a large demonstration at Bad Harzburg on 10–11 October 1931 seemed to hold promise in accomplishing this goal. However, Hitler's behavior at the nationalist gathering quickly dashed the Pan-German League's hopes for a united right-wing front.

Heinrich Claß and several other leading Pan-Germans arrived in Bad Harzburg on 10 October. The main public demonstration, including marches by right-wing paramilitary units, speeches, and the declaration of a joint statement against the Brüning government, was to take place the following day on Sunday, 11 October. As Claß finished a late dinner with other attendees on 10 October, he was called to an emergency "leaders' meeting" to be held at 10:00 p.m. Claß and several other attendees quickly moved to the meeting hall only to wait in vain for nearly two hours for Hitler to appear. Finally exasperated with this treatment, Alfred Hugenberg demanded an explanation for Hitler's absence. Nazi representatives Gregor Strasser and Otto Frick apologized but offered no explanation for their leader's behavior. Instead, they informed those present that Hitler now expected several last-minute revisions to the previously agreed-upon joint statement against the Brüning cabinet to be issued the next day. Shocked by this demand but unwilling to jeopardize the entire gathering, Hugenberg and

---

[48]   Kolb, *Weimar Republic,* 115–116, Jones, *German Liberalism,* 408–410, and Patch, *Heinrich Brüning,* 172–184. For a more detailed account of the depression in Germany, see: Harold James, *The German Slump: Politics and Economics, 1924–1936* (Oxford, 1986).

[49]   See: "Fort mit der Tribut-Regierung!" *Deutsche Zeitung,* 8 June 1930, 1.

[50]   SGA, 5 September 1931, BARCH R8048/ 167, 6–11.

other right-wing leaders agreed to some minor revisions in tone and style that seemed to satisfy Strasser and Frick.[51]

Hitler's behavior the following day further frustrated and angered the Pan-Germans and other non-Nazi members present at the Harzburg meeting. Hitler arrived late to the morning parade of paramilitary forces and stayed only long enough to review the Nazi S.A. from his car. He abruptly departed before the other paramilitary groups, including the Stahlhelm, had passed the reviewing stand.[52] Then the Nazi leader refused to attend the joint midday banquet, later claiming to despise such bourgeois meals while so many of his followers fought on with empty stomachs.[53] Finally, Hitler threatened to not to speak at the main assembly later that afternoon. Only as a result of Hugenberg's persuasion did Hitler finally agree to participate. As Claß recalled, the assembly hall that afternoon was torn by a shouting contest featuring "Heil Hitler" and "Heil Hugenberg." "It did not appear," the Pan-German League chairman concluded, "to be a united rally, but rather one of unbridgeable contradictions."[54]

The nationalist movement never overcame the substantial divisions that emerged at the Harzburg meeting between the Nazis and the established Right under Hugenberg. In the following months this relationship only deteriorated further, as Hitler made clear his party's intent to gain power on its own terms, free from ties to the 'old' Right represented by figures like Hugenberg and Claß.[55] Thus many of the Pan-Germans' old concerns about Hitler resurfaced at the end of 1931 and in the beginning of 1932.[56] Despite the NSDAP's tremendous electoral success in September 1930, the party and its leader simply could not be relied on to support the broad nationalist opposition strategy that the League supported. Confronted with this fundamental problem, the Pan-German League's leaders reiterated their support for Alfred Hugenberg as the only real leader that could solve Germany's crisis. After the failed Harzburg meeting,

---

[51]   Claß, *WdS v. II-addendum*, 42–45.

[52]   Leopold, *Alfred Hugenberg*, 102, and Kershaw, *Hitler*, 356.

[53]   Hitler quoted in: Kershaw, *Hitler*, 356.

[54]   Claß, *WdS v. II-addendum*, 47.

[55]   Ibid., 48–49. Claß recounts a series of discussions immediately following Harzburg in which Hugenberg described the details of Hitler's petulant behavior at the gathering. Hugenberg also lamented the fact the Hitler failed again on several occasions to keep appointments with him in the months following the Harzburg Front. For a detailed treatment of the broader context of right-wing politics following the Harzburg meetings see: Larry Eugene Jones, "'The Greatest Stupidity of My Life': Alfred Hugenberg and the Formation of the Hitler Cabinet, January 1933," *Journal of Contemporary History*, 27/1, 1992, 63–87.

[56]   Heinrich Claß to Konstantin Freiherr von Gebsattel, 14 November 1931, BARCH R8048/357, 366, and Claß to Albert Bongartz, 25 November 1931, BARCH R8048/300, 219.

the Pan-Germans could conjure few other solutions to mend the increasingly fractured nationalist movement.[57]

By 1932, the League's attempts to bring about some general agreement between the Nazi Party and the DNVP within the broader framework of the nationalist opposition had broken down entirely. Inter-party feuding, personal animosities, and political differences had overwhelmed Pan-German attempts to secure a united nationalist front. Additionally, the League was losing members at an alarming rate because of the political discord within the German Right and as a result of the economic crisis ravaging the country.[58] It was in this increasingly polarized climate that the League confronted the dilemma of the 1932 presidential election.[59]

After long and complicated negotiations in the first two months of 1932, Germany's major right-wing parties failed to reach agreement on a joint candidate to run against the communist Ernst Thälmann and the sitting president Paul von Hindenburg in the March 1932 presidential elections. The radical Right openly opposed Hindenburg for his support of the Brüning cabinets, yet the divisions that had plagued the Harzburg meeting only months earlier now also prevented Hugenberg, Hitler, and their supporters from agreeing to a common alternative.[60] As right-wing negotiations floundered, the Nazis announced on 22 February that Adolf Hitler would run for the presidency. Later that day the DNVP and Stahlhelm announced Theodor Duesterberg as their candidate for the March elections.[61] Yet again, Germany's two largest right-wing groups failed to find common ground.

The Pan-German League regretted this development as yet another example of the growing division within the ranks of the so-called national opposition.[62] This divided candidacy was even worse, League leaders argued, when one considered the advantage this would likely afford the sitting president in his

---

[57]   SGA, 5–6 December 1931, BARCH R8048/168, 55–56.

[58]   Pan-German leaders actually considered proposals for restructuring the League in December 1931, after losing 2,383 members since September of that year. See the lengthy discussion about this issue in: ibid., 71–77.

[59]   For Claß's discussion of this issue, see: SGA, 20/21 February 1932, BARCH R8048/169, 32.

[60]   On the Right's division generally over this issue, see: Larry Eugene Jones, "Hindenburg and the Conservative Dilemma in the 1932 Presidential Elections," *German Studies Review*, 5, 1997, 235–260, and Leopold, *Alfred Hugenberg*, 107–121.

[61]   Jones, "Hindenburg and the Conservative Dilemma," 240–241.

[62]   Heinrich Claß to Albert Bongartz, 19 February 1932, BARCH R8048/300, 233, Claß to Bongartz, 8 March 1932, BARCH R8048/300, 235, and SGA, 7 May 1932, BARCH R8048/170, 19. The Pan-German leader was convinced that Hugenberg, not Duesterberg, should have run for the presidency.

re-election bid. In spite of Hindenburg's great military service to the nation, the League had come to view him as an abject political failure. The League's relationship with the President had begun to deteriorate already in 1926 when he refused to support Pan-German efforts to appoint Hugenberg head of an emergency government.[63] The League's opinion of Hindenburg declined further after he signed the Young Plan into law and continued to support the Brüning government with emergency powers in spite of vehement nationalist opposition to the chancellor's policies.[64] Now, to the Pan-German League's deep regret, no single nationalist candidate would even stand against Hindenburg in the March elections.

In the first round of presidential balloting, Hindenburg received 49.6 percent of the vote and therefore barely missed the absolute majority needed for election. Hitler finished far behind with 30.1 percent of votes cast. The DNVP/Stahlhelm candidate Theodore Duesterberg performed very poorly, pulling in only 6.8 percent of the votes.[65] Faced with these results, Alfred Hugenberg decided not to present a nationalist candidate for the second round of balloting scheduled to take place on 10 April. Instead, Hugenberg remained neutral and encouraged all of his supporters to do the same.[66]

Faced with the choice of Hitler, Thälmann, or Hindenburg, Heinrich Claß broke with his trusted ally Hugenberg and authorized League members to support Hitler's candidacy. Publicly, Claß justified Pan-German support for Hitler by citing the League's freedom of action as a non-party interest group and the need to oppose Hindenburg's candidacy at all costs.[67] Privately,

---

[63]   See above, Chapter 5. Between 1926 and 1932, the Pan-German League publicly attacked Hindenburg for allegedly betraying the German people. Claß went so far as to label the president the "executor of the Marxist fulfillment policy." See: Claß, *WdS v. II*, 909; and SGA, 7 September 1928, BARCH R8048/155, esp. 7–10. In spite of these repeated public attacks, the Pan-German leadership privately tried to keep open the channels of communication to Hindenburg through League member Prince Otto zu Salm-Horstmar. Oddly, the League hoped they might yet show the president the error of his ways and convince him to dismiss Brüning and appoint a nationalist cabinet before the 1932 presidential elections. Not surprisingly, nothing came of these efforts. See: SGA, 20/21 February 1932, BARCH R8048/169, 30–32; and the detailed correspondence, including copies of letters to Hindenburg from Salm-Horstmar, in: BARCH R8048/454, esp. 80–84, 93–94, and 123–125.

[64]   Heinrich Claß offers a detailed discussion of the League's deteriorating relationship with Hindenburg in: Claß, *WdS v. II*, 906–912.

[65]   Mommsen, *Rise and Fall of Weimar Democracy*, 409, and Leopold, *Alfred Hugenberg*, 111.

[66]   On Hugenberg's decision, see: Leopold, *Alfred Hugenberg*, 111–112.

[67]   SGA, 7 May 1932, BARCH R8048/170, 21–22. See also: Heinrich Claß to Albert

however, Claß believed Hitler had no realistic chance to defeat Hindenburg. By authorizing Pan-German League members to vote for the Nazi leader, Claß believed that they could safely vent their anger against the current government without actually strengthening the Nazi cause. Claß also felt that he could not ask thousands of Pan-German League members to withhold their votes in the presidential runoff and then solicit their support for the DNVP in the upcoming Prussian state elections on 24 April 1932. In Claß's mind, this decision was a calculated gamble rather than a genuine endorsement of the Nazi leader.[68] Nonetheless, Claß's decision temporarily angered Hugenberg and led to some disagreement within the League's own ranks.[69]

For example, at the League's May 1932 business management committee meeting General Arnold von Mohl reported on the Bavarian Pan-Germans' disappointment in the leadership's support for Hitler. Mohl explained that while many local members understood that there was no other nationalist choice and that the League did not endorse Hitler "with enthusiasm," they still could not bring themselves to vote for a man who "did not possess the required training, suitable social status, and the necessary strength of character."[70] Mohl concluded his remarks with the hope that "the Pan-German League will never again allow itself reach the point that it supports a candidate for President that it does not really consider to be suitable."[71]

The Pan-Germans' tenuous support for Hitler's presidential bid marked the last major instance of cooperation between the two forces. Indeed, the relationship between the Pan-German League and the National Socialists worsened significantly after the presidential elections. Between May and December, the League broke off almost all channels of communication with Hitler's movement as it became completely clear that the Nazi Party was determined to move on without further meaningful cooperation with the Claß/Hugenberg axis in the nationalist opposition. During the League's September 1932 business management committee meeting, members aired their deep

---

Bongartz, 19 March 1932, BARCH R8048/300, 241, and Claß to Konstantin Freiherr von Gebsattel. 19 March 1932, BARCH R8048/357, 370–371.

[68]   Claß to Leo Wegener, 13 April 1932, NL Wegener/23, 143. Claß admitted to Hugenberg's confidant Leo Wegener: "If I wanted to keep my people in line for the Prussian election ... then I had to indulge their need to vent their anger and vote in the presidential runoff. [This was] actually harmless because the NSDAP had no chance of winning."

[69]   Hugenberg was upset with Claß's choice and, according to their mutual friend Reinhold Quaatz, Hugenberg even accused the Pan-German leader of stabbing him in the back. See: Weiß and Hoser, *Die Deutschnationalen und die Zerstörung der Weimarer Republik*, 185.

[70]   Ibid., 26.

[71]   Ibid.

concerns about the Nazi Party's direction and Hitler's true political intentions. Three major points of concern stood out in this discussion.

First, Heinrich Claß sharply criticized Hitler's attempt to force his way into the chancellorship on the heels of the Nazi Party's tremendous electoral success in July 1932.[72] He argued that Hitler not only overplayed his hand in rejecting President Hindenburg's offer of the vice-chancellorship on 13 August 1932, but the Nazi leader also clearly demonstrated his commitment to secure total power in Germany without any cooperation from other members of the nationalist front. Claß expressed relief that Germany had been spared such a government under Hitler's leadership.[73]

Second, members expressed disgust with Nazi negotiations with the Center Party for a potential "Black-Brown" coalition government in Prussia.[74] The NSDAP's movement toward the Center Party was yet another example of Hitler's desperate attempt to secure political power at any cost. Claß argued that the Nazi press's recent attacks on Alfred Hugenberg and the DNVP designed to gain favor with the Center Party made the entire affair even more unseemly.[75] One League member even sarcastically pointed out a notable similarity between the NSDAP and the Center Party: "The Center swears by the Pope's infallibility, and the National Socialists swear by Hitler's infallibility."[76]

Finally, some Pan-Germans began to question the very nationalist credentials of Hitler's movement. Paul Bang took issue with the recent trend in the Nazi press that characterized Hugenberg and his allies as "social reactionaries."[77] Underlying this shift, Bang argued, was the Nazi Party's attempt to build up its factory cell organization to gain support from the ranks of the unionized working class. Bang believed that this attempt to undercut the Communists and the SPD was doomed to fail and called into question the NSDAP's entire political strategy. Bang concluded that Marxism in all its forms was a "deadly poison" and the Nazi attempt to "water down" that poison for short-term political gain would certainly fail.[78] Summarizing the growing concerns about Hitler's movement, Heinrich Claß admitted to his fellow Pan-Germans that:

---

[72]   Kolb, *Weimar Republic*, 194–195. The NSDAP scored a massive victory in the July 1932 Reichstag elections, securing 37.3 percent of the vote and 230 seats. This made the Nazis by far the largest single party in the nation. Kolb, *Weimar Republic*, 194–195.

[73]   SGA, 9 September 1932, BARCH R8048/171, 10.

[74]   Ibid., 11–12. On the background to these coalition negotiations see: Orlow, *Weimar Prussia*, 213–224; and Mommsen, *Rise and Fall of Weimar Democracy*, 465–469.

[75]   SGA, 9 September 1932, BARCH R8048/171, 11.

[76]   Ibid., 15.

[77]   For more on this trend see: Beck, *The Fateful Alliance*, 74–76.

[78]   SGA, 9 September 1932, BARCH R 8048/171, 17–18.

Germany has not been in greater danger since the upheaval [of 1918] and today the greatest source of that danger is the NSDAP. One must clearly recognize that even a nationalist mass party is still based on the masses. History demonstrates that a nation can only prosper when it is compelled to its good fortune by the few [the elite].[79]

In the weeks following this statement, the Pan-German League publicly directed its members to cease their support for the NSDAP and devote their time and votes completely to Hugenberg's DNVP.[80]

The League's opinion of Hitler and the Nazi movement declined significantly in the last months before the Nazi seizure of power. Many Pan-Germans were shocked to learn of Nazi cooperation with the Communists in the Berlin transportation strike in November 1932.[81] The League's leadership now believed that Nazism had sold its soul in an all-out quest for political power with disastrous results for the movement. In light of the NSDAP's substantial electoral decline in November 1932, many League members felt that the party was simply too deeply divided to maintain its political momentum.[82] Heinrich Claß concluded: "I am convinced that the NSDAP has essentially run its course ... we can close the book on Hitler's leadership attributes and on the National Socialists' qualifications to lead the government."[83]

These significant misgivings concerning Nazism did not subside with the creation of the Hitler cabinet on 30 January 1933. While Heinrich Claß was away from Berlin taking a health cure in Thuringia from late December 1932 until early February 1933, momentous events transpired in the nation's capital. Several months earlier in May 1932, Heinrich Brüning's government collapsed under the combined weight of the disastrous economic depression, political intrigue surrounding President Hindenburg, and controversial policy decisions including an agricultural resettlement program targeting failing East Elbian

---

[79]   Ibid., 12.

[80]   See: "Der Alldeutsche Verband für die DNVP," *Deutsche Zeitung*, 25 October 1932, 1. In late October 1932, Pan-German Alexander Graf von Brockdorff attacked the Nazis for their recent political maneuvering in a speech to a sizeable crowd in Stuttgart. See: "Die Irrwege der NSDAP. Eine Klarstellung im Alldeutschen Verband," *Süddeutsche Zeitung*, 21 October 1932, 11.

[81]   *Lagebericht* from 17 November 1932, BARCH R8048/551, 150–156. The strike began on 3 November and lased four days. Berlin police fired into a crowd of demonstrators, killing three and wounding eight. The strike brought the capital's public transportation system to a standstill. See: Kershaw, *Hitler*, 390–391, and 714 n73.

[82]   Kolb, *Weimar Republic*, 194–195. In the 6 November 1932 Reichstag elections, the Nazis lost 34 of the previous 230 seats and just over 6 percent of the total vote. By contrast, the DNVP gained 15 seats and improved its vote total by almost 2.5 percent. For the Nazi response, see: Kershaw, *Hitler*, 389–391.

[83]   SGA, 10–11 December 1932, BA Berlin, R8048/172, 43–44.

landed estates.[84] Following Brüning, Franz von Papen presided over a disastrous six-month crisis government, only to be replaced as chancellor in early December 1932 by Kurt von Schleicher. After seemingly endless political intrigue, Schleicher ended his short term in office by resigning on 28 January 1933. Only two days later on 30 January President Hindenburg administered the oath of office to Germany's new chancellor Adolf Hitler. The Nazi leader now headed a nationalist coalition cabinet that included Franz von Papen as vice-chancellor and Alfred Hugenberg as minister of economics and agriculture.[85]

The Pan-German League's situation report for the first week of February 1933 celebrated the victory of the "nationalist front" and singled out Alfred Hugenberg for his continuing efforts to bring about a true nationalist coalition.[86] The League chose to celebrate that accomplishment, but publicly sought to downplay Hitler's role in the events leading to his appointment as chancellor.[87] Privately, Heinrich Claß and several other Pan-German leaders acknowledged the failure of the Pan-German/DNVP strategy to control Hitler. After Claß returned to Berlin from Thuringia in February 1933, he expressed regret both for his untimely absence and for the outcome of the cabinet negotiations. The Pan-German leader told Hugenberg "if I had been [in Berlin], I would have stuck by you to make sure that you did not go along [with the Hitler cabinet]." Reflecting his deep-seated pessimism regarding the new government, Hugenberg responded "Now I am a prisoner."[88]

Between Conformity and Opposition in the Third Reich

After the establishment of the Hitler cabinet in January 1933, Heinrich Claß and other leading Pan-Germans grew concerned about their organization's continued existence. In reality, Nazi officials initially viewed the Pan-Germans

---

[84]   Mommsen, *Rise and Fall of Weimar Democracy*, 431–433. For a comprehensive analysis of the background and causes for the Brüning cabinet's collapse see: Patch, *Heinrich Brüning*, 220–271.

[85]   The historical literature on the creation of the Hitler cabinet is by now sizeable. Larry Jones provides a detailed account of Alfred Hugenberg's role in these events in: Jones, "'The Greatest Stupidity of my Life.'" For a general overview see: Henry Ashby Turner, *Hitler's Thirty Days to Power: January 1933* (Reading, MA, 1996).

[86]   *Lagebericht* from 1 February 1933, R8048/552, 14–15.

[87]   Ibid., 15. The report praised Hugenberg for his "unforgettable service to Germany." "He [Hugenberg] overcame the bitterness and internal strife in the nationalist camp to push forward a government that Germany needed, a government of the nationalist front."

[88]   Claß, *WdS v. II-addendum*, 50.

in 1933 as a largely harmless organization. Because of the League's non-party status as an allegedly apolitical Verband the government did not dissolve the organization like they had other formal political parties. There are several major reasons for this course of action.

First, the League's membership had fallen to about 10,000 by 1933 and consisted overwhelmingly of older members with little prospect for future growth.[89] Second, the League's official press and many of its initial public speeches stressed themes that generally overlapped with Nazi goals. This material frequently focused on well-established Pan-German topics including racial purity and German expansion.[90] Finally, League leaders remained largely on the sidelines as the Nazi regime consolidated its hold on power between January 1933 and President Hindenburg's death in August 1934. The Pan-German leadership focused primarily on the organization's survival in this period, even as Hitler and his associates eliminated all other political opposition, purged their own party, and violently settled scores against old rivals.[91] In the face of this brazen Nazi seizure of power, the League seemed to be wasting away as an irrelevant relic of a bygone nationalist era. However, other internal Nazi security documents paint a different picture.

Between 1936 and 1938, Gestapo agents filed a series of reports on Pan-German speeches and League meetings at various locations throughout Germany. These data were compiled in a lengthy report on the League, finished in 1938, and distributed within the highest levels of the Nazi leadership.[92] By the beginning of 1939, this report, combined with other evidence compiled

---

[89]   For this assessment see: "Sicherheitsdienst des RFSS SD-Hauptamt: Bericht über den Alldeutschen Verband" from April 1938 (hereafter "Bericht 1938") in: BARCH NS 10 *Persönliche Adjutantur des Führers und Reichskanzlers* (hereafter "BARCH NS 10")/411, 30.

[90]   See examples of the League's public speeches in these years in the activity reports from the Pan-German League's Ortsgruppe Dresden in: *Jahresberichte* 1933–38, StADresden ADV-OD/50, 198–206. The Pan-German *Deutsche Zeitung* also continued to publish positive material concerning the regime: "Der Weg in die völkische Zukunft," *Deutsche Zeitung*, 4 September 1933, 1.

[91]   Documents concerning the League's actual stance on specific aspects of the Nazi consolidation of power during 1933 and 1934 are scarce. However, those sources that do exist focus extensively on issues related to the League's survival in this tumultuous period. For example, see the correspondence between the Reich Interior Ministry and local Thuringian officials concerning Pan-German activities in the town of Hildburghausen. BARCH R1501 *Reichsministerium des Innern*/388, 123–129. Local "activity reports" from the Pan-German League's Dresden chapter also focus exclusively on internal issues including League gatherings, speech topics, and organizational questions. See the *Tatigkeitsberichte* for 1933 through 1938 in: StADresden, ADV-OD/50, 198–206.

[92]   Bericht 1938, BARCH NS 10/411, 28–52.

against local Pan-German groups in Thuringia and elsewhere, convinced Nazi leaders that the League posed a sufficiently serious threat to the regime to justify shutting the organization down. The report contained a great deal of revealing information about the Pan-German League's activities during the first years of the Nazi regime.

The 25-page document began with the Nazi view of the Pan-German League's history. It stressed the influence of the League's "national liberal" origins during Imperial Germany, League members' "pronounced bourgeois-intellectual" orientation, their unquestioned monarchist sentiments, and their general elitism. The report accused the Pan-Germans of rejecting the regime's goals and ignoring the Nazi principle of "the common good before individual need" (*Gemeinnutz vor Eigennutz*). Furthermore, the League allegedly viewed the Nazi regime at best as a transitional government that could not be trusted to lead the German people in the long term.[93]

Perhaps most disturbing to the Nazi regime were the League's accusations of Hitler's flawed leadership. The report recounted numerous instances in which Pan-German members criticized the Führer for guiding the country into a position very similar to, if not worse than, the country's supposed encirclement on the eve of World War I. The report supported this contention by focusing on three major areas: 1) internal politics; 2) foreign policy; and 3) economics. In each of these cases, the Gestapo indicated that the League expressed significant opposition to Nazi policy.

On the subject of internal politics, the League supposedly questioned the basis for the Nazi regime's political authority. According to Pan-German statements, Hitler's unprecedented consolidation of power had produced an unstable government dominated by infighting between various power centers. According to the report, League leaders feared that Germany would descend into total chaos if Hitler died and the remaining leaders were left to fight over leadership of the government.[94] In the realm of foreign policy, the report recounted Pan-German claims that Hitler's decisions had isolated Germany and forced the nation to rely increasingly on a weak Italy under Mussolini.[95] Finally, Nazi economic and trade policy was allegedly a frequent target of Pan-German attacks. According to the report, the League's economic experts gave frequent presentations to private gatherings criticizing Nazi economic policy. League members were particularly concerned about the increasing importation of foodstuffs and the artificially inflated employment numbers tied to rapid

---

[93] Ibid., 29.
[94] Ibid., 32–33.
[95] Ibid., 34.

rearmament. According to Gestapo informants, the League concluded that if Nazi policy continued in this fashion, "a catastrophe [would be] unavoidable."[96]

These critiques of regime policy were not the only problem the Nazis had with Pan-German gatherings. According to the report, the League also frequently engaged in personal attacks against Nazi leaders and important regime symbols. For example, Gestapo agents complained of the League's unwillingness to use the Hitler greeting in any fashion. This refusal took the form of both simple omission and open mockery. The Gestapo recorded one occasion where two guests of a Pan-German meeting in Berlin offered the Hitler greeting and received the following reply: "Why are you sticking your hand out here. Is it raining or something?"[97] The League's verbal attacks against the regime also often took the form of dark humor. At one February 1938 meeting, a local Pan-German leader was said to have offered the following joke: "Who is the greatest hereditary farmer? Hitler! He has 65 million sheep, a stall full of fat pigs, and a lame dog."[98] As historian Detlev Peukert has suggested, even simple acts of non-conformity or refusal represented a potential threat to the Nazi regime.[99] Viewed in this context, the Gestapo's fixation on the Pan-Germans' personal attacks and even jokes about the regime's leaders is noteworthy.

Based on these and other examples, the report concluded that "because of its history and its continuing goals, the Pan-German League—both in its basic ideas and its propaganda—stands in opposition to Nazism."[100] To what extent, however, did the regime fear that the League's accusations constituted a real threat? The annual report *Meldungen aus dem Reich* from the SS Security Service (*Sicherheitsdienst*) contains a revealing passage that summarized the Pan-German League's activities throughout 1938:

> The Pan-German League remained a gathering point for rightist regime opponents who failed to find a connection to the [Nazi] Party or its associate institutions. The League still harbored elements of the liberal and intellectual bourgeois circles that always stood in opposition to National Socialism and even today refuse to cooperate with the [Nazi] Party or the government in the spirit of National Socialism. Destructive critiques of the regime appeared openly in the Pan-German League's ranks ... their foreign policy presentations were alarming and in some cases

---

96   Ibid., 35–36.

97   Ibid., 31.

98   Ibid., 41. The last comment was directed at Joseph Goebbels and his clubbed foot.

99   Detlev Peukert, *Inside Nazi Germany: Conformity, Opposition, and Racism in Everyday Life* (English Edition: New Haven, 1987), esp. 81–85.

100   Bericht 1938, BARCH NS 10/411, 30.

constituted a danger to the regime. They presented ideas that directly opposed the government's foreign policy.[101]

This assessment is remarkable for at least two reasons. First, it clearly articulated the regime's belief that the League had the potential to develop as a source of opposition against the Nazi state. Secondly, state security services took this threat seriously and they suggested that some of the League's positions actually threatened the regime. Other reports expressed concern about League members' purported connections to members from groups including the former Stahlhelm and DNVP, Freemasonry, and even the Confessing Church.[102] In short, Nazi security services believed they had more than enough evidence to justify a quick strike against the Pan-Germans. After consultation between Reinhard Heydrich and other top Nazi leaders, the regime moved decisively in March 1939 to close the Pan-German League's offices and outlaw its publications.[103] Thus, the Nazis brought the League's nearly 50-year existence to a sudden and rather surprising end.

Despite fairly significant evidence of Pan-German criticism of the Third Reich, Nazi actions in March 1939 make it impossible to determine the extent to which the League might have ever developed as a potential rallying point for any meaningful opposition to the Nazi state. While these private state security documents suggest that the Nazi leadership believed this might happen and acted quickly to prevent such an occurrence, there is no concrete evidence that the League ever seriously considered specific action against the regime. Nonetheless, as Detlev Peukert has argued and as Nazi actions in 1939 demonstrated, the regime believed that even non-conformist behavior and rejection of some important aspects of Nazi policy was significant cause for concern in such a highly politicized society.

After 1933, the Pan-German League had to confront the legacy of its failed political strategy in the final years of the Weimar Republic. The Pan-Germans helped to radicalize the DNVP after 1928, ensuring the departure of remaining moderate conservatives and reducing the party to a radical nationalist core incapable of competing politically with the NSDAP in the polarized political climate of the Great Depression. Moreover, the League's misguided attempts to produce closer cooperation between the Nazi Party and the so-called nationalist

---

[101]   Heinz Boberach (ed.), *Meldungen aus dem Reich: Die Geheimen Lageberichte des Sicherheitsdienstes der SS. Band 2 Jahreslagebericht 1938 des Sicherheitsamtes* (Herrsching, 1984), 75.

[102]   Bericht 1938, BARCH NS 10/411, 36–37.

[103]   For details of the discussions that led to the Pan-German League's dissolution see: "Alldeutscher Verband-Auflösung März 1939" in BARCH R43 II Reichskanzlei/829, 4–12.

front led by Alfred Hugenberg only exacerbated the growing divisions between Hitler's movement and the non-Nazi Right. While the NSDAP was clearly willing and capable of pursuing its own political path, the DNVP became increasingly marginalized in the final years of the Weimar Republic.

In the wake of Hitler's appointment as chancellor and Alfred Hugenberg's subsequent resignation from the government in June 1933, the League largely resorted to its long-standing elitist view of political power and mistrust of Hitler's leadership abilities.[104] When cast against the backdrop of the Pan-Germans' troubled relationship with the Nazis in the Weimar era, this post-1933 attitude becomes somewhat easier to comprehend. That the League felt emboldened to criticize the Nazi regime and its leaders stemmed in large measure from the Pan-German claim that it stood above the parties and the political process as the supposedly apolitical conscience of the national opposition. However, in Hitler's Germany this claim no longer sufficed to excuse the League's overt criticism of the government. In the Third Reich—a society in which no organization could truly claim to be apolitical—the League finally met its demise. As they had done on numerous occasions from 1929 to 1933, the Pan-Germans seriously misjudged Nazi resolve. By March 1939 the stakes were much higher than ever before, and the outcome of this miscalculation meant not merely a loss of political influence, but the complete destruction of the Pan-German League itself.

---

[104]   On the Nazi campaign against their conservative coalition partners and Hugenberg's resignation see: Leopold, *Alfred Hugenberg*, 139–163; and Beck, *The Fateful Alliance*, 253–293.

Conclusion

In March 1932, Heinrich Claß confided to a fellow Pan-German League member: "It is truly a shame that in this critical time we simply cannot hold the nationalist forces together ... Today one can truly say that it is nationalist disunity that keeps the enemy powers in government."[1] At the time, the Pan-German chairman was lamenting the failure of the Harzburg meeting in October 1931 to produce a durable nationalist front to oppose the Brüning government. More broadly, however, Claß described an important aspect of German right-wing politics that modern historians have begun to take more seriously; namely, the fractured nature of the German Right in the Weimar Republic.

The Pan-German League's history between 1918 and 1939 provides ample evidence of the significant political divisions that existed within the German Right. On the surface, most right-wing groups professed a general aversion to the democratic system, a hatred of the Marxist Left, suspicion of a Jewish threat, and a desire to establish some sort of authoritarian government to replace the Weimar system. The Pan-German League shared many of these same general goals, and clearly articulated them already in the first post-war years in documents like the Bamberg Declaration. However, these broad points of ideological agreement did not guarantee a politically unified Right in the post-war period. As this study has demonstrated, at various critical junctures throughout the Weimar era major right-wing groups simply could not agree about specific strategies for implementing their ideological goals. While this lack of unity spared Germany's fledgling democracy further damage in its early years, the non-Nazi Right's division in the Republic's final phase after 1930 created a dangerous political opportunity for the Nazi Party. In fact, one can argue that Adolf Hitler ultimately became chancellor in January 1933 because his movement had capitalized on a deeply divided right-wing landscape seemingly

---

[1]   Heinrich Claß to Albert Bongartz, 8 March 1932, BARCH R8048/300, 235. Two months later, Claß reiterated this charge stating: "this Republic does not survive because of virtuous Republicans, but rather because of the mountains of mistakes committed by the nationalists." See: SGA, 7 May 1932, BARCH R8048/170, 23.

incapable of producing any effective alternative to the Nazi Party's dynamism and political independence.[2]

This interpretation runs counter to many existing accounts of the League's activity in the post-1918 era. Most of these studies have stressed the Pan-Germans' primary historical importance as an ideological forerunner of National Socialism and as a key point of continuity between Imperial Germany, the Weimar Republic, and the Third Reich.[3] However, these accounts generally do little to explain exactly how these lines of ideological continuity played out in concrete political terms. While identifying the Pan-German League as one of several important sources of Nazi ideology is a significant aspect of German historiography, it has, to this point, largely obscured the much more complex and often contradictory history of the League's political behavior in the Weimar era. This is perhaps most evident in the Pan-Germans' surprisingly contentious relationship with Adolf Hitler and the Nazi Party beginning in 1920 and ending nearly two decades later in 1939.

How, then, can we assess the Pan-German League's impact on the development of right-wing politics in Weimar Germany? To be sure, the League was one of the first radical nationalist organizations to reject categorically the new Weimar Republic and to advocate an authoritarian government led by nationalist elites who would supposedly restore German honor and power in Europe. The Pan-Germans' early attempts to implement this strategy did not, however, meet with much broad-based success. For example, the Pan-German League's *Deutschvölkischer Schutz- und Trutzbund* (SuTB) quickly developed a large initial following yet failed to translate its radical agenda into a practical political movement that successfully challenged the Weimar Republic's authority.[4] The same is true of the Kapp Putch, the first major right-wing assault against the government which took place in 1920. The Pan-German League's refusal to support Kapp's assault on the government further illustrates the growing divide between right-wing forces even in the first years of the Weimar Republic.

The surprisingly intense conflict between the Pan-German League, Erich Ludendorff, and the leaders of the German Völkisch Freedom Party (DVFP) confirmed the general lack of political cooperation even among radical nationalist

---

[2]   See: Larry Eugene Jones, "Why Hitler Came to Power: In Defense of a New History of Politics," in Konrad Jarausch, Jörn Rüsen, and Hans Schleier (eds), *Geschichtswissenschaft vor 2000. Perspektiven der Historiographiegeschichte, Geschichtstheorie, Sozial- und Kulturgeschichte. Festschrift für Georg G. Iggers zum 65 Geburtstag* (Hagen, 1992), 259–270.

[3]   See: Meinecke, *German Catastrophe*; Mosse, *Crisis of German Ideology*; and Hering, *Konstruierte Nation*.

[4]   Lohalm, *Völkischer Radikalismus*, 210–272.

groups that seemed to share very similar ideological goals. This right-wing infighting carried over to the Pan-German League's early attempts to integrate Adolf Hitler and the Nazi Party into the League's stated nationalist campaign against the Republic between 1920 and 1923. Hitler's rejection of Pan-German control and the League's elitist desire to direct the supposedly inexperienced and unrefined Nazi movement set the tone for the future relationship between these two prominent right-wing groups.

By 1924, the Weimar Republic had survived numerous attempts to destroy it. While the Kapp and Hitler Putsches revealed the lengths to which radical nationalist forces were prepared to go in order to overthrow Germany's fragile democracy, their failure also revealed the deep divisions within the various groups that ultimately undermined these efforts. After surviving these critical initial years, the Republic stabilized to a certain degree and parliamentary party politics took on a much greater role in the Weimar system. The Pan-German League also recognized this political shift and adjusted its plans accordingly. Unable to coordinate a successful right-wing assault on the Weimar system in its early years, by 1924 the League devoted its remaining political clout to the realm of party politics.

Above all else, the League targeted Germany's largest conservative party, the DNVP, in an effort to influence right-wing party politics. Between 1924 and 1930, the Pan-Germans tried to force the DNVP away from any meaningful cooperation with the Weimar system and they strove to purge the party of all moderate conservatives who rejected the League's radical agenda. The Pan-German League's campaign to promote Alfred Hugenberg as party leader helped transform the DNVP into a monolithic radical nationalist block, while Kuno von Westarp and other prominent moderate conservatives split from the party in 1929 and 1930. These events fatefully divided the conservative movement as Adolf Hitler's Nazi Party was beginning to make substantial strides.[5] Although the League's leaders claimed to work for the good of the radical nationalist movement as a whole, the Pan-Germans in fact promoted only their own narrow vision of political power that excluded anyone who did not support their specific goals.

This arrogant, elitist strategy, combined with the League's efforts to discredit DNVP members who did not conform to the League's agenda, helped to undermine the development of a moderate, state-supporting, mass-based conservative party, and thus further destabilized the Weimar Republic after 1930. The Pan-German campaign for Alfred Hugenberg also included a second attempt to draw the Nazi movement into closer cooperation with

---

[5]   For a broader perspective of the significance of the moderate defections from the DNVP, see: Thomas Mergel, "Das Scheitern des deutschen Tory-Konservatismus. Die Umformung der DNVP zu einer rechtsradikalen Partei 1928–1932," *Historische Zeitschrift*, 276, 2003, 323–368.

the Pan-Germans and their DNVP allies. Particularly in 1930 and 1931, the League's leaders were strangely confident that they could convince Hitler to join Alfred Hugenberg in a broad nationalist front against President Hindenburg and the Brüning government. In believing that the Nazi leader would willingly bind himself to the DNVP and the staid political strategies of the established Right, however, the League again displayed its fundamentally elitist conception of political power and its basic misunderstanding of Hitler's revolutionary movement. The Pan-Germans' total faith in Alfred Hugenberg as the only suitable statesman of the nationalist movement blinded them to the realities of the shifting balance of political power within the German Right.

After the Harzburg Front gathering in October 1931, the Pan-Germans again questioned Hitler's loyalty to the common nationalist cause. By the end of 1932, the League's leaders regarded the Nazi movement as a serious threat to the nation's stability because it appeared that Hitler was willing to sacrifice his nationalist principles in order to acquire political power. By the time the Pan-Germans finally understood this basic reality of Hitler's approach to politics, their earlier machinations had already taken effect.

Throughout the Weimar period, the DNVP had been the only other right-wing political party capable of balancing Hitler's radical politics with a potentially more moderate nationalist message. The Pan-German inspired radicalization of that party left it politically weakened and incapable of offering any meaningful challenge to the NSDAP. While the League's leaders reveled in their contribution to the purge of German's largest conservative party, they simply failed to understand that the very party they had helped to create would be quickly overtaken by the far more dynamic National Socialist movement that combined radical nationalist rhetoric with real electoral success and a massive populist political base.[6] Ultimately, the Pan-German League's actions worked to destabilize and further divide the non-Nazi Right, thereby making possible Hitler's appointment as chancellor with the League's conservative allies as junior partners.

After the creation of the Hitler cabinet on 30 January 1933, the Pan-Germans came face-to-face with the final legacy of their earlier political missteps. The League's turbulent relationship with Adolf Hitler and the Nazi movement took a final bizarre turn in the years that led up to the outbreak of World War II. In the context of traditional historical scholarship that highlighted the ideological continuities between the League and the Nazi regime, the government's decision to outlaw the Pan-German League and ban its publications in 1939 seems

---

6   Roger Chickering also identifies this process in the conclusion to his study of the Pan-German League in Imperial Germany. See: Chickering, *We Men Who Feel Most German*, 300–301.

rather incongruous. However, this decision can be more easily understood when viewed within the broader context of right-wing infighting and conflict that characterized the Pan-German League's entire history in the inter-war period. Seen in this light, the Nazi decision to dissolve the Pan-German League simply marked the final chapter in the contentious relationship between the two organizations.

Commenting in 1926 on Heinrich Claß's impact on right-wing politics, a moderate conservative author concluded that:

> [Heinrich] Claß, the chairman of the Pan-German League, is the most influential and powerful of all the political leaders who claim to stand above official party and parliamentary ties ... His fundamental rejection of the republic and of parliamentary democracy is, however, limited to dividing the nation between a leadership elite and the masses ... as a result, his abilities work to destroy, rather than build up [the nationalist movement].[7]

This quote truly summarizes the role of Heinrich Claß and the Pan-German League in the history of the German Right between 1918 and 1939. Far from ensuring the long-term continuity of radical nationalist power from Imperial Germany to the Third Reich, the Pan-German League's elitist approach to political power contributed in significant ways to the divisions and infighting that characterized the German Right and helped create the circumstances in which the Nazi seizure of power became a reality.

---

[7] "Claß und Hugenberg," *Die Wirklichkeit*, June 1926, 2–3.

Bibliography

Archival Sources

Bundesarchiv Berlin-Lichterfelde

90 Ge 4 Nachlass Konstantin Freiherr von Gebsattel
N 2203 Nachlass Reinhard Mumm
N 2329 Nachlass Kuno von Westarp
N 2353 Nachlass Gertzlaff von Hertzberg
NS 10 Persönliche Adjutantur des Führers und Reichskanzlers
R 30.01 Reichsjustizamt/ministerium
R 43 Reichskanzlei
R 72 Stahlhelm-Bund der Frontsoldaten
R 1501 Reichsministerium des Innern
R 1507 Reichskommisar für die Überwachung der Öffentlichen Ordnung
R 8005 Deutschnationalen Volkspartei
R 8034 II Reichslandbund Pressearchiv
R 8048 Alldeutscher Verband

Bundesarchiv Koblenz

N 1003 Nachlass Leo Wegener
N 1034 Nachlass Gottfried Gok
N 1059 Nachlass Gottfried Traub
N 1211 Nachlass Otto Schmidt-Hannover
N 1231 Nachlass Alfred Hugenberg
N 2368 Nachlass Heinrich Claß

Gedenkstätte Deutscher Widerstand, Berlin

Sonderarchiv Moskau 500-3-569 Gestapo files on the Pan-German League

Hessisches Staatsarchiv-Darmstadt

G12 B Gestapo/SS Sicherheitsdienst files on the Pan-German League

Niedersächsisches Staatsarchiv-Osnabrück

Erw. C1 DNVP Landesverband Osnabrück

Politisches Archiv des Auswärtigen Amts-Berlin

Nachlass Gustav Stresemann

Privatarchiv-Kuno Graf von Westarp-Gaertringen

Nachlass Kuno von Westarp

Sächsisches Hauptstaatsarchiv-Dresden

12751 Nachlass Albrecht Philipp

Stadtarchiv Dresden

Alldeutscher Verband, Ortsgruppe Dresden und Oberelbgau

Württembergisches Landesbibliothek

Ernst Marquardt, *Kämpfer für Deutschlands Zukunft und Ehre. Umrisszeichnungen aus der Geschichte der deutschnationalen Volkspartei Württembergs.*
Unpublished manuscript.

Newspapers/Journals

Alldeutsche Blätter
Berliner Lokalanzeiger
Berliner Neuste Nachrichten
Berliner Tageblatt
Das Deutsche Tageblatt
Der Tag
Deutsche Tageszeitung

Deutsche Zeitung
Deutschlands Erneuerung
Deutschvölkische Blätter
Die Freiheit
Dresdner Anzeiger
Dresdner Nachrichten
Frankfurter Zeitung
Germania
Mecklenburger Warte
Münchner Neuste Nachrichten
Neue Preußische Kreuz-Zeitung
Sächsische Volkszeitung
Tägliche Rundschau
Vorwärts
Vossische Zeitung

Primary Sources

Alter, Junius [Frantz Sontag]. *Nationalisten. Deutschlands nationales Führertum der Nachkreigszeit.* Leipzig, 1930.

Arnim, Hans von and Georg von Below, eds. *Deutschnationale Köpfe.* Leipzig, 1928.

Bang, Paul. *Volkswirtschaft und Volkstum.* Langensalza, 1924.

Bang, Paul. *Die Deutschen als Landsknechte.* Dresden, 1926.

Bang, Paul. *Staat und Volkstum.* Langensalza, 1930.

Bonhard, Otto. *Geschichte des Alldeutschen Verbandes.* Leipzig, 1920.

Bonhard, Otto. *Jüdische Geld- und Weltherrschaft?* Berlin, 1926.

Brüning, Heinrich. *Memoiren, 1918–1934.* Stuttgart, 1970.

Claß, Heinrich. *Wider den Strom. Vom Werden und Wachsen der nationalen Opposition im alten Reich.* Leipzig, 1932.

Dinter, Artur. *Die Sünde wider das Blut: Ein Zeitroman.* 4th/5th edn, Leipzig, 1919.

Einhart (pseud. Claß, Heinrich). *Deutsche Geschichte.* 9th edn, Leipzig, 1921.

Erdmann, Karl Dietrich., ed. *Akten der Reichskanzlei-Weimarer Republik: Die Kabinette Luther I und II, Bd. 1 Januar 1925 bis Oktober 1925, Bd. II Oktober 1925 bis Mai 1926.* Bopard am Rhein, 1977.

Freytagh-Loringhoven, Axel Freiherr von. *Bügerliche und sozialistische Weltanschauung.* Published in the series of lectures and pamphlets by the *Deutschnationale Volkspartei-Landesverband Schlesien.* Breslau, 1919.

Freytagh-Loringhoven, Axel Freiherr von. *Politik. Eine Einführung in Gegenwartsfragen*. Munich, 1919.

Freytagh-Loringhoven, Axel Freiherr von. *Deutschnationale Volkspartei*. Berlin, 1931.

Fryman, Daniel (Heinrich Claß). *Wenn ich der Kaiser wär'*. Leipzig, 1912.

Goltz, Rüdiger Graf von der. "Die vaterländischen Verbände." In B. Harms, ed., *Volk und Reich der Deutschen*, vol. 2. Berlin, 1929: 155–177.

Harms, Bernhard, ed. *Volk und Reich der Deutschen*. Berlin, 1929.

Hindenburg, Paul von. *Aus meinem Leben*. Leipzig, 1927.

Hitler, Adolf. *Mein Kampf*. Boston, 1939.

Hugenberg, Alfred. *Streiflichter aus Vergangenheit und Gegenwart*. Berlin, 1927.

Ludendorff, Erich. *Vernichtung der Freimauerei durch Enthüllung ihrer Geheimnisse*. Munich, 1928.

Ludendorff, Erich. *Kriegshetze und Völkermorden in den letzen 150 Jahren*. Munich, 1931.

Ludendorff, Erich. *Auf dem Weg zur Feldherrenhalle. Lebenserinnerungen an die Zeit des 9.11.1923*. Munich, 1937.

Mahraun, Arthur. *Gegen getarnte Gewalt. Weg und Kampf einer Volksbewegung*. Berlin, 1928.

Oldenburg-Januschau, Elard von. *Errinerungen*. Leipzig, 1936.

Pabst, Waldemar. "Das Kapp-Unternehmen." In Wulf Bley, ed., *Revolutionen der Weltgeschichte*. Munich, 1933.

Rabenau, Friedrich von. *Seeckt. Aus seinem Leben 1918–1936*. Leipzig, 1941.

Reventlow, Ernst zu. *Deutscher Sozialismus. Civitas Dei Germanica*. Weimar, 1930.

Röhm, Ernst. *Die Geschichte eines Hochverräters*. Munich, 1933.

Stresemann, Gustav. *Vermächtnis. Der Nachlaß in drei Bänden*, ed. H. Bernhard. Berlin, 1932.

Vietinghoff-Scheel, Leopold von. *Grundzüge des völkischen Staatsgedankens*. Berlin, 1924.

Weiß, Hermann and Paul Hoser, eds. *Die Deutschnationalen und die Zerstörung der Weimarer Republik. Aus dem Tagebuch von Reinhold Quaatz 1928–1933*. Munich, 1989.

Weiß, Max, ed. *Taschenbuch der Deutschnationalen Volkspartei*. Berlin, 1927.

Westarp, Kuno von. *Am Grabe der Parteiherrschaft. Bilanz des deutschen Parlamentarismus von 1918–1932*. Berlin, 1932.

Westarp, Kuno von. *Konservative Politik im Übergang vom Kaiserreich zur Weimarer Republik*, ed. Friederich Freiherr Hiller von Gaertringen, Karl Meyer, and Reinhold Weber. Düsseldorf, 2001.

Wulle, Reinhold. *Deutsche Politik 1925*. Berlin, 1925.

Wulle, Reinhold. *Das Schuldbuch der Republik. 13 Jahre deutsche Politik.* Rostock, 1932.

Secondary Sources

Albrecht, Thomas. *Für eine wehrhafte Demokratie. Albert Grzesinski und die preußische Politik in der Weimarer Republic.* Bonn, 1999.

Allen, William S. *The Nazi Seizure of Power: The Experience of a Single German Town 1922–1945.* 2nd edn, New York, 1984.

Beck, Hermann. *The Fateful Alliance: German Conservatives and Nazis in 1933: The Machtergreifung in a New Light.* Oxford and New York, 2008.

Behrens, Reinhard. *Die Deutschnationalen in Hamburg, 1918–1933.* Ph.D. diss., University of Hamburg, 1973.

Benz, Wolfgang. *Süddeutschland in der Weimarer Republik: Ein Beitrag zur deutschen Innenpolitik 1918–1923.* Berlin, 1970.

Berg-Schlosser, Dirk and Jakob Schissler, eds. *Politische Kultur in Deutschland. Bilanz und Perpektiven der Forschung. Politische Vierteljahresschrift,* 28, Sonderheft 18. Opladen, 1987.

Berghahn, Volker. *Der Stahlhelm. Bund der Frontsoldaten 1918–1935.* Düsseldorf, 1966.

Berghahn, Volker. "Das Volksbegehren gegen den Young-Plan und die Urspünge des Präsidialregimes, 1928–1930." In Dirk Stegmann, Bernd Jürgen Wendt, and Peter Christin Witt, eds, *Industrielle Gesellschaft und politisches System. Beiträge zur politischen Sozialgeschichte. Festschrift für Fritz Fischer zum siebzigsten Geburtstag.* Bonn, 1978: 431–446.

Berglar, Peter. *Walter Rathenau. Seine Zeit. Sein Werk. Seine Persönlichkeit.* Bremen, 1970.

Bessel, Richard. *Political Violence and the Rise of Nazism: The Storm Troopers in Eastern Germany, 1925–1934.* New Haven, 1984.

Blackbourn, David and Geoff Eley, *The Peculiarities of German History: Bourgeois Society and Politics in Nineteenth-Century Germany.* New York, 1984.

Blinkhorn, Martin, ed. *Fascists and Conservatives: The Radical Right and the Establishment in Twentieth-Century Europe.* London, 1990.

Boberach, Heinz, ed. *Meldungen aus dem Reich: Die Geheimen Lageberichte des Sicherheitsdienstes der SS. Band 2 Jahreslagebericht 1938 des Sicherheitsamtes.* Herrsching, 1984.

Bracher, Karl Dietrich. *Die Auflösung der Weimarer Republik: Eine Studie zum Problem des Machtverfalls in der Demokratie.* 2nd edn, Stuttgart and Düsseldorf, 1957.

Brammer, Karl. *Attentäter. Spitzel und Justizrat Claß – Der Seeckt – und Hardenprozess.* Politische Prozesse, heft V, ed. Robert Breuer. Berlin, 1924.

Bruch, Rüdiger vom. "Wilhelminismus-Zum Wandel von Milieu und politischer Kultur." In Uwe Puschner, Walter Schmitz, and Justus H. Ulbricht, eds, *Handbuch zur Völkischen Bewegung 1871–1918.* Munich, 1999: 3-41.

Carsten, Francis L. *Reichswehr und Politik 1918–1933.* Cologne and Berlin, 1964.

Cary, Noel D. "The Making of the Reich President, 1925: German Conservatism and the Nomination of Paul Hindenburg." *Central European History*, 23 (1990): 179–204.

Chamberlin, Brewster Searing. *The Enemy on the Right: The "Alldeutsche Verband" in the Weimar Republic 1918–1926.* Ph.D. diss., University of Maryland, 1972.

Chamberlin, Brewster Searing. "The Pan-German League in Austria." *Studies in Modern European History and Culture*, 3 (1977): 37–74.

Chanady, Attila. "The Disintegration of the German National People's Party 1924–1930." *Journal of Modern History*, 39 (1967): 65–91.

Chickering, Roger. *We Men Who Feel Most German: A Cultural Study of the Pan-German League, 1886–1914.* Boston and London, 1984.

Clemens, Gabriele. *Martin Spahn und der Rechtskatholizismus in der Weimarer Republik.* Mainz, 1983.

Coetzee, Marilyn S. *The German Army League: Popular Nationalism in Wilhelmine Germany.* New York, 1990.

Deuerlein, Ernst, ed. *Der Hitler-Putsch, Bayerische Dokumente zum 8./9. November 1923.* Stuttgart, 1962.

Diehl, James M. *Paramilitary Politics in Weimar Germany.* Bloomington, 1977.

Diehl, James M. "Von der 'Vaterländspartei' zur 'Nationalen Revolution', die 'Vereinigten Vaterländischen Verbände Deutschlands' (VVVD) 1922–1932." *Vierteljahrshefte für Zeitgeschichte*, 33 (1985): 617–639.

Dorpalen, Andreas. *Hindenberg and the Weimar Republic.* Princeton, 1964.

Dörr, Manfred. *Die Deutschnationale Volkspartei 1925 bis 1928.* Ph.D. diss., University of Marburg, 1964.

Duesterberg, Theodor. *Der Stahlhelm und Hitler.* Wölfenbüttel, 1949.

Eley, Geoff. "Conservatives and Radical Nationalists in Germany: The Production of Fascist Potentials." In Martin Blinkhorn, ed., *Fascists and Conservatives: The Radical Right and the Establishment in Twentieth-Century Europe.* London, 1990: 50–70.

Eley, Geoff. *Reshaping the German Right: Radical Nationalism and Political Change after Bismarck.* 2nd edn, Ann Arbor, 1991.

Eley, Geoff. *From Unification to Nazism: Reinterpreting the German Past.* London, 1992.

Erdmann, Karl Dietrich. *Die Weimarer Republik.* 9th edn, Munich, 1989.

Erger, Johannes. *Der Kapp-Lüttwitz-Putsch: Ein Beitrag zur deutschen Innenpolitik, 1919/1920.* Düsseldorf, 1967.

Evans, Richard J., ed. *Society and Politics in Wilhelmine Germany.* London, 1978.

Evans, Richard J. *The Coming of the Third Reich.* New York, 2004.

Falter, Jürgen, Thomas Lindenberger, and Siegfried Schumann. *Wahlen und Abstimmungen in der Weimarer Republik: Materialien zum Wahlverhalten 1919–1933.* Statistische Arbeitsbücher zur neueren deutschen Geschichte. Munich, 1986.

Falter, Jürgen W. "The Two Hindenberg Elections of 1925 and 1933: A Total Reversal of Voter Coalitions." *Central European History,* 23 (1990): 225–241.

Feldman, Gerald D. *Army, Industry and Labour in Germany, 1914–1918.* Princeton, 1966.

Feldman, Gerald D. "Big Business and the Kapp Putsch." *Central European History* 4 (1971): 99–130.

Feldman, Gerald D., ed. *Die Nachwirkungen der Inflation auf die deutsche Geschichte 1924–1933.* Schriften des Historischen Kollegs, Kolloquien 6. Munich, 1985.

Fenske, Hans. *Konsevativismus und Rechtsradikalismus in Bayern nach 1918.* Bad Homburg vor der Höhe, 1969.

Fest, Joachim. *Hitler.* New York, 1974.

Finker, Kurt. "Vereinigte vaterländische Verbände Deutschlands." In Dieter Fricke, ed., *Lexikon zur Parteiengeschichte,* vol. 4. Köln and Leipzig, 1986: 314–321.

Fischer, Conan. *The Ruhr Crisis, 1923–1924.* Oxford, 2003.

Fischer, Fritz. *From Kaiserreich to Third Reich: Elements of Continuity in German History, 1871–1945.* Translated by Roger Fletcher. London, Boston, and Sydney, 1986.

Fischer, Heinz-Dietrich. *Handbuch der politischen Presse in Deutschland 1480–1980.* Düsseldorf, 1981.

Flemming, Jens. "Konservatismus als 'nationalrevolutionäre Bewegung'. Konservative Kritik an der Deutschnationalen Volkspartei 1918–1933." In *Deutscher Konservatismus im 19. Und 20. Jahrhundert: Festschrift für Fritz Fischer zum 75. Geburtstag und zum 50. Doktorjubiläum.* Bonn, 1983: 295–331.

Frankel, Richard. *Bismarck's Shadow: The Cult of Leadership and the Transformation of the German Right, 1898–1945.* New York, 2005.

Franz-Willing, Georg. *Krisenjahr der Hitler-Bewegung 1923.* Preußisch Oldendorf, 1975.

Franz-Willing, Georg . *Putsch und Verbotszeit der Hitlerbewegung: November 1923– Februar 1925.* Preußisch Oldendorf, 1977.

Freisel, Ludwig. *Das Bismarckbild der Alldeutschen.* Oldenburg, 1964.

Fricke, Dieter, ed. *Die bürgerlichen Parteien in Deutschland.* Leipzig, 1969.

Fricke, Dieter, ed. *Lexikon zur Parteiengeschichte. Die bürgerlichen und kleinbürgerlichen Parteien und Verbände in Deutschland (1789–1945).* 4 vols. Leipzig, 1983–1986.

Friedenthal, Elisabeth. *Volksbegehren und Volksentscheid über den Young Plan und die deutschnationale Sezession.* Ph.D. diss., University of Tübingen, 1957.

Friedensburg, Ferdinand. *Lebenserrinerungen.* Frankfurt am Main, 1969.

Fritzsche, Peter. *Rehearsals for Fascism: Populism and Political Mobilization in Weimar Germany.* Oxford, 1990.

Fritzsche, Peter. "Victory and Popular Festivity in Weimar Germany: Hindenberg's 1925 Election." *Central European History,* 23 (1990): 205–224.

Fritzsche, Peter. "Breakdown or Breakthrough? Conservatives and the November Revolution." In Larry E. Jones and James N. Retallack, eds, *Between Reform, Reaction, and Resistance: Studies in the History of German Conservatism from 1789 to 1945.* Providence and Oxford, 1993: 299–329.

Fröhlich, Elke, ed. *Die Tagebücher von Joseph Goebbels: sämtliche Fragmente,* part I: 1924–1941, vol. I. Munich, 1987.

Ganyard, Clifton. *Artur Mahraun and the Young German Order: An Alternative to National Socialism in Weimar Political Culture.* Lewiston, 2008.

Garnett, Jr., Robert Stephen. *Lion, Eagle and Swastika: Bavarian Monarchism in Weimar Germany, 1918–1933.* New York and London, 1991.

Gatzke, Hans W. *Stresemann and the Rearmament of Germany.* Baltimore, 1954.

Gessner, Dieter. *Agrarverbände in der Weimarer Republik. Wirtschaftliche und soziale Voraussetzungen agrarkonservativer Politik vor 1933.* Düsseldorf, 1976.

Geyer, Michael. *Aufrüstung oder Sicherheit: Die Reichswehr in der Krise derMachtpolitik 1924–1936.* Wiesbaden, 1980.

Goodspeed, Donald J. *Ludendorff: Solider, Dictator, Revolutionary.* London, 1966.

Gordon, Jr., Harold. *The Reichswehr and the Weimar Republic, 1919–1926.* Princeton, 1957.

Gordon, Jr., Harold. *Hitler and the Beer Hall Putsch.* Princeton, 1972.

Granier, Gerhard. *Mangus von Levetzow. Seeoffzier. Monarchist und Wegbereiter Hitlers: Lebensweg und ausgewählter Dokumente.* Schriften des Bundesarchivs, Boppard, 1982.

Grathwol, Robert P. *Stresemann and the DNVP: Reconciliation or Revenge in German Foreign Policy*. Lawrence, 1980.

Grünthal, Günther. *Reichsschulgesetz und Zentrumspartei in der Weimarer Republik*. Düsseldorf, 1968.

Guratsch, Dankwart. *Macht durch Organisation. Die Grundlegung des Hugenbergschen Presseimperiums*. Düsseldorf, 1973.

Hagenlücke, Heinz. *Deutsche Vaterlandspartei. Die Nationale Rechte am Ende des Kaiserreiches*. Düsseldorf, 1997.

Hamel, Iris. *Völkischer Verband und Nationale Gewerkschaft. Der Deutschnationale Handlungsgehilfen-Verband 1893–1933*. Frankfurt am Main, 1967.

Hamilton, Richard F. *Who Voted for Hitler?* Princeton, 1982.

Hartung, Günter. "Völkische Ideologie." In Uwe Puschner, Walter Schmitz, and Justus H. Ulbricht, eds, *Handbuch zur Völkischen Bewegung 1871–1918*. Munich, 1999: 3–41.

Hartwig, Edgar. *Zur Politik und Entwicklung des Alldeutschen Verbandes von seiner Gründung bis zum Beginn des Ersten Weltkrieges (1891–1914)*. Diss. Phil., Jena, 1966.

Hayes, Peter. "'A Question Mark with Epaulettes'?: Kurt von Schleicher and Weimar Politics." *Journal of Modern History*, 52 (March 1980): 35–65.

Heinemann, Ulrich. *Die verdrängte Niederlage: Politische Öffentlichkeit und Kriegsschuldfrage in der Weimarer Republik*. Göttingen, 1983.

Held, Joseph. *Heinrich Held. Ein Leben für Bayern*. Regensburg, 1958.

Herf, Jeffrey. *Reactionary Modernism: Technology, Culture, and Politics in Weimar and the Third Reich*. Cambridge, 1984.

Hering, Rainer. *Konstruierte Nation. Der Alldeutsche Verband 1890 bis 1939*. Hamburg, 2003.

Hermand, Jost. *Der alte Traum vom neuen Reich: Völkische Utopien und Nationalsozialismus*. Frankfurt am Main, 1988.

Hertzman, Lewis. "The Founding of the German National People's Party (DNVP), November 1918–January 1919." *Journal of Modern History*, 30 (1958): 24–36.

Hertzman, Lewis. *DNVP: Right-Wing Opposition in the Weimar Republic*. Lincoln, NE, 1963.

Hiller von Gaertringen, Friedrich Freiherr. "Die Deutschnationale Volkspartei." In Erich Matthias and Rudolf Morsey, eds. *Das Ende der Parteien 1933*. Düsseldorf, 1960: 543–652.

Hiller von Gaertringen, Friedrich Freiherr. "'Dolchstoß'-Diskussion und 'Dolchstoß'-Legende im Wandel von vier Jahrzehnten." *Aus Politik und Zeitgeschichte*, 16 (1963).

Hoftadter, Richard. *The Paranoid Style in American Politics and Other Essays.* Cambridge, 1996 (original edn 1952).

Holzbach, Heidrun. *Das "System Hugenberg." Die Organization bürgerlicher Sammlungspolitik vor dem Aufstieg der NSDAP.* Stuttgart, 1981.

Hornung, Klaus. *Der Jungdeutsche Orden.* Düsseldorf, 1958.

Hussmann, Josephine. *Die Alldeutschen und die Flottenfrage.* Diss. Phil., Freiburg, 1945.

Iggers, Georg. *The German Conception of History.* Middletown, 1968.

Jablonsky, David. *The Nazi Party in Dissolution: Hitler and the Verbotszeit 1923–1925.* London and Totowa, 1989.

Jäckel, Eberhard and Axel Kuhn, eds. *Hitler: Sämtliche Aufzeichnungen 1905– 1924.* Stuttgart, 1980.

James, Harold. *The German Slump: Politics and Economics, 1924–1936.* Oxford, 1986.

Jansen, Marlies E. *Max Maurenbrecher: der weltanschaulich-politische Weg eines deutschen Nationalisten 1900–1930.* Düsseldorf, 1964.

Jarausch, Konrad, Jörn Rüsen, and Hans Schleier, eds. *Geschichtswissenschaft vor 2000. Perspektiven der Historiographiegeschichte, Geschichtstheorie, Sozial- und Kulturgeschichte. Festschrift für Georg G. Iggers zum 65 Geburtstag.* Hagen, 1992.

Jasper, Gotthard. *Der Schutz der Republik. Studien zur staatlichen Sicherung in der Weimarer Republik 1922–1930.* Tübingen, 1963.

Jochmann, Werner. *Nationalsozialismus und Revolution: Ursprung und Geschichte der NSDAP in Hamburg, 1922–1933, Dokumente.* Frankfurt am Main, 1963.

Jonas, Erasmus. *Die Volkskonservtiven 1928–1933.* Düsseldorf, 1965.

Jones, Larry E. "'The Dying Middle': Weimar Germany and the Fragmentation of Bourgeois Politics." *Central European History,* 5 (1972): 23–54.

Jones, Larry E. "Inflation, Revaluation, and the Crisis of Middle-Class Politics. A Study in the Dissolution of the Weimar Party System, 1923–1928." *Central European History,* 12 (1979): 148–152.

Jones, Larry E. *German Liberalism and the Dissolution of the Weimar Party System, 1918–1933.* Chapel Hill and London, 1988.

Jones, Larry E. "'The Greatest Stupidity of My Life': Alfred Hugenberg and the Formation of the Hitler Cabinet, January 1933." *Journal of Contemporary History,* 27/1 (1992): 63–87.

Jones, Larry E. "Why Hitler Came to Power: In Defense of a New History of Politics." In Konrad Jarausch, Jörn Rüsen, and Hans Schleier, eds, *Geschichtswissenschaft vor 2000. Perspektiven der Historiographiegeschichte,*

Geschichtstheorie, Sozial- und Kulturgeschichte. Festschrift für Georg G. Iggers zum 65 Geburtstag. Hagen, 1992: 259–270.

Jones, Larry E. "The Limits of Collaboration: Edgar Jung, Herbert von Bose, and the Origins of the Conservative Resistance to Hitler, 1933–34." In Larry Eugene Jones and James N. Retallack, eds, *Between Reform, Reaction, and Resistance: Studies in the History of German Conservatism from 1789 to 1945.* Providence, 1993: 465–501.

Jones, Larry E. "Hindenburg and the Conservative Dilemma in the 1932 Presidential Elections." *German Studies Review*, 5 (1997): 235–260.

Jones, Larry E. "Saxony, 1924–1930: A Study in the Dissolution of the Bourgeois Party System in Weimar Germany." In James Retallack, ed., *Saxony in German History: Culture, Society, and Politics, 1830–1933.* Ann Arbor, 2000: 336–355.

Jones, Larry E. "Nationalists, Nazis, and the Assault against Weimar: Revisiting the Harzburg Rally of October 1931." *German Studies Review*, 29 (2006): 483–494.

Jones, Larry E. "German Conservatism at the Crossroads: Count Kuno von Westarp and the Struggle for Control of the DNVP, 1928–1930." *Contemporary European History*, 18 (2009): 147–177.

Jones, Larry E. and James N. Retallack, eds. *Between Reform, Reaction, and Resistance: Studies in the History of German Conservatism from 1789 to 1945.* Providence and Oxford, 1993.

Jones, Larry E. and Wolfram Pyta, eds. *"Ich bin der Letzte Preusse." Der politische Lebensweg des konservativen Politikers Kuno Graf Westarp (1864–1945).* Cologne, 2006.

Jung, Dietrich. *Der Alldeutsche Verband und die Marokkofrage.* Diss. Phil., Bonn, 1934.

Kennedy, Paul and Anthony Nichols, eds. *Nationalist and Racialist Movements in Britain and Germany Before 1914.* London, 1981.

Kershaw, Ian. *The "Hitler Myth": Image and Reality in the Third Reich.* Oxford, 1987.

Kershaw, Ian. *Hitler: 1889–1936 Hubris.* New York, 1999.

Kiiskinen, Elina. *Die Deutschnationalen Volkspartei in Bayern (Bayerische Mittelpartei) in der Regierungspolitik des Freistaats während der Weimarer Zeit.* Munich, 2005.

Klemperer, Klemens von. *Germany's New Conservatism: Its History and Dilemma in the Twentieth Century.* Princeton, 1957.

Klotzbücher, Alois. *Der politische Weg des Stahlhelm, Bund der Frontsoldaten, in der Weimarer Republik. Ein Beitrag zur Geschichte der "Nationalen Opposition" 1918–1933.* Ph.D. diss., University of Erlangen, 1965.

Kolb, Eberhard. *The Weimar Republic*. London, 1988.

Kolditz, Gerhard. *Die Ortsgruppe Dresden des Alldeutschen Verbandes von ihrer Entstehung bis zum Verbandstag 1906*. Diplomarbeit, Humboldt Universität Berlin, 1989.

Krebs, Willi. *Der Alldeutsche Verband in den Jahren 1918 bis 1939: ein politisches Instrument des deutschen Imperialismus*. Diss. Phil., Berlin, 1970.

Kruck, Alfred. *Geschichte des Alldeutschen Verbandes, 1890–1939*. Wiesbaden, 1954.

Krumeich, Gerd and Joachim Schröder, eds. *Der Schatten des Weltkrieges. Die Ruhrbesetzung 1923*. Essen, 2004.

Kurlander, Eric. *The Price of Exclusion: Ethnicity, National Identity, and the Decline of German Liberalism, 1898–1933*. New York, 2006.

Lamberti, Marjorie. *The Politics of Education: Teachers and School Reform in Weimar Germany*. New York and Oxford, 2002.

Lapp, Benjamin. *Revolution from the Right: Politics, Class, and the Rise of Nazism in Saxony, 1919–1933*. Atlantic Highlands, 1997.

Large, David Clay. *Where Ghosts Walked: Munich's Road to the Third Reich*. New York and London, 1997.

Lauter, Anna-Monika. *Sicherheit und Reparationen. Die französische Öffentlichkeit, der Rhein und die Ruhr (1919–1923)*. Essen, 2006.

Lebovics, Herman. *Social Conservatism and the Middle Classes in Germany, 1914–1933*. Princeton, 1969.

Leopold, John A. *Alfred Hugenberg: The Radical Nationalist Campaign Against the Weimar Republic*. New Haven and London, 1977.

Levy, Richard S. *The Downfall of the Anti-Semitic Political Parties in Imperial Germany*. New Haven and London, 1975.

Liang, Hsi-Huey. *The Berlin Police Force in the Weimar Republic*. Berkeley, 1970.

Liebe, Werner. *Die Deutschnationale Volkspartei, 1918–1924*. Düsseldorf, 1956.

Lohalm, Uwe. *Völkischer Radikalismus. Die Geschichte des Deutschvölkischen Schutz- und Trutzbundes 1919–1923*. Hamburg, 1970.

Malinowski, Stephan. *Vom König zum Führer. Sozialer Niedergang und politische Radikalisierung im deutschen Adel zwischen Kaiserreich und NS-Staat*. Berlin, 2003.

Maser, Werner. *Hindenburg. Eine politische Biographie*. Rastatt, 1990

Matthias, Erich and Rudolf Morsey, eds. *Das Ende der Parteien 1933*. Düsseldorf, 1960.

Meinecke, Friedrich. *The German Catastrophe: Reflections and Recollections*. English edition: Boston, 1963 (originally published in 1950).

Mergel, Thomas. "Das Scheitern des deutschen Tory-Konservatismus. Die Umformung der DNVP zu einer rechtsradikalen Partei 1928–1932." *Historische Zeitschrift*, 276 (2003): 323–368.

Mitchell, Allen. *Revolution in Bavaria, 1918–1919: The Eisner Regime and the Soviet Republic*. Princeton, 1965.

Mohler, Arnim. *Die konservative Revolution in Deutschland 1918–1932: Grundriss ihrer Anschauungen*. 3rd edn, Darmstadt, 1989.

Moeller, Robert G. *German Peasants and Agrarian Politics, 1914–1924: The Rhineland and Westphalia*. Chapel Hill, 1986.

Mommsen, Hans. *From Weimar to Auschwitz*. Princeton, 1991.

Mommsen, Hans. "Government Without Parties: Conservative Plans for Constitutional Revision at the End of the Weimar Republic." In Larry Eugene Jones and James N. Retallack, eds, *Between Reform, Reaction, and Resistance: Studies in the History of German Conservatism from 1789 to 1945*. New York, 1993: 347–373.

Mommsen, Hans. *The Rise and Fall of Weimar Democracy*. Translated by Elborg Forster and Larry Eugene Jones. Chapel Hill, 1996.

Mosse, George. *The Crisis of German Ideology: Intellectual Origins of the Third Reich*. New York, 1964.

Müller, Markus. *Die Christlich-Nationale Bauern- und Landvolkpartei 1928–1933*. Düsseldorf, 2001.

Neliba, Günter. *Wilhelm Frick: der Legalist eines Unrechtstaates: eine politische Biographie*. Paderborn, 1992.

Neuberger, Helmut. *Freimauerei und Nationalsozialismus: Die Verfolgung der deutschen Freimauerei durch völkische Bewegung und Nationalsozialismus 1918–1945*. Hamburg, 1980.

Nipperday, Thomas. *Die Organization der deutschen Parteien vor 1918*. Düsseldorf, 1961.

Orlow, Dietrich. *The History of the Nazi Party: 1919–1933*. Pittsburgh, 1969.

Orlow, Dietrich. *Weimar Prussia 1918–1925: The Unlikely Rock of Democracy*. Pittsburgh, 1986.

Orlow, Dietrich. *Weimar Prussia 1925–1933: The Illusion of Strength*. Pittsburgh, 1991.

Patch, Jr., William L. *Christian Trade Unions in the Weimar Republic, 1918–1933: The Failure of "Corporate Pluralism"*. New Haven, 1985.

Patch, Jr., William L. *Heinrich Brüning and the Dissolution of the Weimar Republic*. Cambridge, 1998.

Peck, Abraham J. *Radicals and Reactionaries: The Crisis of Conservatism in Wilhelmine Germany*. Washington, D.C., 1978.

Peters, Michael. *Der Alldeutsche Verband am Vorabend des Ersten Weltkrieges (1908–1914)*. Frankfurt am Main, 1992.

Petzold, Joachim. "Claß und Hitler. Über die Förderung der frühen Nazibewegung durch den Alldeutschen Verband und dessen Einfluß auf die Nazi Ideologie." *Jahrbuch für Geschichte*, 21 (1980): 247-288.

Peukert, Detlev. *Inside Nazi Germany: Conformity, Opposition, and Racism in Everyday Life*. New Haven, 1987.

Puhle, Hans-Jürgen. *Agrarische Interessenpolitik und preßischer Konservatismus im wilhelminischen Reich, 1893–1914*. Hannover, 1966.

Puschner, Uwe. *Die Völkische Bewegung im wilhelminischen Kaiserreich. Sprache-Rasse-Religion*. Darmstadt, 2001.

Puschner, Uwe, Walter Schmitz, and Justus H. Ulbricht, eds. *Handbuch zur "Völkischen Bewegung" 1871–1918*. Munich, 1999.

Pyta, Wolfram. *Hindenburg: Herrschaft zwischen Hohenzollern und Hitler*. Berlin, 2007.

Repp, Kevin Douglas. *Westarp, Hugenberg and Control of the DNVP: Toward Understanding Contemporary and Historical Perspectives*. M.A. Thesis, Washington State University, 1987.

Retallack, James N. *Notables of the Right: The Conservative Party and Political Mobilization in Germany, 1876–1918*. Boston, 1988.

Richter, Ludwig. *Die Deutsche Volkspartei 1918–1933*. Düsseldorf, 2002.

Rohrkrämer, Thomas. *A Single Communal Faith? The German Right from Conservatism to National Socialism*. New York and Oxford, 2007.

Sabrow, Martin. *Die Verdrängte Verschwörung. Der Rathenaumord und die deutsche Gegenrevolution*. Frankfurt am Main, 1999.

Scheck, Raffael. *Alfred von Tirpitz and German Right-Wing Politics, 1914–1930*. Atlantic Highlands, 1998.

Scheck, Raffael. *Mothers of the Nation: Right-Wing Women in Weimar Germany*. New York, 2004.

Schödl, Günter. *Alldeutscher Verband und deutsche Minderheitenpolitik in Ungarn 1890–1914: Zur Gechichte des deutschen "extremen Nationalismus."* Frankfurt am Main, 1978.

Schönhoven, Klaus. *Die Bayerische Volkspartei 1924–1932*. Düsseldorf, 1972.

Schuker, Steven A. *The End of French Predominance in Europe: The Financial Crisis of 1924 and the Adoption of the Dawes Plan*. Chapel Hill, 1976.

Schulze, Hagen. *Weimar. Deutschland 1917–1933*. Berlin, 1982.

Smith, Woodruff D. *The Ideological Origins of Nazi Imperialism*. Oxford, 1986.

Stegmann, Dirk. *Die Erben Bismarcks. Parteien und Verbänden der Spätphase des Wilhelminischen Deutschlands*. Cologne, 1970.

Stegmann, Dirk, Bernd-Jürgen Wendt, and Peter-Christian Witt, eds. *Deutscher Konservatismus im 19. Und 20. Jahrhundert. Festschrift für Fritz Fischer.* Bonn, 1983.

Stern, Fritz. *The Politics of Cultural Despair.* Berkeley, 1972.

Stoltenberg, Gerhard. *Politische Strömungen im schleswig-holsteinischen Landvolk 1918–1933. Ein Beitrag zur politischen Meinungsbildung in der Weimarer Republik.* Düsseldorf, 1962.

Striesow, Jan. *Die Deutschnationale Volkspartei und die Völkisch-Radikalen, 1918–1922.* Frankfurt, 1981.

Struve, Walther. *Elites against Democracy: Leadership Ideals in Bourgeois Political Thought in Germany, 1890–1973.* Princeton, 1973.

Stupperich, Amrei. *Volksgemeinschaft oder Arbeitersolidarität: Studien zur Arbeitnehmerpolitik in der Deutschnationalen Volkspartei 1918–1933.* Göttingen, 1982.

Stürmer, Michael. *Koalition und Opposition in der Weimarer Republik 1924–1928.* Düsseldorf, 1967.

Thimme, Annelise. *Flucht in den Mythos: Die Deutschnationale Volkspartei und die Niederlage von 1918.* Göttingen, 1969.

Thimme, Roland. *Stresemann und die Deutsche Volkspartei 1923–1925.* Lübeck, 1961.

Thoß, Bruno. *Der Ludendorff-Kreis 1919–1923: München als Zentrum der mitteleuropäischen Gegenrevolution zwischen Revolution und Hitler-Putsch.* Munich, 1978.

Trippe, Christian F. *Konservative Verfassungspolitik, 1918–1923. Die DNVP als Opposition in Reich und Ländern.* Düsseldorf, 1995.

Turner, Jr., Henry A. *Stresemann and the Politics of the Weimar Republic.* Princeton, paperback edn, 1965.

Turner, Jr., Henry A. *German Big Business and the Rise of Hitler.* New York, 1985.

Turner, Jr., Henry A.. *Hitler's Thirty Days to Power: January 1933.* Reading, MA, 1996.

Vogelsang, Thilo. *Reichswehr, Staat und NSDAP. Beiträge zur deutschen Gechichte 1930–1932.* Stuttgart, 1962.

Waite, Robert G.L. *Vanguard of Nazism: The Free Corps Movement in Postwar Germany 1918–1923.* Cambridge, MA, 1952.

Walkenhorst, Peter. *Nation-Volk-Rasse. Radikaler Nationalismus im Deutschen Kaiserreich 1890–1914.* Göttingen, 2007.

Walker, D.P. "The German Nationalist People's Party: The Conservative Dilemma in the Weimar Republic." *Journal of Contemporary History*, 14 (1979): 627–647.

Wehler, Hans Ulrich. *The German Empire, 1871–1918.* Providence, 1985.

Wehner, Siegfried. *Der Alldeutsche Verband und die deutsche Kolonialpolitik der Vorkriegszeit.* Diss. Phil., Greifswald, 1935.

Werneke, Klaus and Heller, Peter. *Der vergessene Führer. Alfred Hugenberg, Pressemacht und Nationalsozialismus.* Hamburg, 1982.

Werner, Lothar. *Der Alldeutsche Verband 1890–1918.* Berlin, 1935.

Wertheimer, Mildred S. *The Pan-German League, 1890–1914.* New York, 1924.

Wheeler-Bennett, John W. *The Wooden Titan: Hindenburg in Twenty Years of German History.* New York, 1967.

Williamson, John G. *Karl Helfferich, 1872–1924: Economist, Financier, Politician.* Princeton, 1971.

Winkler, Heinrich August. *Weimar 1918–1933. Die Geschichte der ersten deutschen Demokratie.* Munich, 1998.

Wright, Jonathan. *Gustav Stresemann: Weimar's Greatest Statesman.* Oxford, 2002.

Wulff, Reimer. *Die Deutschvölkische Freiheitspartei 1922–1928.* Ph.D. diss., Marburg University, 1968.

Index